The Unraveling of the West

The Unraveling of the West

The Rise of Postmodernism and the Decline of Democracy

DONALD N. WOOD

Westport, Connecticut
London

Library of Congress Cataloging-in-Publication Data

Wood, Donald N., 1934–
    The unraveling of the West : the rise of postmodernism and the decline of
democracy / Donald N. Wood.
      p. cm.
    Includes bibliographical references and index.
    ISBN 0–275–98104–5 (alk. paper)
    1. Postmodernism—Social aspects.   2. Democracy.   I. Title.
    HM449.W66   2003
    303.4—dc21   2003048803

British Library Cataloguing in Publication Data is available.

Library of Congress Catalog Card Number: 2003048803
ISBN: 0–275–98104–5

First published in 2003

Praeger Publishers, 88 Post Road West, Westport, CT 06881
An imprint of Greenwood Publishing Group, Inc.
www.praeger.com

Printed in the United States of America

The paper used in this book complies with the
Permanent Paper Standard issued by the National
Information Standards Organization (Z39.48–1984).

10 9 8 7 6 5 4 3 2 1

Copyright Acknowlegments

The author and publisher gratefully acknowledge permission to use excerpts from the
following material:

From *Consilience* by Edward O. Wilson, copyright © 1998 by Edward O. Wilson. Used by
permission of Alfred A.Knopf, a division of Random House, Inc.

For Marie
Your years of devotion, support, research assistance, and constructive
criticism cannot be measured. Only treasured. Thank you, Breeze.

Contents

Illustrations

Acknowledgments

In pulling together the ideas and particulars of this book, I owe a great deal to numerous scholars, writers, students, colleagues, friends, and family members, who have inspired, challenged, questioned, and supported me over the past several years. I am heavily in debt to numerous philosophers, researchers, and social critics who furnished material that contributed to my synthesis. Although I could not attempt to mention everyone who helped me, I do want to recognize the following persons who were especially instrumental in providing information, assistance, and encouragement: Andy Bingham, Eric Goodman, Axel Granered, Mike Hermann, Thomas Humphrey, Wallace Jackson, Rodney Kling, Al Koning, Ants Leps, Howard Passell, George Rebane, Jerry Rees, George Reeves, Nina Pearlstein Skaya, Dik Van Iten, Brian Wood, and members of my "Solutions for a Small Planet" class at the Duke Institute for Learning in Retirement. To all, I express my thanks. But I insist on taking full credit for all the mistakes, misinterpretations, and shortcomings the reader may find.

Introduction

The ongoing curse of mankind is this: we can envision what we should be, we know what we should do, and yet we constantly fail to achieve those ideals. We repeatedly fall short in our attempts to better ourselves. We know how to live in peace, but we continue to do battle with our neighbors. We aspire to be selfless and altruistic, but we act out of materialism and self-centeredness. We say we love our brothers and sisters of all races and creeds, but again and again we act with prejudice and bigotry. We say we believe in a God of love and tolerance, and then we kill those who believe differently than we do. We know we must preserve the biosphere, yet we continue to drain the wetlands and bulldoze the forests. We know we must conduct our affairs with reason and responsibility, but we are guided by our animal lusts and greeds. If we had no more intelligence than the butterfly, no more insight than the baboon, we would be content with our place in the cosmos. But we know better. We are philosophers and theorists, thinkers and problem-solvers, moralists and preachers. And yet we constantly sabotage our intellectual efforts to improve ourselves and better our world. This is our tragedy, our unending frustration: we aspire to elevated heights—but we continually pull ourselves down to the lower depths.

Modern Western civilization came into being about three centuries ago as an *intellectual* vision—the belief that human beings could conduct their social, economic, and political matters with reason and responsibility. It was conceived out of the idea that men and women were rational, were able to think for themselves, were committed to logic and scientific inquiry, and would be able to govern themselves in a responsible manner.

We knew what we wanted to do, we saw what we should become. Today, however, we are not managing our affairs in an intellectual manner. We have evolved into a chaotic *post-intellectual* culture.

The West's greatest threat comes not from terrorists' bombs and stealth warfare, not from nuclear missiles, not from chemical and biological weapons smuggled through our porous borders—but it comes from within, from its deteriorating intellectual infrastructure. The unraveling of the West is an insidious phenomenon that has been eroding our intellectual climate for much of the twentieth century.

This book is a follow-up to my earlier work on *post-Intellectualism*.[1] The notable addition to this volume is the integration of an analysis of postmodernism—a reality that must be explored if we are to understand the phenomenon of post-intellectualism. The term *postmodernism* generally strikes the average citizen as a deliberately vague and pompous academic term that bears little relation to the real world. But the certainty of our postmodern world is very much with us.

THE FABRIC OF AN INTELLECTUAL CULTURE

Our modern culture is a rich tapestry, woven over a period of a couple hundred years. The warp and woof of this sturdy fabric consist of two threads—reason and responsibility. But this magnificent tapestry, our intellectual heritage, is unraveling. America is evolving from the intellectual stimulus of the eighteenth and nineteenth centuries into a post-intellectual state of cultural disarray. Western culture was an outgrowth of the Enlightenment, roughly the seventeenth and eighteenth centuries.[2] It was during this era of intellectual ferment that philosophers, economists, scientists, and political theorists gradually drafted a blueprint that would outline a new, *modern* approach to human culture. This enlightened view was based on scientific empiricism, humanism, reason, individualism, personal and social responsibility, libertarian democratic principles, exploration, capitalism, growth, and progress. We determined that human beings were rational enough and responsible enough to govern themselves. Quite a revolutionary idea. We enjoyed an intellectual awakening that powered a cultural transformation and the industrial revolution. This modern libertarian project replaced centuries of Old-World authoritarian practice—domination by the church and assorted monarchs and dictators.

European scholars theorized about Enlightenment ideas; and the American founders put them into practice, a pragmatic test of lofty eighteenth-century philosophizing. We proceeded under the libertarian assumption that the citizenry would evolve into an increasingly intellectual populace, and hence could be entrusted with more and more responsibility for its own destiny. During the nineteenth and twentieth centuries, however, this modern paradigm of scientific and humanistic reason gradually lost some of its cohesiveness and its sense of inevitable destiny. Romanticism, existentialism, urbanization, capitalistic exploitation, Marxism, scientific uncertainties, global warfare, enveloping technology, and international politics all contributed to the erosion of Enlightenment idealism.

We sense today that something has gone amiss. Many of our intellectually based institutions—schools, business enterprises, the judicial system, churches, the family, government, indeed the very idea of democracy itself—are no longer functioning the way they were originally envisioned. We feel safer on the streets because we have locked up so many of our suspected troublemakers—but we question whether this really is the right path to a sane society. We send increasing numbers of our youngsters on to higher education—but we know that our schools are not turning out citizens who can cope with our increasingly incoherent society. We rush down the path to embrace new advances in digital and genetic technologies—but we are not clear in what direction this path is leading us.

POSTMODERN TURMOIL

We have entered into a new and unstable postmodern era of post-intellectualism. We have reined in scientific reason and rationalism in favor of spontaneity and passion; we have swapped our commitment to privacy for the promise of security; we have downplayed competition in order to foster sensitivity; we have embraced technology while surrendering control of our own destiny; we have sacrificed our individualism on the altar of retribalization; we have had to give up a broad liberal-arts intellectual perspective in order to focus on specialized vocational training; we have abandoned our quest for universal Truth and have adopted a loose form of moral relativity. *Whatever.* As a result, our modern civilization has evolved into a postmodern rejection of reason and structure. As we liberated ourselves from the tyranny of history and the rigidity of truth-seeking, we also liberated ourselves from responsibility. We have engineered a new era of abandon and ambiguity. This vague sense of loss of coherence is what characterizes the phenomenon that has been identified as postmodernism. John Ralston Saul defines for us the uncertainty of our times:

It is a curious sort of confusion. Organized and calm on the surface, our lives are lived in an atmosphere of nervous, even frenetic agitation. Hordes of essential answers fly about us and disappear, abruptly meaningless. Successive absolute solutions are provided for major public problems and then slip away without our consciously registering their failure. Neither the public and corporate authorities nor the experts are held responsible for their own actions in any sensible manner because the fracturing of memory and understanding has created a profound chaos in the individual's sense of what responsibility is.[3]

It may be that what we are witnessing at the dawn of the twenty-first century is actually the end of modernity itself.

While I champion the cause of a modern, intellectual culture, I must accept that we do live in a postmodern society—it is not merely an abstruse academic abstraction to be scoffed at. It is real. It permeates every aspect of our societal being. I also must note that there are some positive things to say in support of nonintellectual values. While the pursuit of reason is to be promoted, we must also see the importance of spontaneity, passion, religious faith, cooperation, tribal loyalties, community, compassion, playing with your dog, and other nonintellectual qualities. Humans do not live by reason alone.

Basically, this is a "Why" book. It is not a "How To" book (although Part IV, Chapters 19 to 23, does offer a number of recommendations and proposals to get the reader agitated). The book is primarily concerned with understanding and analyzing a problem. As outlined in Chapter 3, the first step in any problem-solving endeavor is a thorough analysis of the problem—its definition, background, causes, and effects. Before you can fix something that isn't working right, you've got to examine why it isn't working. As Garrett Hardin puts it, "In general, a great deal of looking for causes must precede the finding of remedies."[4] This is my purpose in this book—to engage in a "looking for causes," to gain an understanding of our cultural problems and uncertainties at the beginning of the twenty-first century. This book is about what it was we wanted to become, and why we have fallen short.

PART I

The Problem:
Trying to Define What's Wrong

As the twenty-first century dawns,
American culture is, quite simply, in a mess.

—Morris Berman

The present crisis is not ordinary but extraordinary. It is not merely an economic or political maladjustment, but . . . it consists in a disintegration of a
fundamental form of Western culture and society dominant for the last four
centuries.

—Pitirim A. Sorokin

Terrorism is a problem. Economic recession is a problem. Children born out
of wedlock are a problem. Potholes on the freeway are a problem. Virtually
every unwanted situation we face can be defined as a problem. The format
of this book basically follows a problem-solving model (as outlined in
Chapter 3). The first step in any problem-solving or decision-making exercise is to clarify and define the problem. This is what Part I (the first seven
chapters) is all about—analyzing and defining the issue. In particular I want
to investigate the underlying source of much of our current societal
stupor—the phenomenon I have identified as *post-intellectualism*. Part II
(Chapters 8 through 12) explores the causes of our post-intellectual malaise.
Part III (Chapters 13 to 18) is concerned with the effects—examined as six
crises of the twenty-first century. And Part IV (the final five chapters) is an
attempt to suggest some possible solutions.

CHAPTER 1

A Culture in Disarray

This book is not to convince the reader that all is lost. I predict no apocalyptic ending of the human race. (If that were the case, I would not bother taking the time to write this book; I would be spending the End Time frolicking in a condominium on Maui.) In fact, some days I am downright optimistic. We beat back Nazism. Soviet Communism fell apart of its own accord. Florida got some new voting machines. And we're getting things under control in the Middle East. (Well, maybe not quite yet.)

The fact is that many aspects of Western culture are not working as they should. Although religious terrorists feel the need to destroy modern civilization, our greatest danger is the threat of self-destruction. Historians and social writers have been analyzing the deterioration of Western culture throughout most of the twentieth century. They include voices from the left and from the right—scientists and artists, politicians and media pundits, teachers, preachers, and atheists.[1] Many of these writings and prognostications argue that what we are facing today is the end of modernity itself. That, in essence, is what this book is about—the unraveling of Modern Civilization. Specifically, it is our *intellectual* culture that is failing. Not just our schools and colleges, but the entire way we think and process information and make decisions. Our country may have the world's smartest weapons and the fastest Internet servers, but our intellectual infrastructure is disintegrating. And as our intellectual environment breaks down, so too does the idea of modern civilization.

DEFINITION OF THE PROGRESS PARADOX

This is the Progress Paradox: *The more progress we make—materialistically and technologically—the more problems we create.* With each technological and material advancement—making faster computers, utilizing resources more efficiently, automating our manufacturing processes, and building larger houses—we generate new problems and perils. Every advance triggers unanticipated consequences—fresh problems and dilemmas that arise as the result of the new solutions that we have implemented. Increased progress results in increased complexities, and as systems get more complex there are more things to go wrong. This is why you have more trouble with your computer than you do with your TV set. So it is also with our reliance on bureaucratic progress. Increasingly complicated corporate maneuverings and government programs only lead to further complexities and more problems.

Scientists and technicians have succeeded in making incredible black boxes, fancy gizmos, and things that go boom in the night. Yet we are unable to solve the basic problem of maintaining an orderly and just society. Why do we still have so much racial injustice, environmental degradation, stupidity in the classroom, and cupidity in the boardroom? In making the argument that things are not going so well, let us list briefly a few symptomatic issues.

Technological Insecurities

Technological progress is wondrous to behold. And worrisome. We are seeing incredible advances in computers, genetic breakthroughs, nanotechnology, and digital tools. But do all these whiz-bang technologies really make us more comfortable and secure, give us more leisure, increase our intellectual productivity, satisfy our spiritual yearnings, strengthen our family relations, and make us better citizens? Or do they give us a vague unsettled feeling of apprehension and increased anxiety? Perhaps Henry David Thoreau was right when he observed 150 years ago that "men have become the tools of their tools."[2] This is the definition of technological determinism—a theme we shall explore throughout the book.

One casualty of our technological progress is environmental devastation. Consider just the following: Air pollution levels in every one of the world's twenty largest cities exceed guidelines established by the World Health Organization. Over half of the major rivers on the planet are polluted or are actually drying up. We destroy between 90,000 and 100,000 acres of forest every day. Global warming is a reality. And all our ecological woes are compounded by the suffocating global population crunch. More in Chapter 16.

Medical advances and setbacks are one of the most perplexing examples of the Progress Paradox. As our modern miracle drugs proliferate, we see an increase in drug-resistant diseases and other health problems. Increased air travel and congested urban centers add to an increase in maladies from malaria and yellow fever to bubonic plague and tuberculosis.

We overdose ourselves with powerful antibiotics, resulting in the faster evolution of new superbugs—viral, bacterial, and fungal mutants—that promise numerous new forms of unknown and unanticipated diseases. More than 30 new diseases have cropped up in the last 30 years. Additionally, we rely increasingly upon psychotic and mood-altering drugs and call it good health. We move ahead with new forms of gene therapy, while suppressing a wary concern about the unintended consequences of genetic tampering. We compound these problems with our lifestyle corruptions: we grow fatter; we exercise less. And contemporary stress and anxiety have led to higher rates of depression and suicide.[3]

Social Problems

We exist in a truly liberated age. We enjoy freedom of the press (and more tabloid sensationalism than we could ever digest), freedom of religion (and the resulting intolerance of those who disagree with us), freedom of expression (and the glories of unbridled sexual permissiveness), freedom of job opportunities (and the right to declare bankruptcy at the drop of a stock ticker), freedom of artistic creation (and expanding opportunities for all categories of pornography), and freedom from family responsibilities—in a country where roughly half of all marriages end in divorce.[4] Starting in the 1970s, quality-of-life indexes such as the Fordham University Index of Social Health and the Genuine Progress Indicator out of San Francisco show a steady decline in measurements such as child poverty, health care coverage, and teenage homicide.[5]

In 1980, CEOs of America's largest corporations earned 45 times as much as their production and nonsupervisory workers. Twenty years later the CEOs were making 460 times as much as their production and non-supervisory workers.[6] About 35 million Americans live below the poverty line. In terms of living standards, community cohesiveness, educational opportunities, and medical services, these inequities lead to considerable weakening of our social fabric. And worldwide, billions of inhabitants of underdeveloped countries exist in squalor and destitution.

The national debt is now close to $7 trillion. That's more than $125,000 dollars for every family of five in the United States. Whenever politicians talk about an eventual debt-free America, they are talking only of the *external debt*—the amount owed to institutions, individuals, and foreign countries that have purchased Treasury securities. In order to pay down this external debt, Washington is borrowing heavily from the temporary surpluses of Social Security and other trust funds—which will eventually have to be paid back by raising taxes, by cutting back on other federal programs, or by continuing to raise the national debt. In addition, our projected fiscal deficit for the next decade is another $7 trillion.[7]

Racial discrepancies are evident in virtually every economic or social indicator you look at. Blacks comprise about 13 percent of the total U.S. population; yet they make up 26 percent of all persons living below the poverty line. Between 1990 and 2000, housing segregation increased in almost every large suburban area in the country. Expand this inventory of inequities to include Hispanics, Native-American Indians, Asians, Middle-easterners, and other ethnic identities, and we can see how far we are from achieving racial justice.

Violent crime increased 80 percent from 1973 to 1992. Crime levels then declined slightly over the next decade—but at what cost? Including those who are on probation or parole, we have 6.6 million convicted criminals under penal supervision—that's about one out of every 32 adults in the country. In 1990, for every 100,000 Americans there were 292 sentenced inmates in state and federal prisons; in ten years this number had risen to 465 per 100,000—an increase of over 59 percent. The United States now has a higher percentage of its citizens behind bars than any other country in the world. In any case, we should note that in the first years of the new millennium the number of homicides and other violent crimes started creeping up again.

We are processing more and more students through our schooling systems, but the resulting end product is increasingly disappointing. In his eye-opening 1984 *Megatrends*, John Naisbitt stated, "The generation graduating from high school today is the first generation in American history to graduate less skilled than its parents."[8] That is quite a damning indictment. And the situation has only gotten worse in the ensuing two decades. SAT scores have dropped over ten percent in the past 35 years.[9] The functional illiteracy rate in the United States is about 30 to 35 percent.[10] A 1999 study by the National Assessment Governing Board concluded that only one-fourth of America's school children (in fourth, eighth, and twelfth grades) have mastered the knowledge and skills to write proficiently. And across the country, colleges and universities have had to institute "writing proficiency exams" to ensure that their graduates could write at least three or four coherent paragraphs in a row.

Democratic Reversals

We accept that government is controlled by lobbyists, corporate giants, trade unions, and other special interests (to be continued in Chapter 18). Less than 50 percent of the U.S. electorate votes in major elections. And when we turn to global hopes for the spread of democracy, we must contend with the fact that about one-third of the world's population identifies primarily with some tribal or native nation—rather than with political nation-states. Following the demise of overt colonialism, and with the disintegration of the global communist monolith, we witness country after country unable to cope with the corruption and chaos of sudden freedom.

One of the ironies of the Progress Paradox is that as we Americans succeed materialistically and technologically, we generate more and more tension and bitterness among other nations. Our successes trigger the revulsion of those who are not succeeding. One of the deepest challenges we face is to reconcile modern Western values with the premodern religious and ethnic tribalism that dominates much of the globe. How are we to coexist rationally with cultures that do not want to coexist rationally?

It is as if we in America are riding into the twenty-first century in a giant upscale, armored motor home. We are safely ensconced in our luxury Winnebago, self-contained, with all of the necessities and conveniences we could ask for—refrigeration and air conditioning, modern plumbing, comfortable living and sleeping quarters, and all the electronic entertainments we can imagine. We are completely isolated and protected from the devastation and poverty outside our bubbled existence. We comfortably navigate our well-appointed mobile mansion through the deserts created by deforestation, past the remnants of broken cultures, around the potholes of poverty, through the shantytowns and destitution of the Third World. We are thoroughly shielded in our opulent self-contained environment, oblivious to the rest of the planet. We try not to worry about the fact that eventually we will have to stop and negotiate with the natives when we need to refuel; we will have to find potable water from time to time; we must stock up on groceries now and then; we must occasionally pull off the road and dump the sewage from our holding tanks. All of these necessities demand contact with the rest of the world. And, as armored and protected as we feel, some terrorist will find a way to shoot out our tires.

In summarizing the Progress Paradox, we could look also at political malfeasance, corporate corruption, drug abuse, increasing materialism, decreasing church attendance, violations of privacy, violence in the media, and many other issues—which we shall do throughout the book. The point in this quick review is that, despite our material wealth and comfortable surroundings, the fabric of Western culture is indeed unraveling. We are violating our intellectual covenant and as a result we are losing our sense of direction, our confidence that we know what we are doing.

A FAILURE OF OPTIMISM AND CONFIDENCE

At the beginning of the twentieth century, there existed an undeniable sense of progress and optimism. America was on the brink of a brand-new cultural and technological renaissance. Science and industrialization promised a new era. We had reached the west coast, conquering both the wilderness and the Native-Americans. We could manipulate and control the natural environment to suit our expansionist desires. A technological utopia beckoned—fueled by electricity, the automobile and airplane, indoor plumbing and sewers, the telephone and wireless telegraphy, radio and moving pictures.

At the beginning of the twenty-first century, however, we aren't quite so sure where we're headed. We question our environmental shortcomings, our global involvements, our political wanderings, our electronic diversions, our expansionist policies. Instead of moving straight ahead in a clear linear direction, we find ourselves stumbling around in a web of uncertainties. We have lost faith both in our leaders and in our establishment organizations. Popular polls show that from the 1960s on, the public says each year that it has less faith in both government and corporate institutions.[11]

With the attacks on the World Trade Center and the Pentagon, our loss of confidence and optimism was shattered further. As the twin towers came down, so too did our vision of immortality and our sense of innocence. Simultaneous with the overt terrorist attack came the Enron implosion. Our confidence in our institutions of commerce was demolished. Our twin towers of capitalistic hubris—exploitation and expansion—were knocked to the ground. What does this say for the rationality of the free marketplace? The responsibility of corporate America? Enron and WorldCom were not anomalies; their corporate mentality represented the norm. Numerous other companies demonstrated the same corporate sleight-of-hand deception.

If we can't trust our corporate boards of directors and top executives, in whom can we then place confidence? Perhaps the clergy? But then come the public revelations of priestly pedophilia and the widespread cover-up by the Catholic hierarchy. Maybe we should place our trust in our historians and scholars—if it weren't for the accusations of plagiarism and fabrication leveled at a half-dozen of our most prominent writers.[12] Neither our politicians, business executives, religious leaders, stock brokers, media pundits, business attorneys, auditors, social workers, nor our academicians, it seems, can be counted on to restore confidence in the modern dream. Even Martha Stewart failed us.

Loss of Control

Our greatest anxiety, perhaps, is loss of control. We don't understand what's happening with our schools today. The stock market is beyond comprehension. Government has gotten too big—and it doesn't know what it's doing anyway. All of our automated systems run our lives without our understanding what's going on. We simply don't have the certainty, the security, that we can run our own lives anymore. And it leaves us with a disquieting sense of enfeeblement.

In a preliterate tribal culture, people accepted that they were not in charge of their own affairs. Their lives were dictated by the gods, by chiefs and priests. With the ascendance of a monotheistic culture, people's destinies were still determined by God, by their kings and popes. Then for a few giddy centuries—starting with the Reformation and the Enlightenment—people were wrapped up in the modern idea that they were in charge of their own lives; they could govern their affairs and direct their destinies. But in the postmodern late twentieth century we began to sense that we once again were not in control of our lives. This time it is not the gods and dictators that have taken charge of our lives; but it is the faceless bureaucracies and the encroaching technologies.

We are discarding the certainty of an intellectually oriented modernity and are rushing into an ill-defined, post-intellectual, chaotic postmodern reality. In *The Twilight of American Culture,* Morris Berman sums up our state: "As the twenty-first century dawns, American culture is, quite simply, in a mess."[13] After a lengthy analysis, he concludes,

American civilization is in its twilight phase, rapidly approaching a point of social and cultural bankruptcy. The gap between rich and poor has never been greater; our long-term ability to pay for basic social programs is increasingly in question; the level of ignorance and functional illiteracy in this country is so low as to render us something of an international joke; and the takeover of our spiritual life by McWorld—corporate/consumer values—is nearly complete.[14]

Loss of a Cultural Narrative

Ever since our earliest Paleolithic ancestors sat around the evening campfire pondering the forces of nature and questions of mortality, we human beings have felt the need for some sort of explanation of who we are, how we originated, how our culture is structured, what rules we follow, what determines our values system. We crave a mythology, a cultural history, a story, a vision, a narrative. In *Consilience,* E. O. Wilson reminds us that people "yearn to have a purpose larger than themselves. We are obliged by the deepest drives of the human spirit to make ourselves more than animated dust, and we must have a story to tell about where we came from, and why we are here."[15]

Such a narrative usually is based on some spiritual or religious foundation—the story of the creation, the roles played by the gods, the penalties to be rendered by offended spirits. But it also may be based upon secular cultural history—faith in scientific rationalism, racial superiority, manifest destiny, unrestrained capitalism, or any other belief system that gives purpose to our cultural structure. A cultural narrative does not need to be factually true in a scientific and anthropological sense. It merely has to provide a set of guidelines, an explanation, a framework that its people accept as their underlying structure. The narrative must give its citizens a sense of meaning. But today we lack a sense of structure—an explanation of what our cultural institutions are all about and how they relate to each other. As a people, we are not sure what to expect of our houses of worship, our halls of learning, our temples of government, our machinery of commerce.

Western civilization as a whole no longer has a unifying explanation of who we are and where we are headed. In our pluralistic culture, that is to be expected. We have no shared mythic heritage, no universal set of mores or values. We cling to vestigial myths of capitalism, democracy, materialism, or splintered religiosity as a guiding principle. But we sense that each of these narratives fails to fully satisfy us as a people. It is this lack of a cultural narrative that—to a great extent—defines our current societal malaise, that explains our loss of cohesion and coherence.

IN TERMS OF CULTURAL GOALS, we have replaced morality with materialism; we confuse liberty with license; and we have rejected responsibility in favor of opportunism. The promise of democracy is riddled with hypocrisy. Columnist Hal Crowther gives us a striking simile: "The death of a culture is a lot like the death of a tree. There's no heart-stopping moment when the line on the monitor goes flat. Each season there are more dead limbs. The foliage grows mangy, the bark turns dry and scaly, creatures burrow deep inside and eat away at the heart. The tree's profile changes, its roots contract. And then one spring there are no new leaves."[16]

Meanwhile, our luxury Winnebago rolls on; we are insulated from most of the rest of the planet's problems, the market appears sound, the police are out in force, and the Internet beckons. Thus, unless you feel vaguely ill at ease with the direction of our materialistic culture, our faith in technological panaceas, the nature of your offsprings' pastimes, or the state of our democracy, you might as well close this book, check your stock portfolio, set your security alarms, and enjoy a good night's sleep.

CHAPTER 2

Modernism: Defining the Intellectual Roots

The ideals upon which Western Civilization was established were fairly well defined about three or four hundred years ago—what we refer to as the *modern* period of human development. Most scholars and historians designate this modern era, or age of *modernity,* as starting roughly in the early seventeenth century. The intellectual ideals we began to assemble then are the criteria by which we can evaluate our current cultural disarray. To understand what went wrong, we need to look at the intellectual building blocks of our modern Western culture.

VOICES OF REASON AND ENLIGHTENMENT

The earliest human societies were authoritarian. The assumption was that individuals, if left to their own instincts and animalistic drives, would not have the intelligence and self-control to run their own affairs. Ordinary men and women must be governed by authorities who know what is best for them: tribal chiefs, religious priests, military leaders, emperors, and potentates. These authoritarian sovereigns and dictators ruled over their subjects with little or no input from the masses. Then the early Greeks devised their initial version of democracy (literally "popular government") which amounted to decision-making by a small handful of citizens—probably 20,000 or so out of a population of 350,000 in Athens. This was government by an elite class that excluded women, slaves, farmers, and other toilers. Rome followed with a system of consuls elected by a senate that represented more-or-less popular opinion. After that, with competing popes and kings fighting for dominance throughout the Middle Ages, there was very little concept of popular rule for the next few centuries.

Renaissance, Reformation, and Reason

Gutenberg gave us the printing press around 1456, which eventually led both to the creation of the modern nation-state and, as we shall see, to the concept of individualism. Columbus confirmed that there were lands waiting to be exploited beyond the western horizon—promoting mercantilism and the promise of growth and development. Some Renaissance minds stretched the medieval boundaries in art, literature, and religion without breaking entirely with tradition or the church—Leonardo da Vinci and Desiderius Erasmus, for example. Others challenged the church and establishment dogma: Nicolaus Copernicus who dared to claim that the Earth was not the center of the universe; and Martin Luther who argued against the more outrageous practices of the church and thereby inadvertently launched the Reformation. These were among the scholars and thinkers who paved the way for the Age of Reason.

Libertarian thinkers—countering the centuries-old domination of the authoritarians—slowly began to piece together a philosophy which argued that human beings were reasonable enough and responsible enough to govern themselves. In the long story of *Homo sapiens*, this was perhaps the most significant paradigm shift ever. This piecemeal revolution marked the transition from a premodern social structure to modern societies. The reverberations of the clash between authoritarianism and libertarianism echo today throughout every corner of the globe— dictatorships versus democracies, socialism versus capitalism, the pope versus humanists. And the most devastating conflict today—religious fundamentalism and terrorism versus Western civilization.

Science and Mathematics

The Age of Reason was nowhere better illustrated than in the advancement of science—with its resulting challenge to established authority. One of the earliest thinkers to foster scientific methodology was Francis Bacon who, in his *Meditationes Sacrae* (1597), came up with his famous slogan, "Knowledge is power." He was one of the first to actively promote scientific investigation, he defined modern inductive reasoning, and he declared that the future of mankind lay in science and technology. Bacon drew up the outline; René Descartes filled it in with his *Discourse on Method* (1637) and his *Meditations* (1641). He defined philosophical rationalism, refined the scientific method, created analytic geometry, and gave us modern deductive reasoning. In 1632 Galileo published his *Dialogue Concerning the Two Chief World Systems* (contrasting Ptolemaic and Copernican astronomy). He came to represent those who would choose scientific reason over traditional authority, and his imprisonment by the Inquisition only served to secure his position as a crusader for freedom of inquiry.

Isaac Newton represented the pinnacle of Enlightenment scientific thinking. In 1687 he published his *Philosophiae naturalis principia mathematica* ("Mathematical Principles of Natural Philosophy"), combining elements of gravity, laws of motion, calculus, and optics. It was an intellectual landmark that dominated scientific thinking for more than two hundred years. Newton's genius was testimony to the Enlightenment faith in the mind of *Homo sapiens*. And his *Principia* demonstrated that, when great minds were allowed to question and reason freely, truth would ultimately be found.

Literature and Freedom of Speech

In the world of arts and letters, inspired writers and philosophers helped define the emerging era of rationalism and libertarianism. John Milton was a vigorous voice in opposition to the established church and early defender of free speech. His *Areopagitica* (1644) was a rousing treatise against censorship, arguing that Truth "needs no policies, nor stratagems, nor licensings to make her victorious."[1] This credo formed the cornerstone for Enlightenment-libertarianism thinking.

In France, a diverse group of thinkers comprised the *philosophes*. Their works promoted critical reason and tolerance; they challenged traditional authority; and they displayed confidence that progress would prevail. Prominent among them was Voltaire who typified the intellectual mind— curious about all things. He was a poet, essayist, playwright, historian, philosopher, and social reformer. With his sense of irony, he fought for class justice, warned against the dangers of arbitrary power, condemned the greed of the privileged classes, analyzed the nature of evil, and campaigned against the intolerance of religious fanaticism.

One of the primary components of intellectualism (as we shall define it in Chapter 3) is the acquisition of knowledge. To this end, two philosophes, Denis Diderot and Jean Le Rond d'Alembert, compiled their awe-inspiring *Encyclopædie*, published during the years from 1751 to 1772, to give us the first comprehensive modern encyclopedia. More than just a reference work, however, the *Encyclopædie* exemplified Diderot's dedication to the power of reason and his distrust of unquestioned authority.

Social and Political Thought

Perhaps the most important legacy of the Enlightenment was the social, political, and economic heritage that emerged. Although Thomas Hobbes supported the view that a strong central government was necessary to protect mankind from anarchy and self-destruction (his *Leviathan* in 1651 is essentially a justification of an absolute monarchy), the key idea in Hobbes' construct was that such a system would be supported by *individual rational choice*. The legitimacy of any government could be maintained only with the consent of the governed.

Later Enlightenment writers argued for more of a libertarian state. One of the most important of these was John Locke. In his *Second Treatise on Civil Government* (1690), three doctrines stand out. First, human beings are essentially rational and just. Contrary to authoritarian dogma, citizens are capable of self-government. Second, Locke advanced the idea of basic natural rights. Men and women are endowed with certain unalienable rights—including life, freedom, the right to hold property, and the right to express themselves uncensored. This principle found its way into both the American *Declaration of Independence* and the French *Declaration of the Rights of Man and of the Citizen*. Third, government exists only with the permission of the people who created and maintain it. People come together freely to establish a state because there are certain works that can only be achieved by collective action—maintaining a militia, building a highway system, or launching a mosquito-abatement program. It follows that the government has no right to impose any obligations on the people other than what the people ask the state to do. These anti-authoritarian tenets are the foundations of every democratic system of government.

Perhaps the most perplexing of all Enlightenment writers was Jean Jacques Rousseau. A contemporary of Voltaire and Diderot, he was considered one of the brightest of the *philosophes* in his early years—swept up in the euphoria of Enlightenment thinking. In the mid-eighteenth century, however, he began attacking civilization as a corrupting influence. He argued that man in a natural (ungoverned) state was basically a good being; he cared about his fellow men and women and was capable of self-sacrifice. However, when placed in a civil state, men become more competitive and less trusting; society alienates men from their natural state and from each other. Rousseau subsequently quarreled with Diderot and the *philosophes* and distanced himself from the mainstream Enlightenment thinkers. Along with Hobbes and Locke and others of the period, Rousseau pondered the nature of the *social contract*, the essence of which is summed up by Jacques Barzun: "Man in Nature has every right that his individual power affords—no limits, no prohibitions. But this violent free-for-all proves inconvenient, so he enters into an agreement with his fellows to set up an authority that will restrain violence and settle disputes."[2] In *The Social Contract* (1762), Rousseau outlines plans for a state in which citizens must subvert their individual persona to become part of the "general will." All persons must submit to this communal essence. In other works Rousseau spells out specific steps the state must take in order to ensure that the individual will be conditioned to comply with the general will.

Adam Smith defined modern capitalism. His *An Inquiry into the Nature and Causes of the Wealth of Nations* (1776) is the classic source for all subsequent free-enterprise advocates. Allow every individual to compete freely to the best of his or her ability—without any government intervention. No wage and price controls, no tariffs, no subsidies, no antitrust interventions, and no bailouts. Get off Microsoft's back and let the laws of supply and demand do their thing. Society thrives when every individual works for his or her own enlightened long-term self-interest. This economic theory has become one of the cornerstones of libertarian thinking.

INTELLECTUAL LEGACIES OF THE ENLIGHTENMENT

We must be careful not to paint too homogeneous a picture of the Enlightenment thinkers. They were a diverse lot, reflecting a variety of national and cultural biases, writing at different times, and coming from several different perspectives. Nevertheless, there are certain universal themes and intellectual legacies we can find woven throughout the Enlightenment. These are the criteria against which we can evaluate our current culture.

Reason, Science, and Humanism

Following Bacon and Descartes, the process of scientific reasoning was established as a cornerstone of modern culture. Men and women no longer would have to depend on divine guidance, witchcraft, astrology, and Ouija boards. They could now determine their affairs rationally. This becomes the guiding principle for all decision-making and problem-solving. Scientific methodology dictated new standards for impartial research and objective experimentation. Bacon encouraged us to believe that we could use science to discover new directions for society; we could actually improve society by applying science. The age of technology was born—using science for the mastery of nature and the improvement of the human condition. We would turn the wild and inhospitable planet into a garden of bounty for human benefit.

Humanism does away with supernaturalism and proclaims the essential worth and dignity of the human being on its own terms; men and women have the capacity to achieve self-realization through the use of reason and scientific methodology. Humans can determine their own fate without recourse to an omnipotent God. Secular values and standards gradually replaced spiritual guidelines and dictates. Kurt Vonnegut gives us a succinct summary: "I am a humanist, which means, in part, that I have tried to behave decently without any expectation of rewards or punishment after I am dead."[3] Thus we moved from a God-centered culture to a human-centered culture.

Individualism, Personal Responsibility, and Privacy

In the premodern world, your identity was defined essentially as a member of a particular village or tribe. You were simply part of a larger organic whole. No man or woman had any separate existence. With modern thinking came the modern *individual*. The printing press made it feasible for individual scholars and researchers to have access to personal copies of great works of history and literature. Persons could read and contemplate and evaluate and think independently. Prior to the Enlightenment, ordinary citizens and peasants didn't have much occasion to worry about self-esteem or individual recognition. Personal validation was a non-issue.

The need for individual responsibility was significantly heightened as a result of Enlightenment thinking. If men and women were going to claim more freedoms for themselves, they would have to accept more responsibility for their actions. In premodern cultures, individuals had relatively little control over their lives. Their destinies were determined by the gods and the tribal medicine men, by the monarchs and the pope. If the church or the state has complete control over your life, you have little responsibility but to obey the dictates of those in charge. However, once the people adopt a humanistic code that says they have free will and they are capable of making their own decisions and running their own affairs, they also have to accept responsibility for the consequences of those decisions.

In premodern tribal cultures there is no concept of privacy. There is no individual identity to be kept apart from others. There are no secrets, nothing to hide from anyone else. Everyone stands naked in front of the tribe. As individualism crept into our being, however, there came also a sense that we needed to keep certain aspects of our selves private. Architecture began to give us rooms where we could sit alone, read a book in isolation, define our own persons. As we learned to think independently, we also learned to value our physical independence and privacy.

Capitalism, Progress, and Geographic Exploration

The emergence of free enterprise is one of the key features of Western culture. Modern capitalism—with its contractual arrangements, banking procedures, and marketing structures—was established as an intellectual enterprise. The rise of a truly fluid middle class signaled the creation of a new social structure: independent manufacturers, wholesalers, bankers, insurers, managers, agents, and retailers. From this point on, economic structures and priorities dominated the structure of Western civilization.

Exploration gave us a new global perspective. Voyagers from Columbus and Magellan to Tasman and Cook probed every corner of the seven seas in search of raw materials and expanding markets. Whether the impetus for exploration was capitalist opportunism, missionary zeal, military conquest, colonization, or just intellectual curiosity, the result was the same— reinforced faith in the ability of the human animal to reach out, to expand, to develop and conquer new horizons.

With the modern age, the idea of *progress* was defined in a way that would have been utterly incomprehensible to our premodern ancestors. We could change. We could grow. We could expand and develop. We would find new lands to exploit, new industrial techniques, new markets for our increasingly modern products. The idea of progress became, in the words of Garrett Hardin, "the ruling paradigm of Western society."[4] This concept of continual growth and development dominated modern thinking, largely unchallenged, until the last half of the twentieth century.

Universal Education, Equality, and Civil Rights

If men and women were to be able to set up their own systems of self-government, they must be enlightened enough to engage in collective decision-making. All citizens must be knowledgeable in all arenas of civic affairs—economics, agriculture, jurisprudence, foreign affairs, scientific research, social policies, and industrial zoning. This demanded a system of universal schooling focused on the liberal arts—a commitment to public education that would encompass every child in the realm. Such a schooling system would stress analytic thinking and social criticism. Future citizens must be educated to think rationally and independently.

Another legacy of Enlightenment thinking was the concept of equality and human rights—a commitment to egalitarianism. This was imbedded in our Declaration of Independence: *all men are created equal.* This was one of the three rallying cries of the French revolution: *Liberté! Égalité! Fraternité!* All persons, regardless of station or rank, are to be accorded the same privileges under the law. After all, this is rational; this is the logical thing to do. The laws of justice, of trade, and of politics shall apply to all equally. With such equality, however, is again the notion of responsibility. All men and women shall maintain their claim to liberty and equality only by behaving in a responsible manner—treating all others with respect, providing for one's own sustenance, taking care of one's family, obeying all laws, working to promote the general welfare, and participating in the process of self-governance.

Democracy and the Nation-State

The invention of the printing press made it financially feasible to mass-produce books and other materials in the popular vernacular languages spoken by common people. No longer would great books be printed only in Latin, Hebrew, and Greek. Once printed materials were available in French, Italian, German, Spanish, and English, individuals began to identify more closely with those who shared the same language, culture, and provincial customs. The modern nation-states began to evolve. The map of Europe was to be changed forever.

The Enlightenment gave us the legacy of self-government. Men and women could determine their own political structures and run their own affairs without the guiding hand of God or Big Brother. As Francis Fukuyama writes, "Blind obedience to authority would be replaced by rational self-government."[5] Out of this intellectual ferment of the Enlightenment was created the United States of America. Our nation was founded by a cabal of intellectuals—a gang of idealistic visionaries who deemed that human beings were rational enough and responsible enough to govern themselves. They would engage in collective decision-making. They would promote the general welfare, ensure domestic tranquility, and provide for their common defense.

Fukuyama presents the argument rather convincingly in *The End of History* that—despite the short-term problems that beset us—the idea of liberal democracy has been generally accepted worldwide. He argues that,

a remarkable consensus concerning the legitimacy of liberal democracy as a system of government [has] emerged throughout the world over the past few years, as it conquered rival ideologies like hereditary monarchy, fascism, and most recently communism. More than that, however, . . . liberal democracy may constitute the "end point of mankind's ideological evolution" and the "final form of human government," and as such constituted the "end of history."[6]

This is a heady hypothesis: liberal democracy represents the final stage in human cultural evolution. There is no higher political or social system to which we can aspire. The ideals of Western democracy signify the End of History, the final chapter of *Homo sapiens'* journey. This is a strong endorsement of Enlightenment principles.

NOT ALL OF THESE INTELLECTUAL LEGACIES of the Enlightenment are congruent or totally complementary. They overlap, they tug at each other, they pull in conflicting directions. Equality and civil rights don't always mesh easily with individualism and economic competition. Skepticism and tolerance represent opposing mindsets. Capitalism and democracy are not the same thing; they overlap, they are somewhat compatible, but they spring from different urges. Capitalism promotes the accumulation of wealth; democracy is more likely to favor equitable distribution.

If there is one overriding principle bequeathed from the Enlightenment, it is this: *Men and women are to think for themselves.* We are free to come to our own conclusions, to make our own decisions. Then we are to be free to act upon those decisions. This means we must be *responsible* for our decisions. In effect, we are in charge of our own destiny. No agency is to tell us what we may or may not think individually. No state totalitarianism. No church dictatorship. No cultural dogma that denies individuals the right to reason independently. We are on our own. This thinking has far-reaching implications for women's rights, for tolerance of homosexual lifestyles, or for the right-to-choose in reproductive decisions. No wonder that religious zealots feel so threatened.

I cannot help but agree with E. O. Wilson that "the Enlightenment thinkers of the seventeenth and eighteenth centuries got it mostly right the first time."[7] And America's founders got it remarkably right—establishing a governmental framework that has stood up well over two centuries. Specifically, what we inherited from those bewigged Enlightenment thinkers were reason and rationality, personal responsibility, scientific methodology, humanism, and democracy. These were the objectives to be realized in the new American experiment. These are the criteria by which our modern Western civilization is to be evaluated.

When I argue that our intellectual culture is unraveling, that somehow we are losing what we once had, I am not arguing that all citizens ever achieved a true intellectual mindset. But, nevertheless, that was our *objective,* our goal, the standard by which we wished to be judged. We believed that humans were *capable* of building an intellectual society. But today that goal has been clouded as we strive to adapt to population pressures, technological and bureaucratic determinism, information hubris, capitalistic abuses, global entanglements, and the reality of finite physical limits. Our modern vision is obscured by postmodern realities.

CHAPTER 3

Intellectualism: Defining the Twin Pillars

Our legacies from the Enlightenment are based on the assumption that humans are capable of thinking—that they will analyze, evaluate, and make rational decisions. Men and women would be committed to acting with reason in all their personal, political, economic, and cultural affairs. Alexis de Tocqueville observed that in the young democracy, "Argument is substituted for faith, and calculation for the impulses of sentiment."[1] Although we still pay lip service to the intellectual principle that men and women are to think for themselves, we have—in our postmodern turmoil—evolved into a post-intellectual mindset.

FOUR COMPONENTS OF INTELLECTUALISM

In defining the cognitive aspects of *intellectualism*, there are four related components to be considered: a liberal-arts perspective, acquisition of knowledge, rational problem-solving or scientific thinking, and social criticism.[2] These are the four intellectual attributes that underlie Enlightenment thinking. These are the specific things I am talking about when I use the term *intellectualism*.

Liberal-Arts Perspective

Among other definitions, the Oxford English Dictionary interprets the adjective *Intellectual* as "Given to pursuits that exercise the intellect." Those pursuits consist of philosophy, history, science and mathematics, social sciences, literature and language, and the arts and humanities—in effect, all the disciplines one associates with Liberal Arts. These are the studies that an educated person must be comfortable with in order to remain *at liberty,* functioning as a free individual in a self-governing state. Citizens, if they are to participate in decision-making on all issues facing the nation, must be informed about all cultural matters—from economics and international relations to genetics research and space exploration. If the citizen cannot navigate the waters of these diverse subjects, then the political decisions must be turned over to an elite corps of informed specialists, bureaucrats, and technocrats.

This liberal-arts orientation requires the mindset of the generalist, rather than of the specialist or narrowly focused professional. One thinks of the "Renaissance man"—knowledgeable in all fields of human endeavor— Leonardo, Bacon, Voltaire, Rousseau, Franklin, and Jefferson. Indeed, America's founders formed their new republic on the premise that the citizen-participants would be persons of intellectual breadth. Citizens must be liberally educated, even before they acquire the specialized vocational skills needed to earn a living. The resourcefulness and self-discipline of a broad liberal-arts background would enable them to participate in the collective decision-making of the emerging republic.

Historically, the university has been at the center of the cultural tradition of liberal arts. In recent decades, however, the university has been pulled away from that center—to the left by its postmodern fixation on political correctness and to the right with an emphasis on federal and corporate fund-raising. Russell Jacoby points out that our educational systems must provide a certain insulation from business concerns and vocational training: "Thinking, reading, and art require a cultural space, a zone free from the angst of moneymaking and practicality. Without a certain repose or leisure, a liberal education shrivels."[3] The post-intellectual university has lost sight of its traditional liberal-arts orientation.

Acquisition of Knowledge

Another component of intellectualism is the acquisition of knowledge: "Placing a high value on or pursuing things of interest to the intellect, especially the higher or more abstract forms of knowledge."[4] The intellectual is one who wants to seek out information, to compare and contrast differing ideas, to satisfy one's curiosity, to revel in new experiences and novel situations, to learn for the sake of learning—as opposed to earning college units, improving one's marketable skills, or meeting some other externally imposed obligation. This intellectual curiosity is what leads one to take a guided nature walk, to read Churchill's *History of the English-Speaking Peoples,* to travel to exotic locales, to watch PBS or the Discovery channel, and to audit extension classes.

This acquisition of knowledge does not mean simply the accumulation of bits and pieces of unrelated items and memorization of trivia. Acquisition without coherence may make for neat parlor tricks—and a shot for an appearance on *Jeopardy*—but it does not necessarily guarantee an intellectual turn of mind. It is important to distinguish among four terms—*Data, Information, Knowledge,* and *Wisdom. Data* are the raw bits and pieces of reality, the isolated details and disembodied facts. Data consist of advertisments, news headlines, names, Post-it notes, telephone numbers, glimpses of billboards, fragments of conversations, almanac entries, weather reports, and the list of state capitals. We are exposed to thousands of pieces of disconnected data every day.

When data have been organized into a meaningful pattern, we have *Information.* We may define information as data that have been structured and categorized into some sort of systematized and accessible storehouse or library. Such repositories include not only books and libraries, but also computer disks, personal diaries, office filing systems, the kitchen recipe box, and so forth. Thus, the definition of a word may be a datum; once it is inserted into a dictionary it becomes information. The bits and pieces of digital code on your computer's hard drive are data; when made accessible by proper programming and a directory system, you have information.

The next step is the assembling of information into *Knowledge,* which may be defined as the internalization and comprehension of external information by the human brain. Information exists in storehouses; knowledge exists in one's head. The assembling of information into knowledge is the mark of a true intellectual.

Finally, we consider *Wisdom.* This is the discerning and judicious use of knowledge in critical thinking or decision-making. This is where we put knowledge to work—where we use the information we have access to, filter it through the knowledge we have accumulated, and make our decisions. In his electronic newsletter, David Bennahum reminds us of the dangers of confusing data-gathering and information-sharing with the processes of acquiring knowledge and demonstrating wisdom:

The proliferation of data is . . . a serious challenge, requiring new measures of human discipline and skepticism. We must not confuse the thrill of acquiring or distributing information quickly with the more daunting task of converting it into knowledge and wisdom. Regardless of how advanced our computers become, we should never use them as a substitute for our own basic cognitive skills of awareness, perception, reasoning, and judgment.[5]

This definition of wisdom—intelligent decision-making—gets us into the realm of analysis and reasoning.

Rational Problem-Solving and Scientific Methodology

A common dictionary definition of *intellectualism* is "The development and use of the ability to think, reason, and understand."[6] This is the capacity to think logically, to analyze, to figure things out rationally. This process shows up in many professions and disciplinary pursuits: science (scientific method, medical diagnosis); education (lesson plans, instructional design, programmed instruction); philosophy and literature (critical thinking, literary analysis, Reflective Thinking[7]); law (criminal investigations, judicial proceedings), politics (legislative debate, national diplomacy), and business (program-planning-budgeting systems, management-by-objectives, labor-management negotiations). What all these applications have in common is the orderly sequencing of logical steps in the thinking or decision-making process.

These models typically follow some variation of the following steps: (1) Define the problem. Document the extent of the difficulty. (2) Examine the background and history of the problem. How did we get where we are today? What are the causes of the current situation? What are the immediate effects, or the long-term ramifications, if nothing is done? (3) Clearly define what it is you want to accomplish. What do you want a solution to do? State your purpose or hypothesis. What are your objectives? What criteria do you want your solution to meet? Consider cost and time constraints. Consider also the negative criteria (What are the bad things that you want *not* to happen as a result of your solution?). (4) Consider all possible alternative answers. List all possible solutions. Brainstorm. Keep all options open at this point. (5) Assess the proposed courses of action. Measure each possible solution against each listed objective or criterion. Which solutions have the best chances of meeting your objectives? This step is the cost/benefit or cost/effectiveness analysis. (6) Choose a course of action. Select the best solution—or combination of solutions. Make a decision. I often use the terms *problem-solving* and *decision-making* interchangeably. The overall pattern I am describing here might be called a problem-solving pattern; but this specific step in the process is clearly the decision-making point. (7) Implement your solution. Carry out your decision. (8) Evaluate the success of the course of action. Ask simply, *Did the solution meet the objectives?* No rational problem-solving process is complete without evaluating whether or not your solution worked. Did you make the right decision? If not, go back to step one and repeat as necessary.[8]

For purposes of simplification, I've condensed this process down to a four-step model I call the *Analytic Thinking Pattern:* Problem definition, Objectives determination, Solutions, and Evaluation (see Figure 1).[9] Or as Abraham Lincoln so eloquently put it, "If we could first know *where* we are, and *whither* we are tending, we could then better judge *what* to do,

Figure 1
The Analytic Thinking Pattern

- PROBLEM
  - Definition
  - Background
  - Causes
  - Effects
- OBJECTIVES AND CRITERIA
- SOLUTIONS
  - Listing all possible solutions
  - Measuring each solution against each criterion
  - Selection of the best solution(s)
  - Implementation
- EVALUATION

and *how* to do it."[10] In Chapter 15, where we look at the failure of our cultural problem-solving efforts, we discuss this process in more detail.

The Western liberal thinker tries to maintain an open mind; nothing is known for sure until it has been thoroughly sorted out, scrutinized, argued about, and put on trial in the court of rational analysis. A reasoning person does not approach decision-making with a set of ready-made solutions. An intellectual culture is based on the probing, skeptical, questioning, analytic individual—not the self-confident ideologue who knows the answer before examining the issue. This is one of the primary sources of conflict between the Western mind and other cultures. The closed mind, the nonintellectual, knows all the answers before any discussion begins. The answers are handed down from some authority—the Book of Genesis, the Koran, the Communist Manifesto, *Mein Kampf*—or some other infallible source; and therefore no discussion is necessary; no debate is to be tolerated.

Among other things, the commitment to reason results in the ability to deal with abstractions. This is a key element in the modern worldview. In a premodern culture, we worked and traded with people we knew personally—our extended family, community members, and neighboring tribes. We signed no papers. We implicitly trusted those with whom we dealt. With modern, abstract contracts, we could now deal with people we do not know personally—tradesmen, bankers, lawyers, and bureaucrats. We could establish legalistic and contractual arrangements with these strangers. This is a rational thing to do. This would result in an orderly, logical societal structure.

As people began to think rationally and form independent judgments and opinions, true individualism emerged. Today, however, teenagers (and other adolescent minds) pierce their body parts and paint their hair vibrant hues in an attempt to be "individuals." In effect, they are demonstrating their conformity to a particular tribal lifestyle. To be an individual one must think originally and independently—not follow the fads and dictates set by others. One expresses individuality in the uniqueness of one's thoughts, not in the appearance of one's physical features. Others think they are achieving some degree of individualism by embracing the mysticism and murkiness of New Age gurus. They will no longer be a slave to cognitive methodologies that inhibit their free spirit. Morris Berman points to Deepak Chopra and his book *Escaping the Prison of the Intellect,* and observes that "Chopra seems to be addressing an audience that for the most part hasn't managed to find its way into the 'prison of the intellect' in the *first* place. It is one thing to see the limits of the Enlightenment tradition after you have studied it for a few decades. It's another to reject it before you have ever been exposed to it."[11] The true individual is one who has learned to *think* on his or her own, to research and analyze and evaluate—not merely to close one's eyes and wait for some bolt of inspiration to awaken the individual within.

Social Criticism

My definition of intellectualism has one final component—*social criticism.* The intellectual mind is always ready to question what has been assumed up to this point, always ready to challenge what the established authorities have decreed. The more liberally educated the citizenry, the less likely it is to follow the dictates of arbitrary authority. One goal of a liberal education is to teach people to think for themselves, to learn how to question the establishment constructively and responsibly.

The more we examine what we are doing, the more likely that we will find better ways of doing it. But therefore, as William Barrett declared, "Every thinker . . . puts some portion of the stable world in danger as soon as he begins to think."[12] This is one of the paradoxes of an intellectual society. The well-being of the society is dependent upon an intellectual segment of the citizenry constantly questioning the leadership. One must have not only the right but also the appetite for getting on one's soapbox and arguing with the authorities. This is a rational and responsible practice—asking, *Where are we headed? Why are we doing it this way? What if we tried something else?* To question the establishment is not to say that the establishment is always wrong. To challenge authority is not to promote anarchy. It is just to say, *Let's examine what we are doing.*

Societies based on nonintellectual foundations—monarchies, theistic autocracies, military dictatorships—cannot tolerate this kind of open criticism. In totalitarian regimes, intellectual inquiry is not to be allowed: *Don't rock the boat!* In a participatory democracy composed of freethinking individuals, the emphasis is on critical examination of what the government is doing: *Let's find a way to build a better boat!*

John Stuart Mill underscored the value of social criticism also in the sharpening and improvement of the individual mind: "He who does anything because it is the custom makes no choice. He gains no practice either in discerning or in desiring what is best. The mental and moral, like the muscular powers, are improved only by being used."[13] *Use your intellectual prowess to question authority or your mind atrophies.*

TWIN PILLARS OF INTELLECTUALISM: REASON AND RESPONSIBILITY

The four factors outlined above (liberal-arts orientation, acquisition of knowledge, rational problem-solving, and social criticism) all have to do with logical qualities of the mind—*cognitive* skills. They form the essence of reason. But the intellectual mindset has one other component that must be emphasized: the responsibility to *act* with reason—the will, the commitment, to behave in a reasonable manner. One must have the passion to behave dispassionately. This is the *affective* component of intellectualism. One may be able to think logically, to follow a problem-solving model, to conduct a scientific experiment—but if one does not *wish* to act with reason, then that person is not behaving in an intellectually responsible manner. One must have not only the ability to think, but also the commitment to think. These then are our two pillars of intellectualism—*reason* (the ability to act rationally) and *responsibility* (the will to act rationally). These are the two elements that define the intellectual culture.

Responsibility encompasses two factors. First, you must consider the welfare of all your fellow beings, the obligation you have to all humanity—not just to your extended family and tribe members. Second, responsibility includes the long-term commitment you have to future generations; you cannot plan only for short-term profits.

This affective component of intellectualism is crucial because engineering prowess by itself does not guarantee responsible behavior. To exploit workers and consumers in the name of unfettered capitalism might be a rational way to make a profit—but is it responsible? (Even slavery can be justified on a cost/benefit basis). To dig up and squander the earth's resources might be economically defended on rational grounds (in the short run)—but is it environmentally responsible? We may employ high-tech scientific methodology to eke out more agricultural product from a given patch of depleted topsoil—but is that the most responsible way to approach problems of overpopulation and famine? We can use computer-based control and feedback systems to squeeze more vehicles onto a congested stretch of freeway—but is that the most responsible way to handle urban congestion?

Any social contract that asks me to act with reason has to require that others will also act with reason. Thus, Hobbes, Locke, Voltaire, Rousseau, and their peers recognized that it is in our enlightened self-interest to live responsibly—as long as all of mankind is rational enough to do so also. *I'll respect your civil rights—that's a reasonable thing to do—but I must know that you will also respect my civil rights.* Otherwise the whole cultural fabric unravels. Similarly, we give a humanistic twist to the Golden Rule: *I will do unto others as I would have them do unto me because I make the assumption that they will treat me in a like manner.* The libertarian idealism of Enlightenment philosophers is based on the assumption that human beings will decide that they *wish* to act with reason. *I will share an intellectual-democratic society with you only if you agree to follow the intellectually responsible rules.* It is a lack of intellectual responsibility that ails much of our contemporary culture. Columnist Hal Crowther comments, "Libertarianism is politics for responsible adults, [not] for a population of petulant adolescents."[14]

FREEDOM AND RESPONSIBILITY go hand in hand. The goal of an intellectual culture is personal independence—the freedom to be oneself, to develop individually, to enjoy the liberties spelled out in our Bill of Rights. But this freedom can be maintained only by carrying out personal decision-making in a responsible manner. In order to maintain freedom, the intellectual citizen must temper scientific methodology (reason) with restraint (responsibility). You are free to make choices only so long as your choices, your decisions, are responsible. As youngsters, we earned the freedom to cross the street to play with a friend only after we demonstrated that we could make responsible decisions regarding traffic dangers. As teenagers, we earned the right to borrow the family car only after we proved that we were mature enough to handle the vehicle responsibly.

Freedom basically means the right to make decisions—and to be able to act upon those decisions. Whether you are concerned with freedom of the press, freedom of religion, freedom of speech, freedom of assembly, economic freedom, or any other form of personal liberty, it all comes down to this: demonstrate sufficient reason and responsibility in making your personal decisions and you will be able to hold on to your freedoms. Make decisions irresponsibly and your freedoms will be taken away.

Self-restraint is crucial in any kind of civilized culture. Either we must exercise a great deal of personal restraint or restraint will be administered externally—by the state or church. Edmund Burke wrote over two hundred years ago, "Men are qualified for civil liberty in exact proportion to their disposition to put moral chains upon their own appetites. Society cannot exist unless a controlling power on will and appetite be placed somewhere, and the less of it there is within, the more there must be without. It is ordained in the eternal constitution of things, that men of intemperate minds cannot be free."[15] It's that simple. Exercise self-restraint and act with responsibility, or lose your freedoms.

Thus we have the twin pillars of intellectualism—reason and responsibility. We must demonstrate that we have the capacity to think clearly, to make rational decisions. And we must demonstrate that we have the responsibility to act with reason; we must decide to be reasonable. If we fail to maintain these two pillars of intellectualism, we degenerate further into a post-intellectual state.

CHAPTER 4

Exploring Postmodernism

Despite the vague and inaccessible jargon coined by its interpreters and critics, the concept of postmodernism must be tackled if we are to understand our post-intellectual culture. Neil Postman helps to define the idea:

> To begin with, the point of view commonly referred to as "postmodern" covers a vast terrain of cultural expression including architecture, art, film, dance, and music, as well as language. In the broadest sense, it argues that at some point in recent history (it is not clear exactly when) there occurred a striking and irreversible change in the way artists, philosophers, social critics, and even scientists thought about the world. And it is this change that takes the name of postmodernism . . . because it calls into question some of the more significant "modern" assumptions about the world and how we may codify it—in other words, assumptions and ideas inherited from the Enlightenment.[1]

Slogging through the pretentious pedagogy and abstruse obfuscation (postmodernists love terms like those), what it comes down to is this: postmodernists proclaim that we have outlived the Enlightenment ideals of modernity—scientific empiricism, capitalistic growth, individualism, progress, conclusive truth, and participatory democracy. Today we have evolved into a *post*-modern period of cultural chaos and confusion. The bottom line: postmodernism is the refutation of Enlightenment reason and structure.

POSTMODERNISM IN SEVERAL FIELDS

Writing in 1958, prior to the debut of the term *postmodernism* on the world's cultural stage, William Barrett observed that across the domains of science, literature, art, and philosophy, there are major transitions "all of which evince a sense of crisis, breakdown, loss of absolutes and foundations, and dissatisfaction with rationalism."[2] Although just about everybody who discusses postmodernism is describing a different kind of academic animal, there are several consistent themes that show up in these diverse fields: a sense of the limitations of reason, the lack of cohesion and structure, the absence of absolute truth and certainty, and the failure of material progress to satisfy our deepest spiritual needs.

Postmodernism in Science

The modern concepts of Newtonian science—neat and orderly, mechanistically rational—began to fall apart in the nineteenth century. First came the second law of thermodynamics, stating that the energy of the universe is constantly moving from a useful to a useless state. This became known as the Law of Entropy: the cosmic system is running down—gradually, but irreversibly, deteriorating. This may be somewhat of a simplification, but it serves to illustrate what was happening to the perception of the certainty of Newton's modern universe.

Biology was dealt a similar blow when Charles Darwin came along. Up to the publication of Darwin's theories, an uneasy truce existed between scientists and theologians. The concept of divine creation of individual species had been tacitly embraced by most scholars—as an attempt to meld modern scientific thinking with premodern religious precepts. However, Darwin introduced a disturbing measure of uncertainty into a world that had previously been conceived as a comprehensible and uncontested God-given creation.

Like many other pioneers and scientists, Sigmund Freud did not set out to overturn modern science or establish a postmodern philosophy. He was simply pursuing the advance of knowledge in the best intellectual tradition. But his observations that humans were governed by irrational drives and sexual lusts ran counter to the high hopes that Locke and others had held out for the future of the reasoning human animal. Maybe we weren't cut out for rational self-government after all.

In the world of physics, Albert Einstein showed us that no longer are things as they seem. Time became relative. Space bends. Quantum Mechanics followed in the mid-twenties, and in 1927 Werner Heisenberg coined the Uncertainty Principle. By 1931 Kurt Gödel had postulated his "incompleteness theorems" which undermined the stability of rational mathematics. Then his Undecidability Theorem led to Chaos Theory—a butterfly beating its wings over Tokyo would affect weather patterns in London. By the end of the twentieth century, new cosmological observations and theories were revising our view of reality almost on a monthly basis. The modern, coherent clockwork universe recedes further and further from our grasp.

In the latter half of the century we became embroiled in debates about ecology and the increasingly interdependent nature of all our natural systems; the more we learn about our intertwined ecosystem, the more difficult it becomes to grasp the whole. And now we toss into the postmodern mix the uncertainties and debates about genetic manipulation. The picture gets messier and messier. Nothing is as evident and assured as it was when clearly explained by Newton. The certainty of modern science has given way to postmodern turmoil and uncertainty.[3] Philosopher Dik Van Iten sums up the feelings of many:

Rather than bringing us closer to the Truth, this science seems bent on creating its own world, leaving the rest of us to work things out on our own. What does one do when condemned to be ignorant, to live in darkness? I'm inclined to believe that *post-intellectualism* is what one gets when the notion strikes home that not only is the universe—including us—beyond our ken, but we must also find our own way to keep going; we must be self-justifying in a world that some say couldn't care less.[4]

Postmodernism in Literature

The Swiss linguist Ferdinand de Saussure pioneered the study of *structuralism* in the 1920s. To the extent that it focused on functional arrangements of language systems—the structural relationships among the parts and wholes of languages—it could be thought of as a *modern* concept. Modernity, after all, is concerned with the practical, the rational, the structural. The American scientist and theologian Charles Peirce had introduced the term *semeosis* (sign activity) in the late nineteenth century and, along with Saussure, may be considered the cofounder of modern semiotics.

Then there came *post*-structuralism—and the dawning of literary postmodernism. While structuralism seeks to define the underlying systematic structure of meaning or identity, post-structuralism questions whether it is possible to find coherent structure. Underlying poststructuralism is the idea that reality cannot be expressed directly. We deal with it only through a system of codes—language, science, mathematics, art—with their signs and symbols. And these codes or symbols easily can mislead us—intentionally or unintentionally. Postman reminds us that "The codes themselves have a shape, a history, and a bias, all of which interpose themselves between what we see there and what is there to be seen."[5]

Jacques Derrida introduced the term *deconstruction* in the late 1960s. Often derisively described as the literary equivalent of nihilism, the idea of deconstruction is essentially that, in the words of Duke University English professor Wallace Jackson, "we can never know the author's intent and he can never make it fully apparent either to himself or to us."[6] Every text is meaningless until the reader injects his or her own meaning into it. Literary critics deconstruct a text by exposing the linguistic and semiotic devices imbedded within it. Such analysis allows the reader/critic to explain and discount the prevailing cultural biases of the author. Thus, the classic literary canon of Western literature can be dispensed with because these Great Books of the Western World are little more than an affirmation of the cultural prejudices of a Eurocentric worldview, dominated by dead white men. It is the reader, not the author, who creates meaning in a text. The eminent scientist and cultural observer Edward O. Wilson summarizes the movement:

Truth is relative and personal. Each person creates his own inner world by acceptance or rejection of endlessly shifting linguistic signs. There is no privileged point, no lodestar, to guide literary intelligence. And given that science is just another way of looking at the world, there is no scientifically constructible map of human nature from which the deep meaning of texts can be drawn. There is only unlimited opportunity for the reader to invent interpretations and commentaries out of the world he himself constructs.[7]

In literary analysis, there are numerous other schools or *isms* that interpret texts from their particular postmodern viewpoint. Feminist literary criticism, for example, points to the domineering role played by men in decision-making positions in the media, to the exploitation of women as sex objects, and to the stereotyping and subjugation of women in most dramatic works. Feminist critics argue that the essential virtues promoted by modern Western culture—scientific thinking, progress, exploration, economic competition, technology, and industrialization—all have an inherent masculine bias. Thus, modernity itself is sexist and prejudiced against women.

Marxist critical theory maintains that those in control of a nation's media and entertainment infrastructure—the capitalists and bourgeoisie producers—utilize the media channels to promote a subservient consumer culture. Although Marxist political theory has been convincingly discredited, the Marxist critique of capitalism as a means of domination remains quite popular. Indeed, much of the anti-capitalist and anti-materialist momentum from the 1960s to today is rooted in postmodern criticism based on Marxist foundations.

Postmodernism in Art and Architecture

Modernity in art encompasses several *isms*—realism, impressionism, cubism, and expressionism. What defines all these styles as modern is that they retain some structure, they are formal in their approach, and they reflect the creativity of individual artists. Cubism, for example, is modern not because it is something new and unusual, but it is modern in the classical sense because it is rational and carefully constructed. Postmodern art, on the other hand, is often deliberately without structure or meaning—it celebrates the paste-up and the pastiche, the collage and the montage. It copies older works, borrows themes, and rearranges classical motifs. Postmodern art regularly reflects an abandonment of individual creativity. It is the copying of a soup can and putting it in a new frame. Postmodern art rejects originality, composition, order, and interpretation. In music, it is typified by the techno remix or *mash-up*—mixing or crushing together soundtracks from different works, superimposing contrasting rhythms, adding a vocal from one song with an instrumental track from another recording.

Modernism celebrates individuality and competition; it rewards the meritorious. Postmodernism embraces mediocrity; it rewards everyone equally. In a postmodern world, there is little originality or skill displayed. To be neat and orderly, to demonstrate any lyricism or poetry, to have a trained singing voice, or to display any actual talent, is somehow elitist. To gain recognition on the basis of one's ability is somehow not fair. Therefore, much postmodern art is often derided as meaningless non-art and outright trash—punk rock, performance art, spontaneous silliness, "happenings," rap lyrics, art installations, "flash mobs," and so forth. It is deliberately ugly and repulsive. This accounts for much of the ragged dress, smashing of instruments, screaming and ranting, and flagrant vulgarities. To be civil is to be snobbish; to be talented is elitist.

Turning to architecture, the Bauhaus School of the 1920s typified modernism. With its cube-like anonymous public buildings, this *International Style* was functional, rational, and antiseptic—what Jacques Barzun calls, "the silhouette of shoe boxes on end."[8] Best and Kellner in *The Postmodern Turn* observe, "High modernism in architecture fit perfectly with corporate capitalism and provided a useful ideology for its legitimization. The demand to restructure the environment, to destroy all obstacles in the path of modernization, was a perfect ideology for a relentless capitalist development."[9] And thus the 9/11 terrorist attack—while not intentionally architecturally inspired—was directly aimed at these classic modern monuments to "relentless capitalist development."

But we have now moved beyond the modern functionality of the Bauhaus School. Think of Frank Lloyd Wright's Guggenheim Museum, Jørn Utzon's Sydney Opera House, or Frank Gehry's Disney Concert Hall. Curves and graceful arches were reintroduced. Angles and diagonals replaced square boxes. Rough textures and contrasting materials replaced the aluminum and glass facades of modern design. Colors bright and pastel replaced muted concrete surfaces. Best and Kellner sum up the state of postmodern art and architecture: "We now live in a more decentered world, with no artistic core, in which a plurality of styles uneasily coexist, and there is no aesthetic consensus as to what is quality or advanced art. . . . Instead, the art world, like postmodern culture in general, is ruled by fragmentation and the hype of media and consumer culture, with its cacophony of competing trends, works, and artists."[10]

Postmodernism in Philosophical and Social Theory

Modern civilization embraced rationality and reason, certainty and structure. Postmodern social theory recognizes irrationality, doubt, and nihilism. The ideals of the Enlightenment are replaced by the reality of uncertainty. Since Biblical times, we have embraced the dictum that *the Truth shall make you free.*[11] Postmodernists decree that uncertainty reigns; that is the only truth. Therefore, to embrace uncertainty is to be free. Post-modern theory argues that the modern idea of rationality—which was supposed to liberate the human mind—ironically winds up encasing the individual in a rigid cocoon of formalistic and scientific methodology. The modern rationalist is bound by inflexible rules and formats that dictate scientific techniques, educational practices, and condominium agreements. Postmodernists ask, *Where is the spontaneity, the passion? Where is your freedom?* In effect, postmodernists argue, modern rationality demands the curtailment of freedom. Therefore, true freedom means throwing off the restrictions of being rational.

This perspective has its seeds in the religious insights of Søren Kierkegaard, the founder of existentialism. Kierkegaard asserted that humans must suppress their reliance on externally imposed, impersonal, rational rules of ethics and behavior; they must instead nurture their own free, personal spiritual growth. Kierkegaard argued that no authority—that is, the Church—can dictate truth to the individual. Truth is not something that one acquires by memorizing canonical law or by learning one's catechism. Rather, truth exists only as it is experienced subjectively by the individual. Kierkegaard distrusted reason. Logic can be manipulated; scientific "facts" can be twisted. Only a fool allows his life to be governed by reason. Ultimately one must rely on faith. Such thinking was clearly *post*-modern.

Friedrich Nietzsche followed Kierkegaard roughly a generation later. He was one of the earliest to define a multicultural perspective of morality. This viewpoint dominates much of our postmodern social and academic thinking today. *Your culture is as good as mine; my value system is no better than yours.* There is no absolute authority. There is only moral relativity. Nietzsche became a lodestar for a postmodern generation of relativists and deconstructionists.

The social and philosophical thinking of modernity also is charged with abetting an exploitative Western imperialism. *Modern thinkers used science, capitalism, and colonialism to keep native peoples and women from gaining any foothold in the establishment.* T. H. Breen refers to those "contemporary critics of Enlightenment thought—postmodernists and feminists—who argue that the 18th-century regime of reason amounted to little more than an effort by a male ruling class to preserve its own privilege and power. . . . The English Enlightenment thus stands accused of cultural imperialism."[12] This anti-imperialistic reaction has greatly added to postmodern thinking. It has, as well, fueled escalating resentment among non-Western peoples and terrorist attacks by religious extremists.

THE ESSENCE OF POSTMODERNISM

Modern idealists were looking for some logical structure in all fields—the sciences, arts, and our cultural arrangements. Postmodernism recognizes a culture characterized by ambiguity and chaos in all fields. Postmodernists reject the Enlightenment quest for certainty, the search for universal truths. In his analysis of the decline of American culture, Morris Berman defines postmodernism as "the notion that nothing is absolute, that one value is as good as another, that there is no difference between knowledge and opinion, and that any text or set of ideas is merely a mask for someone's political agenda. . . . A philosophy of despair masquerading as radical intellectual chic, postmodernism is, in fact, the ideological counterpart to the civilizational collapse that is going on around us."[13]

There are many inconsistencies within the broad hodgepodge that is postmodernism. While postmodern art tends to play down the creative role of the individual artist, the romantic roots of postmodernism stress the importance of individualism. Modern thinkers (Locke, Voltaire, the American founders) campaigned against the authoritarian state; but both Kierkegaard and Nietzsche also defined a strong anti-authoritarian position. John Gray writes that postmodern theory "is typically one which rejects Enlightenment reason while (like the Romantic movement) retaining its commitment to a humanist emancipatory project—a shallow and ultimately incoherent perspective."[14]

Although they are not identical, postmodernism and post-intellectualism do fit together snugly. Post-intellectualism is *unintentional* erosion of reason and structure; and postmodernism describes a *deliberate* rejection of reason and structure. Postmodernism is a refutation of the intellectual society—as we have defined it. An intellectual society is one in which the standards are set by a relatively small handful of intellectual leaders who want to bring the rest of the populace up to that level; in a postmodern society everyone determines his or her own standards. Our cultural leadership has given up on trying to establish any universal standards—that is, standards that incorporate coherence and structure, the search for truth, universal morality, respect for reason, and acquisition of knowledge. And the individual citizen no longer pledges to try to achieve any intellectual standards. Chaos and relativity become the passwords of the era.

Postmodernism promotes freedom of the individual; but it often does so without recognizing the accompanying requirement for responsibility. Our intellectual covenant demands that the two must go together. The postmodern slogan "Do your own thing" implies a carefree license to follow your own whims without regard to the consequences. To do so, however, results either in (a) universal chaos and anarchy, or (b) your freedoms ultimately being restrained by some outside authority (your parents, God's enforcers, or the ATF knocking on your door). The lack of structure (freedom without responsibility) embraced by postmodernism will ultimately result in either anarchy or totalitarianism. Gray declares that nihilism is "the West's only true universal inheritance."[15]

THE ENLIGHTENMENT SPARKED an optimistic, modern, belief in the possibility of human progress; this would overcome centuries of darkness, oppression, and suffering. This idealism was still the confident outlook that characterized America at the dawn of the twentieth century. With technological breakthroughs and social reform, we could achieve a near-utopian form of self-government. School curricula implicitly preached optimism, can-do initiative, and patriotism. But today the curricula more often reflect doubt, uncertainties, and cultural turmoil.

Modern intellectuals—the Enlightenment thinkers—assumed truth could be found; it was possible ultimately to know everything. Postmodern thinkers believe we can ultimately know nothing.[16] The modern thinker searched for certainty. The postmodern thinker accepts that there is no certainty. The modern thinker felt that we humans were in charge of our own destiny. The postmodernists know that we are not in charge—no one is in charge. Wallace Jackson writes that "expulsion from the Garden of Enlightenment is the tragic fact of postmodernism."[17]

The seeds of postmodernism, ironically, were planted during the Enlightenment. Modern men and women cast aside the religious dogma that had governed their lives; individuals were set free to discover truth for themselves. The idea was that rational beings—following the scientific method and using empirical reasoning—would be able to create the ideal judicious state. That was the plan. In actuality, however, their individualism proved their undoing. Every person started with his or her idiosyncratic set of assumptions and biases, followed his or her own set of instincts, built upon his or her existing tribal and traditional perspectives, and wound up with his or her different version of truth. *Whatever.* Thus, the promise of a modern rational culture gave way to the disorder and uncertainty of a pluralistic postmodern reality. The visionary dream of a modern society was replaced by the chaotic dystopia of a postmodern Kafkaesque nightmare.

The postmodern existentialist accepts life, with all its absurdities, as it is. The postmodernist believes in nothing permanent, nothing structured, nothing universal. We are left with the possibility, in the words of philosopher Richard Bernstein, that "there may be nothing—not God, reason, philosophy, science or poetry—that answers to and satisfies our longing for ultimate constraints, for a stable and reliable rock upon which we can secure our thought and action."[18] We are left with no opening paragraph for our cultural narrative. Your science is as good as my science. Creationism should be taught alongside evolution. Words are used primarily to distort and manipulate. Consumers exist only to be exploited. There are no intrinsic standards for judging art or literature. And no universal philosophical principles can be articulated. What then is left to believe in? God is wounded; science is crippled; and truth is dead.

CHAPTER 5

Exploring Post-Intellectualism

The term *post-intellectualism* implies that we have moved beyond the Age of Intellectualism (as inherited from the Enlightenment) and that we are now enveloped in something past intellectualism. It's not that we have suddenly gone stupid—our brains have not disintegrated. It's just that our cultural environment no longer is based on that intellectual vision that has been the anchor of modern society for more than three hundred years.

My definition of post-intellectualism takes the four components of intellectualism identified in Chapter 3 (liberal arts, acquisition of knowledge, rational problem-solving, and social criticism) and examines the antithesis of each component. I then come up with four attributes of post-intellectualism: *Specialization* (the opposite of a liberal-arts perspective), *Ignorance* (the shrinking of knowledge), *Dumbth* (the lack of reasoning capability), and *Establishmentism* (the disinclination to engage in constructive social criticism).[1]

SPECIALIZATION

The intellectual mind is interested in everything—that is the liberal-arts perspective. The post-intellectual mind has been forced to become more and more specialized, focusing on a narrow range of knowledge or expertise. Specialization does not imply a lessening of individual virtue; we are not bad people just because we have had to develop a degree of specialization in order to earn a living and function in our complicated social and political environment. Specialization is an inevitable outgrowth of increased information and societal complexity; it is an unavoidable result of the modern intellectual search for knowledge. In our educational pursuits and in our vocational endeavors, we have had to become specialists in order to survive in an increasingly complex culture.

Much of this specialization is the result of the narrowly focused professional training that increasingly dominates higher education. John Ralston Saul points out that most professional schools seek out students who are talented and predisposed to focus on some specific area of interest—be it business, engineering, art, law, or medicine. Thus, "most people are equipped with an unbalanced distribution of talents," and the professional curriculum "actively seeks students who suffer from the appropriate imbalance and then sets out to exaggerate it."[2]

Specialization leads to two distinct problems. First is the loss of the big picture; individuals no longer have a clear grasp of everything that's going on around them. Second, we experience loss of autonomy; individuals have lost a sense of self-sufficiency and can no longer cope on their own.

Loss of the Big Picture

The more specialized we become, the less each of us can comprehend the whole. The more we rely on specialists the more we lose the perspective of the generalist—the liberally educated person who can see the big picture. We have become a society of twig authorities and leaf experts, but few can understand the whole tree—let alone the entire forest.

Enron boasted that it hired only the best and the brightest—the best specialists, that is: the top MBAs, the best accountants, the sharpest engineers, and the shrewdest managers. Every specialist was then so absorbed with his or her own particular projects and specific dealings that no one stepped back and tried to perceive where their corporate impetus was taking them. As bureaucrats and lawyers and accountants get more insulated and locked up in their single-minded specialties, it becomes increasingly difficult to maintain perspective. It becomes easier to justify shortcuts and questionable procedures that serve their particular jobs—while ignoring the implications for the bigger picture. Enron would have been better served had it sprinkled among its executive ranks some philosophers and history majors—some intellectuals to examine where they were headed, to ask what they were doing. To question authority. It needed a few poets and ecologists along with the engineers and technicians.

Writing of his own profession, E. O. Wilson laments that the education of the vast majority of scientists "does not orient them to the wide contours of the world. . . . The most productive scientists, installed in million-dollar laboratories, have no time to think about the big picture and see little profit in it."[3] Surveying the rest of the intellectual landscape, he continues: "The same professional atomization afflicts the social sciences and humanities. The faculties of higher education around the world are a congeries of experts." To be a successful scholar today is to be so narrowly focused on nineteenth-century German poets or recombinant gene-splicing, that one no longer can grasp even where to turn to get a glimpse of the big picture. The problem we are concerned with is, in the words of English author and scientist C. P. Snow, "the overspecialization of the educated elite."[4]

Our concern is the vitality and viability of a democratic culture. Enlightened citizens are to come together in an arena of clear-headed discussion to engage in collective decision-making. If individuals acquire only the particularized skills needed to function in one specialized job, then how do these specialists develop the broad understandings and insights they need to be an informed and involved electorate? Citizens are to be knowledgeable about all the issues and problems they must make decisions about: foreign affairs, fiscal policies, education programs, genetic research, energy alternatives, urban blight, international terrorism, pollution, and overpopulation. These are Wilson's "wide contours of the world" that must be understood and debated by the citizenry at large. Otherwise, governmental decision-making becomes so specialized that the individual citizen no longer can pretend to be participating.

Loss of Autonomy

A second problem with specialization is the loss of a sense of individual self-sufficiency. This is the underpinning of all personal freedom. Self-sufficiency means independence. In the *pre-intellectual* world, humans were dependent upon the authoritarian rulers—tribal chiefs, priests, and assorted monarchs. In an *intellectual* culture, humans are self-sufficient, relying on reason and objective research to make decisions and solve their problems. But in today's *post-intellectual* reality, we have returned to an era of dependence upon outside sources—this time the engineers and bureaucrats, the lawyers, and technocrats.

To the extent that you don't understand what someone else is doing—with your legal affairs, your computer programs, your financial matters, and your job—you are not in charge of your own life. The more technology we have and utilize, then the more that we have to rely on specialists to install, explain, modify, update, and repair that technology for us. Just a couple generations ago, most homeowners were able to fix their own furnace, handle their car's routine maintenance, deal with a simple real-estate transaction, build a room addition, or replace a vacuum tube in their radio. Today, however, most of us are increasingly dependent upon repairmen, agents, and contractors to handle these chores for us.

We have become a loophole society. Much of our legislation, corporate maneuvers, legal procedures, and accounting sleight-of-hand are deliberately designed to keep the citizenry at bay and the specialists in control. The IRS loophole labyrinth, for example—with its thousands of regulations and definitions that are devised to provide singular exemptions and hidden benefits for special interests—force us to call in the accountants and tax lawyers to handle our affairs. The tax code is a calculated refutation of an intellectual culture.

The same sense of debilitation becomes evident in the workplace. Adam Smith, the modern champion of specialization, declared in one of his *Lectures on Jurisprudence* that specialization would ultimately lead to certain drawbacks—specifically, "The minds of men are contracted and rendered incapable of elevation, education is despised or at least neglected, and heroic spirit is almost utterly extinguished."[5] Each individual would be restricted to a smaller and smaller sphere of operation and competence. Each individual knows less and less about the overall job. As we are rendered increasingly incapable of handling our own affairs, what does this do to the individual human spirit? Our sense of self-worth? Are we not individually diminished when we are less able to cope on our own? *We are not in control.*

IGNORANCE

Every few weeks we are presented with some new survey underscoring the relative ignorance of the American populace—from elementary school through adulthood. One nationwide survey of seniors at 55 of the top colleges and universities in the country (including Harvard and Princeton) concluded that 80 percent of those surveyed received the equivalent of D or F on a test regularly used by the National Assessment of Education Progress given to high school students.[6] In a National Geographic poll, less than a quarter of U.S. citizens could find the Pacific Ocean on a world map. And in a science survey, less than half of American adults knew that the earth orbits the sun once a year, that electrons are smaller than atoms, or that dinosaurs were extinct by the time humans appeared.[7] But it is not altogether unexpected that we come up short in history, geography, and science. After all, there is so much more to learn about history, geography, and science than there was a couple generations ago.

If we think of knowledge as the "internalization and comprehension of external information by the human brain" (Chapter 3), then each of us is able to conceptualize as knowledge a smaller and smaller percentage of the total amount of information that exists. The world's *information* is expanding exponentially; the total amount of *knowledge* we can hold in our individual heads is relatively constant; therefore *ignorance*—the amount of information that each of us personally does not have a grasp of—is growing. My ignorance expands as more information is generated, collected and stored—but remains out of my personal knowledge storehouse.

It's stuff that someone *else* knows about; therefore my relative knowledge is diminished. I remain increasingly ignorant of what is going on.

Imagine your brain as the size of a ping-pong ball (let's say metaphorically that's the space that is devoted to storing knowledge). About 40,000 years ago, the total amount of information that existed in the world would fill one tennis ball. Information at that time consisted of hunting and fishing techniques, shelter construction, some religious ceremonies and tribal taboos, rudimentary first aid, and a few other miscellaneous items. Each individual actually would be able to conceptualize quite a bit of the existing world information in his or her ping-pong-ball-sized knowledge reservoir. All persons would be pretty knowledgeable about the world in which they lived. Today, however, the total amount of information that exists would take enough tennis balls to fill Yankee Stadium several times over. Yet, your ping-pong-ball capacity for internalizing knowledge has not increased significantly. Therefore, you can comprehend but a very tiny portion of the total amount of information that exists today. You are relatively ignorant—compared to your hunter-gatherer ancestors of 40,000 years ago. Wendell Berry puts it this way: "In living in the world by his own will and skill, the stupidest peasant or tribesman is more competent than the most intelligent workers or technicians . . . in a society of specialists."[8]

But, you say, you have *access* to all that information in the several Yankee Stadiums. You can use search engines on the Web; you know how to navigate a computer-based library catalog; you know how to look things up in the thousands of professional journals that exist; you can download millions of files from around the globe. True. But you still don't have that information as knowledge in your head. You don't have the perspective and experience to analyze the incoming data; you cannot place all the new information you pick up into some sort of relevant context. You cannot read the latest piece of research and compare it to all other pertinent research in the same area. And you can't confidently sort out all of the Internet data to determine which information is valid and which is garbage. As Daniel Boorstin, former Librarian of Congress, puts it, "Information tends to drive knowledge out of existence."[9] More poetically, T. S. Eliot writes, "All our knowledge brings us nearer to our ignorance, . . ."[10]

Not to worry, you say. That's what we have experts for—the stock analysts and the accountants. They can pull together the relevant pieces of information that are needed and make some intelligent decisions. Back to the specialists. But if we are to rely on the specialists and technocrats for governmental decision-making, how are we to continue pretending that we citizens participate in collective decision-making? Besides, do we really want to blindly trust the advice of the stock analysts and accountants?

Too much information also gets in the way of personal reflection and examination. We are swamped with data input. We are so occupied with gathering information that we have less and less time for analyzing what we take in. It is as if our internal computers are so busy downloading data (overloading our Input/Output capability) that our gray matter (the CPU) has little computing capacity free to process the data. Columnist G. D. Gearino comments, "Information hasn't supported thinking; it has replaced it."[11] Which gets us into the topic of *Dumbth*.

DUMBTH

In a 1948 speech, Albert Einstein lamented the lack of reason in our political affairs: "For all of us who are concerned for peace and the triumph of reason and justice must today be keenly aware how small an influence reason and honest good-will exert upon events in the political field."[12] To this sad commentary on the absence of reason in the political field, we could add that we also aren't doing very well with rational problem-solving in any other cultural or social field. Looking at the business world, Scott Adams, creator of *Dilbert*, puts it succinctly: "After careful analysis I have developed a sophisticated theory to explain the existence of this bizarre workplace behavior: People are idiots."[13]

The title for this section is taken from an insightful book written by Steve Allen in 1989, *Dumbth: And 81 Ways to Make Americans Smarter*. He writes, "Mountains of evidence—both in the form of statistical studies and personal testimonies—establish that the American people are suffering from a new and perhaps unprecedented form of mental incapacitation for which I have coined the word *Dumbth*."[14] Humans just do dumb things: suburbanites buy tank-sized SUVs to bring home their high-calorie groceries; people engage in risky behaviors they know can lead to AIDS; Americans spend an average of $159 per person on lottery tickets each year. The failure of critical thinking, the abandonment of reason: this is dumbth, the third component of post-intellectualism. Much of the explanation for the Progress Paradox is this tautology or circular reasoning: *We are experiencing so many societal problems because we are not doing a very good job of problem-solving*. We simply aren't adequately following the Analytic Thinking Pattern—reasoning, critical thinking, decision-making. In Chapter 15 we explore a number of reasons for this intellectual meltdown.

One difficulty is that we have come to rely on both technology and the experts to solve our problems, to do our thinking for us. Why bother to figure things out for yourself if the mental work can be done by some other person? Or some machine or computer program? One hallmark of the modern intellectual age was the nurturing of individualism—which includes thinking independently. But today we live in an age that does not particularly value independent thinking. We put our faith in group projects, committee efforts, and consultant teams.

The United States, founded on intellectual principles, paradoxically has devolved into a postmodern culture of anti-intellectualism. We don't take time to deliberate and think. And we don't reward those who do think. We reward the corporate overlords and pop idols—not the intellectuals. Think of the financial prizes and celebrity status we lavish upon our entertainers and sports stars. But where are the rewards for the philosophers, the poets, the artists? Even the teaching profession—the one field that more than any other is dedicated to facilitating and promoting the art of thinking—is one of the poorest paid.

Numerous critics point to the public schools as the source of many of our cultural problems—including the de-emphasis on thinking skills. While the schools may be indicative of our anti-intellectual slide, they are as much a victim of the postmodern cultural landscape as they are a cause. The schools reflect the uncertainties, the fuzzy sensitivities, the garbled goals, and the conflicting priorities of society at large. Students are taught the mechanics of how to get along in today's society, but they are not given the necessary tools for thinking independently. One indication of the lower level of intellectual activity in our classrooms is the falling SAT scores mentioned in Chapter 1. The average verbal score dropped from 478 in 1963 to 424 in 1995 (on a scale from 200 to 800). The decline was so tangible and definitive that the College Board (which administers the exam) *recentered* the scoring—that is, the Board simply declared that henceforth 424 was to be considered "average" (it had been 500). When you no longer can meet your objectives, you simply set your objectives lower.

ESTABLISHMENTISM

I am defining the term *Establishmentism* as the unquestioned acceptance of the establishment just as it is. The true intellectual is one who thinks for himself or herself, one who does not automatically accept what "they" say. John Stuart Mill, in his famous 1859 essay *On Liberty*, emphasized that in our search for truth nothing can be accepted at face value; all beliefs and positions must be critiqued and rationally challenged before we can accept any proposition as valid. Unless any opinion "is vigorously and earnestly contested, it will, by most of those who receive it, be held in the manner of a prejudice, with little comprehension or feeling of its rational grounds."[15] The intellectual is always looking for a clearer idea of what we are doing, a more cogent definition of where we want to go, a better way to get things done. The intellectual is always questioning the establishment.[16]

The post-intellectual, on the other hand, accepts what the establishment says partly because things have gotten so complex that the average individual no longer has any comprehension of what is going on: *Therefore, the specialists—the technocrats and priests—must know better than I do.* Postman and Weingartner observe that "the price of maintaining membership in the Establishment is unquestioning acceptance of authority."[17] It is this uncritical acceptance of authority's dictate (for example, Hitler's concept of racial superiority or bin Laden's interpretation of the Koran) that leads to inevitable culture clashes. Establishmentism also is the foundation of all religious fundamentalism. Andrew Sullivan explains: "In a world of absolute truth, in matters graver than life and death, there is no room for dissent and no room for theological doubt. Hence . . . the ancient Catholic insistence on absolute church authority. Without infallibility, there can be no guarantee of truth. Without such a guarantee, confusion can lead to hell."[18]

Up through the 1950s, our coffee houses and academic corridors were populated by idealistic bohemians, sipping their brews and debating broad philosophical issues and abstract political and social theories—critiquing society. Today these same watering holes are political outposts where single-interest activists debate how best to get their specialized agenda implemented. The intellectual has been replaced by the post-intellectual lobbyist. Politicians may haggle over how best to shore up Social Security, what we should do about tax cuts or tax increases, what level of federal funding there should be for public education, and so forth—but (aside from the libertarians and the socialists) few politicians are seriously questioning the design of the system. Russell Jacoby notes how the meaning of the term *intellectual* has mutated in recent years: "Intellectuals live less as independent writers or poets and more as professional groups, interest coalitions, perhaps classes. . . . Today intellectuals travel with curricula vitae and business cards; they subsist by virtue of institutional backing."[19] Many of those who today are identified as "intellectuals" are, in effect, actually specialists and post-intellectual shills for establishment interests. True intellectuals would shun institutional validation.

SUMMING UP POST-INTELLECTUALISM, we could contrast the intellectual mindset with the post-intellectual perspective. The intellectual is broadly educated; *the post-intellectual is a specialist.* The intellectual seeks knowledge; *the post-intellectual is overwhelmed by the information explosion.* The intellectual solves his or her own problems; *the post-intellectual calls in consultants and sets up committees.* The intellectual challenges the establishment; *the post-intellectual embraces the establishment and merely asks for a larger piece of the pie.* These four components of post-intellectualism do not necessarily represent intentional abandonment of intellectual principles. *Specialization* is a result of our commitment to unending progress; *Ignorance* comes as a result of our expanding information base; *Dumbth* is indicative of our increasingly complex and chaotic social environment;

and *Establishmentism* represents a lack of any clear-cut alternative visions. Ironically, as we shall explore in Chapter 8, many of these post-intellectual symptoms are the inevitable consequences of intellectual ideas pursued to the extreme.

On the other hand, as we shall see in the next two chapters, much of what happens under the banner of post-intellectualism is a throwback to pre-intellectual thinking. The pre-intellectual culture was characterized by authority, stability, law, and order. *Don't rock the boat.* To a great extent, these are the same attributes that characterize part of the post-intellectual mindset (as opposed to an intellectual culture that emphasizes conflict, change, and competition). To some degree, part of our post-intellectual experience is a recycling of our pre-intellectual culture.

CHAPTER 6

Three Periods of Intellectual Evolution

In this chapter, we look at three periods of cultural evolution—using both *modern* and *intellectual* models. There are several obvious parallels between a premodern-modern-postmodern analysis of human culture and a similar breakdown of pre-intellectualism, intellectualism, and post-intellectualism. However, we aren't dealing strictly with historical periods. Intellectualism can be defined as a specific mindset, as well as an historical age. There were elements of intellectual inquiry in the ancient world, just as there are many pre-intellectual cultures on the globe today.

THREE PERIODS DELINEATED

Historians, geologists, and scholars in general love to break things down into identifiable time frames—eons, eras, periods, epochs, ages, and so forth. And for good reason. These historical file folders generally help us put history in a clearer perspective. For the purpose of our analysis, this section will briefly summarize our cultural evolution in terms of three periods or classifications.

Pre-Intellectualism

From ancient times to the fifteenth century or thereabouts, the story of mankind has often been defined as the premodern culture. This was a world of superstition and astrology, religious rites and rituals, clannish allegiances and customs. It was an era of authoritarian societies—tribal cultures, religious kingdoms, and medieval fiefdoms—wherein the authorities decreed that people were not capable of self-government. Under any kind of authoritarian regime, the rules and conventions were well established, usually based on deep spiritual and religious beliefs. The cultural narrative was unquestioned. Critical thinking, alternative lifestyles, nonconformist social ideas—even individualism—could not be tolerated. There was little occasion to voice one's opinion, to differ with the leadership. Freedom of choice could only lead to confusion and uncertainty. What men and women needed in such tribal cultures was the assurance of truth, unquestioned faith in the established order.

The Cyclical Culture

In such societies, there was little difference from one generation to the next. Indeed, the whole idea of *change* would be abhorrent. Each generation was raised to repeat the cycle of its preceding generations—to perpetuate the culture of its elders. There was no social, economic, or scientific incentive to encourage progress or expansion. This was a *cyclical* culture. Historian L. S. Stavrianos describes this cyclical mindset: "Primitive humans were basically ahistorical and nonevolutionary in their attitudes towards themselves and their society. They assumed that the future would be identical to the present, as the present was to the past. Consequently there was no notion of change, and hence no inclination to criticize or to tamper with existing institutions and practices."[1]

Intellectualism

Then there gradually evolved the intellectual culture, or modernism. Conceived in Classical Greece, nurtured in the Renaissance, blossoming during the Enlightenment, and coming of age with the Industrial Revolution, this intellectual spirit was the core of the modern age. Scientific thinking replaced superstition and astrology; capitalism succeeded bartering; and humanism threatened traditional authoritarian religion. Agriculture became more specialized. Population pressures demanded larger cities. Geographic discoveries stimulated new economic patterns. And society became more libertarian.[2] The Western world would never be the same. We could never return to a cyclical culture.

The Linear Culture

This intellectual mindset resulted in a *linear* culture. Instead of preserving and perpetuating the existing social structure in an endless cycle, we would now evolve and grow in an unending linear fashion—always moving ahead, expanding and discovering new horizons, developing new tools and technologies. We would follow Bacon's injunction to use science to discover new knowledge and continually improve the social condition.

We invented progress.[3] Jacques Barzun writes, "Modernist Man looks forward, a born future-ist, thus reversing the old presumption about ancestral wisdom and the value of prudent conservation."[4]

This was perhaps the most monumental transformation of human society ever experienced. It is a culture clash continuously repeated today—wherever the developed Western linear cultures (think zealous missionaries, colonial imperialists, and post-colonial exploiters) try to impose upon premodern Third World cyclical cultures the ideas of social development, democracy, capitalism, religious reform, and fast-food chains. The resulting turmoil and chaos are played out over and over again. Terrorist attacks on Western civilization are triggered by the collision of premodern and modern cultures, conflicts between the authoritarian and the liberal, between the religious fanatic and the secular humanist.

Post-intellectualism

But now we witness the intellectual modern age stumbling to a halt. We no longer have a clear linear idea where we are headed.[5] We have progressed; we have expanded; we have subdued nature. What next? More growth? More colonization? More subjugation of nature? Karen Endicott, editor of the *Dartmouth Alumni Magazine*, sums up much of the transition:

Don't rely on Reason, Science, Truth, and the steady march of Progress—all those Enlightenment articles of faith that underscore modernism. Why? Because, say postmodernists, unquestioning confidence in these ways of thinking about the world led to the kind of dogmatic notions that gave us . . . the bomb, the Cold War, environmental degradation, and other man-made woes. As . . . professor Gerald Auten points out, "It's hard to learn about the twentieth century and think of it as progress."[6]

We discard the idea that science and progress will inevitably lead to a more secure and equitable world. We mistrust the notion that research and information-gathering will necessarily result in objective truth.

The Web Culture

Today we aren't sure in what direction to turn. We want progress, but without pollution or depletion of our resources. We embrace technology, although we have lost faith in the veneration of science. We espouse capitalism, but we criticize corporate abuses and the exploitation of labor. We want to escape the squalor of urban living, but we lament the loss of open space as we push development further into rural areas. We build rational frameworks for all our dealings, but rely on intuition and instinct to make decisions. We find ourselves today flailing about uncomfortably in what can best be described as a postmodern *Web Culture*—contrasted with a cyclical or a linear culture. Radiating in all directions, strands of our web extend up and down, left and right, forward and backward. Connections stretch out every which way. And we aren't sure which way to go. We are encouraged to *try this. No, that. Do this first. No, back up and try that. Push on. Turn around.*

We have been living in a web culture for a number of years—arguably for three or four decades. When I refer to the "web culture," I am not talking about only the World Wide Web, but about all the discontinuous links and channels that characterize our culture today. It encompasses all our transient networks and fleeting relationships: corporate mergers and splits, temporary employment patterns, vacillating government policies, social revolutions and counterrevolutions, short-lived educational reforms, religious upheavals, nontraditional families, cyber-connections, and information mazes. The quivering strands of our jittery web culture provide no firm foundation or secure footing—no sense of values from which we can get our bearings.

We no longer are guided by an intellectual mindset that gives us clear answers. We make this connection, then that. We form this alliance, then that. New patterns are perceived, explored, then abandoned. We are pulled this way, then that way. We are not sure where we should be headed as we explore our web up this strand and down that one. We relocate geographically with a rapidity that would have been inconceivable to earlier generations. We cohabit, marry without commitment, then walk out when the relationship gets uncomfortable. We switch careers at the drop of a training program. We capitalize a new venture, declare bankruptcy, then move on.

The web culture represents rootlessness, a sense of impermanence, a loss of orientation, and no enduring values. We have lost the certainty of both the cyclical culture and the linear culture. In a cyclical culture we knew what to do (*preserve and perpetuate the culture of our forefathers*). In a linear culture we knew what to do (*keep going in the same expansive direction that our fathers pointed us*). In a web culture we aren't sure at all in what direction to head. *Try something. Or don't try anything. Just chill out. Whatever.*

PARALLEL PATTERNS AND PARADIGMS

Numerous historians and theorists have described this three-part analysis from diverse viewpoints. A few of these terms and perspectives are illustrated in Figure 2. The same three-part breakdown shows up in many academic fields. Three of them are relevant to our discussion at this point.

Media Studies

Media scholars have long used a three-part breakdown of media development that closely parallels premodernism, modernism, and post-

Figure 2
Comparison of Three Intellectual Periods

PRE-INTELLECTUALISM	INTELLECTUALISM	POST-INTELLECTUALISM

Society and Culture

Premodern/Ancient	Modern	Postmodern
Cyclical culture	Linear culture	Web culture
Oral tradition	Written word	Electric media
Ideational	Sensate	Idealistic
Social stability	Progress	Social chaos
Group identity	Individualism	Ethnic retribalization
Yin (feminine)	Yang (masculine)	Yin/Yang balance

Science, Technology and Religion

Tool-using culture	Technocracy	Technopoly
Tradition	Analytic thinking	Intuition
Superstition	Scientific method	New Age mysticism
Faith	Reason	Secularism
Religion	Humanism	Fundamentalism
Divine authority	Existentialism	Agnosticism/Atheism

Governance and Economics

Authoritarianism	Libertarianism	Elitism
Dictatorship	Democracy	Communism
Tribes	Nation-states	Regional alliances
Cooperation	Competition	Affirmative Action
Group security	Self-reliance	Victimization
Bartering	Capitalism	Socialism
Feudal economy	Free enterprise	Exploitation

Art and Education

Folk art	Fine art	Popular art
Religious indoctrination	Scholarly inquiry	Specialization
Practical education	Liberal arts	Social relevance
Collective wisdom	Individual research	Information anarchy

modernism. These are the divisions of the Oral Tradition, the Written Word, and the Electric Media.

The Oral (and Pictorial) Tradition

Over tens of thousands of years, early subhuman grunts and growls gradually evolved into what we would recognize today as the spoken word. Although many media scholars refer to this period as the age of Oral Communication, we should also include the pictograph. Cave paintings—depicting family trees, religious ceremonies, and records of successful hunts—were the prerequisite step before the alphabet would be invented.

There was little abstract thinking or philosophical musing during this premodern period. Not much thought was given to the acquisition of knowledge above and beyond what was needed for social maintenance and survival; and this was easily handled with oral instruction. This is one reason it took thousands of years for the idea of the alphabet to emerge. In a cyclical culture, it simply was not needed. If necessity is the mother of invention, then lack of need is the barrier to invention.

The Written Word (and the Printing Press)

Slowly the cave paintings and pictographs became more stylized and abstract; and notational symbols gradually evolved. By 800 b.c. or so, we had the basic Greek alphabet. With the revolutionary technology of the alphabet, our social fabric was completely rewoven. The scribe's pen replaced the memory of the village elder; the secular administration of the government supplanted the authority of the church. Marshall McLuhan and Quentin Fiore colorfully sum up the impact of the written word: "The goose quill put an end to talk. It abolished mystery; it gave architecture and towns; it brought roads and armies, bureaucracy. It was the basic metaphor with which the cycle of civilization began, the step from the dark into the light of the mind. The hand that filled the parchment page built a city."[7]

The printing press magnified tremendously the power of the written word. The widespread printing of books in vernacular languages gave rise to the eventual creation of new nation-states; and by placing books directly in the hands of individual scholars and researchers, the printing press fostered the intellectual ideas of independent thinking, privacy, and individualism. The printing press was the catalyst that facilitated the linear culture. The stability and authority characteristic of the oral tradition were ravaged by the ferment and challenge of the printed word—the quest for knowledge, the exchange of ideas, the promotion of critical thinking, and the spirit of exploration of new worlds. The modern age was created on the platen of Gutenberg's crude press.

Within this context, the media are seen primarily as a way of facilitating the Search for Truth. The print media would foster change, not continuity. They would serve the individual, not the state. The press is an avenue for questioning authority—providing a forum to bring the populace together in its collective decision-making process. Clearly, this is a modern, intellectual use of the media.

The Electric Media and Computer Culture

Today we are immersed in what McLuhan labeled "the electric media"—encompassing everything from the telegraph and telephone to audio recordings and television.[8] The term now includes all electronic communication, computer-based technologies, and other digital advances. We are plunged into a nonintellectual whirling, dazzling, reeling display of colors, images, sound-bites, and disconnected data. Spontaneity and emotion have pushed aside contemplation and rational discourse.

The clearest manifestation of the electric web culture is the Internet, with its millions of web sites and chat rooms. A person could spend a lifetime bouncing around in the cyberspace web of specialized information sources, shopping outlets, gossip channels, opinion vehicles, stock trading portals, dating services, entertainment leads, professional contacts, pornography, library catalogs, auction sites, and casinos. The Internet is a continually changing paradigm of the web culture. It is everywhere and nowhere. It exists only as hundreds of millions of users make fleeting contacts with anybody and everybody else.

The cyclical culture was typified by *one-to-one* interpersonal communication; virtually all discourse was conducted on a face-to-face personal level. The linear culture introduced *one-to-many* transmission; mass communication was born with the printing press. With the web culture we have entered an era of *many-to-many* communication; everyone is trying to communicate with everyone else. Our focus is constantly shifting. Rather than reading a linear passage to absorb a coherent message, we are aimlessly flipping the pages of an ever-evolving electronic almanac. We find ourselves wandering around in cyberspace, lost in a technological fog.

Sorokin's Analysis

Pitirim A. Sorokin was an early twentieth-century sociologist who explained that every great society has been dominated by one of three prevailing cultural systems. It is the interplay of these three cultural precepts that accounts for the historical fluctuations and crises of all great civilizations.

The **ideational** society is a "unified system of culture based upon the principle of a supersensory and superrational God as the only true reality and value."[9] Everything in the culture revolves around this one overriding idea or belief system. Family structure, education, political structures, healing practices: these are all dictated by one dominant doctrine—religious faith. Belief in an omnipotent God determines every aspect of culture. Authoritarian and tradition-bound, this clearly is a pre-intellectual cyclical culture. The ideational culture was stable. Traditions were set in stone. Values and mores were immutable. The tribe's cultural narrative is straightforward and readily accepted by all members of society.

The **sensate** civilization, on the other hand, holds that "the true reality and value is sensory. Only what we see, hear, smell, touch, and otherwise perceive through our sense organs is real and has value."[10] This is what gives rise to empiricism and scientific thinking. All our cultural institutions are based upon rational determinations and concrete knowledge. We must observe and experiment, handle and experience, in order to know what is real. This scientific rationality leads to materialism in the purest sense—what exists is the material, sensate world. This is the modern worldview, an intellectual linear culture. With the sensate culture, truth was constantly being redefined as new scientific facts were uncovered. New theories emerged; new social paradigms were devised and implemented. Tradition and authority were no longer written in indelible ink. This instability eventually would lead to pluralism and relativism. Our cultural narrative becomes fragmented and temporal. This is the path that ultimately would lead to postmodernism.

Sorokin identified his third culture as the *idealistic*. This is a synthesizing culture, a harmonious blending of the sensate and ideational. Its major premise is that "the true reality is partly supersensory and partly sensory—that it embraces the supersensory and superrational aspect, plus the rational aspect and, finally, the sensory aspect, all blended into one unity."[11] This is a synthesis that would be both intellectual and passionate, an idealistic fusion that has occurred perhaps only twice in human history—during the Golden Age of Greece and during the Renaissance. It would be reassuring to feel that our postmodern turmoil might ultimately result in another idealistic culture—an exquisite blending of religious morality and scientific reality. It is too early, of course, to determine if that idealistic juncture is where the twenty-first century will wind up. Our unifying cultural narrative has yet to be written.

Postman's Paradigm

In his insightful *Technopoly: The Surrender of Culture to Technology*, Neil Postman defines three distinct cultures in terms of their tools and technologies. The premodern society is a *Tool-Using Culture*. People used basic tools—from weapons and plows to the water wheel and the clock—to solve problems of their daily existence and to support the efforts of their particular culture. The tools did not intrude on the form and function of their society. The tools "did not attack (or, more precisely, were not intended to attack) the dignity and integrity of the culture into which they were introduced."[12] The intent was not to modify the shape of the culture. The tools were just to be used to make life a little easier. The premodern cyclical culture would be preserved.

With the Age of Reason and the Enlightenment, European societies evolved into a *Technocracy*. They began to use tools to define and transform their cultures. Bacon gave us the insights that knowledge is power, progress is good, and science and technology are to be used to improve society. We can move forward; we can expand and build a better world.

This intellectual cornerstone of modernism led to the concept of *technocracy*, which has dominated Western culture for the past four centuries. Postman explains: "Technocracy filled the air with the promise of new freedoms and new forms of social organization. Technocracy also speeded up the world. We could get places faster, do things faster, accomplish more in a shorter time."[13]

Postman defines his third period as **Technopoly**. We now enter a post-intellectual stage—a culture where the technologies have determined their own place in society and define their own roles. Human intellect no longer is the driving force. Postman defines technopoly or "totalitarian technology" as "the submission of all forms of cultural life to the sovereignty of technique and technology."[14] Jerry Mander refers to the same concept as *Megatechnology* in which computers, television, satellites, corporations and banks, space technology, genetics, nanotechnology, and robotics intersect and merge with one another so that "they are forming something new, almost as if they were living cells; they are becoming a single technical-economic web encircling the planet."[15]

Just as the automobile, the airplane, television, the split atom, the satellite, and the computer shaped the twentieth century, so will genetic engineering, alternate energy sources, nanotechnology, new materials synthesis, virtual reality, fusion, superconductivity, and other unforeseen technologies dictate the direction of the twenty-first century. This post-intellectual phenomenon—technopoly, megatechnology, or *technological determinism*—is an underlying theme throughout the book.

In the pre-intellectual or cyclical culture, men and women accepted the fact that they were not in charge of their own lives; their destinies were dictated by God and by the various sovereigns that ruled over them. In the modern linear, intellectual culture, people came to assert their independence and declare that they were in charge of their own lives; it was an exhilarating period of cultural evolution. But in the post-intellectual web culture, we feel once again that we are not in charge. Technological and bureaucratic forces beyond our power and comprehension have taken over. This is the essence of our postmodern angst. *We are not in control.*

We have evolved through two vast ages (by whatever definition) and are now embarking upon a third great human adventure. On one hand, a new and entirely unknown future awaits us. On the other hand, it appears that in some ways we are returning to many of the dynamics that characterized the premodern or pre-intellectual age. Which is it? Are we moving forward? Or backward? Or are we trying to do both simultaneously as we flounder around in our web culture? This is the theme we investigate in Chapter 7.

CHAPTER 7

Two Faces of Post-Intellectualism

Postmodernism is a hodgepodge of numerous trends and tendencies. The postmodern worldview is that there is no unifying worldview. But there are some theorists who have discerned at least two categories of postmodernism. Hal Foster described a "postmodernism of reaction" which Teresa Ebert suggested should be labeled *ludic postmodernism* (from the Latin *ludus*, "play" or "sport").[1] This is an approach that celebrates the superficial and playful, fun with form and appearance—what Best and Kellner describe as "reveling in puns, parody, and pastiche."[2] In other words: making fun of modernism.

But also we have what has been called "postmodernism of resistance," which takes itself much more seriously. This is postmodernism that is focused on denouncing and attacking modernism in all its manifestations—artistic, linguistic, and political. Postmodernists of this bent seek actively to undermine the structures of a modern society. In the words of Best and Kellner, this version of postmodernism "seeks to engage political issues and to change the existing [modern] society."[3] The 9/11 terrorist attacks represent this postmodernism of resistance carried to the extreme—an assault on modern civilization.

HYPER AND COUNTER DIRECTIONS

Up to this point, we have been discussing post-intellectualism as if it were a coherent, unified identifiable phenomenon—a single entity that could be placed in a proper pigeonhole. But it's not that simple. Like postmodernism, post-intellectualism is not a distinct, easily defined matter. We need to examine post-intellectualism as it splits into two separate paths. And as these two post-intellectual paths have deviated from the modern or intellectual ideal, they have resulted in two quite dissimilar phenomena.

One of these two thrusts is what we might call *hyper-intellectualism*—an attempt to extend modernism and move forward with an uncompromising determination.[4] The other facet is *counter-intellectualism*. This would be somewhat analogous to "postmodernism of resistance"—a deliberate attempt to return to an earlier era. (Although counter-intellectualism might be compared to "postmodernism of resistance," hyper-intellectualism is in no way analogous to ludic postmodernism.) Francis Fukuyama summarizes these two paths: "On the one hand, there is the ever-increasing homogenization of mankind brought about by modern economics and technology [hyper-intellectualism] . . . On the other hand, there is everywhere a resistance to that homogenization, and a reassertion, largely on a sub-political level, of cultural identities that ultimately reinforce existing barriers between people and nations [counter-intellectualism]."[5] The hyper–intellectual thrust would be Sorokin's sensate culture pursued without restraint. Counter-intellectualism would be a return to Sorokin's ideational culture.

Hyper-Intellectualism

One part of our post-intellectual culture wants to push ahead with the economic and technological modern model at any cost—aiming for more capitalistic globalization, urbanization, and continued scientific progress and development. This is hyper-intellectualism—the unbridled linear extension of intellectual endeavors without consideration of ultimate consequences. Pushing forward without thought of the cultural costs. Expanding. Exploiting. Profiteering without moderation. Progress without restraint. Under such a hyper–intellectual push, scientific advances lead to technological determinism, universal education furthers narrow specialization, tolerance breeds amorality, and capitalism breeds greed.

We see more bureaucracy and institutionalism, environmental exploitation, information overload, economic manipulation, and moral deterioration. These are all unintended consequences of unconstrained extensions of intellectual ideas without responsible moral control. This is the Progress Paradox. Pushing forward without clearly thinking through where we are headed—promoting capitalistic goals and free-enterprise competition without due consideration of needed checks and restraints. Individualism over community. Profits over compassion.

In analyzing the evolution and ultimate dissolution of modernity from roughly 1650 to 1950, Stephen Toulmin traces two distinct branches of modern thinking. One is the *doctrinal* or *metaphysical* (flowing from an ideational culture) that eventually leads to counter-intellectualism. The other is the *experiential* or *scientific* (Sorokin's sensate culture). Toulmin writes that, "Over these three centuries, the two aspects of Modernity— doctrinal and experiential, metaphysical and scientific—traced out quite different trajectories."[6] The experiential/scientific aspect is what leads to hyper-intellectualism. We just keep pushing and pushing in the same direction—regardless of consequences. Toulmin explains that the experiential or scientific trajectory of modernity "has headed broadly upward."[7] But it is headed upward without a clear direction or reasonable restraint.

Counter-Intellectualism

The other part of our post-intellectual culture yearns to dissemble the modern dream/nightmare and return to a simpler pre-intellectual model— emphasizing passion, tribal identity, and a revitalized moral center. This is counter-intellectualism. Often this is a deliberate reaction to out-of-control hyper-intellectualism. This is the opposing aspect of modernity that Toulmin describes—the doctrinal or metaphysical: "The formal doctrines that underpinned human thought and practice from 1700 on followed a trajectory with the shape of an Omega, i.e., 'Ω.' After 300 years we are back close to our starting point."[8] This is an ideational counter-intellectual retreat from science and humanism.

The counter-intellectual mindset has dominated much of our cultural landscape since the Luddites of the early 1800s. In Fukuyama's words, "The deliberate rejection of technology and a rationalized society has been suggested by any number of groups in modern times, from the Romantics of the early nineteenth century, to the hippie movement of the 1960s, to Ayatollah Khomeini and Islamic fundamentalism."[9] Counter-intellectualism has long been a force in attempting to reverse the historical push towards modernity. It would be impossible, of course, to return to a premodern, non-technological society. We cannot put the technology genie back into the bottle. We cannot dissemble our bureaucracies. We cannot burn down our storehouses of information. Yet this counter-intellectual push is what drives Islamic extremists in their attempt to destroy Western modernity.

OPPOSING POST-INTELLECTUAL TRENDS IN SEVERAL FIELDS

It may be helpful to examine the distinctions between hyper-intellectualism and counter-intellectualism by looking at the contrasts in several different areas. In each of the fields discussed below, post-intellectualism can be divided into both hyper–intellectual trends and counter-intellectual movements.

Science

Critical thinking and science are the hallmarks of an intellectual culture—tempered with responsibility and restraint. But today we rush to embrace every new technological advance—the latest digital communication and entertainment formats, programmed household systems, automated vehicles, the promise of genetic improvement of the human race, and whatever comes down the pike next week. We seldom hesitate to charge forward wherever technology points. This hyper–intellectual mindset defines technological determinism.

At the same time, we witness a counter-intellectual return to mysticism and superstition—New Age philosophies, magic crystals, and psychic readings. Astrology and the occult are revived. Intuition replaces analysis and reasoning. In school districts across the country vocal citizens' groups insist on incorporating creationism into the curriculum on a par with scientific theories. Columnist Nicholas Kristof cites polls by Gallup and Harris to show Americans are three times more likely to believe in the virgin birth of Jesus than they are to believe in evolution.[10]

Economics

The hyper–intellectual economic trend is unrestrained capitalistic expansion and manipulation—exploitation that supersedes a rational and responsible free market system. The abuse of child laborers and impoverished workers enslaved in Third World sweatshops remains a capitalistic reality. Most of our environmental degradation is a result of hyper–intellectual economic policies. And postcolonial exploitation of the natural resources of developing countries is a provocation for terrorist attacks.

But we also witness counter-intellectual reactions to hyper-capitalist activity: anti-trust laws, truth-in-advertising legislation, labor unions, Affirmative Action, child-labor laws, minimum-wage statutes, wage-and-price controls, import and export tariffs, and so forth. If capitalism were to function with reason and restraint, there would be no need for such legislative remedies. Global movements for various forms of collective enterprise—from Marxism to democratic socialism to tribal communes—all reflect a counter-intellectual trend away from capitalistic competition as the sole economic paradigm. In retail operations we see a counter-intellectual reaction to massive merchandising endeavors—the swap meets, flea markets, arts-and-crafts fairs, yard sales, and farmers' markets that recall a more personal and informal retail environment. Even eBay—which moves about ten billion dollars worth of goods per year—is a vast, postmodern, decentralized, counter-intellectual virtual marketplace.

Education

As soon as widespread public education became a universal goal, we witnessed the inevitable slide into a post-intellectual frame of mind. By the late nineteenth century, according to Frances FitzGerald in *America Revised*, "Administrators and teachers put increasing faith in the notion that vocational training was the democratic alternative to the academic elitism of the European secondary schools. . . . The ideology of the teachers, however, merely reflected the fact that the community at large had no interest in providing intellectual training for the mass of high-school students; its concern was to train skilled workers for industry."[11] This is the hyper–intellectual aspect of post-intellectual education—*schools exist primarily as training centers for the corporate establishment.* We have forsaken the liberal arts in favor of vocational education; we have abandoned the generalist and embraced the specialist.

At the same time, we have the counter-intellectual trend toward "feel-good" education—schooling aimed at self-esteem, self-discovery, and self-acceptance. Multicultural pluralism and social relevance both evolved from this concern with equitable treatment of all individuals. Nobody fails. It may well be, in this day of cultural turmoil and ethnic inequities, that such an emphasis on self-esteem is indeed a needed function of schooling. However, it is not an *intellectual* function.

Scope of Governance

With the mass communication potential of the printing press and the philosophical stimulus of the Enlightenment, we embraced the intellectual idea of creating governmental units greater than the village or tribe. We invented the modern intellectual nation-state. Today we witness the continuing hyper–intellectual push toward world federalism on different levels—the United Nations, the European Union, international alliances, regional economic ventures, and so forth. We see the need for global cooperation in law enforcement, environmental protection, and international peacekeeping. This is a clear hyper–intellectual trend, recognizing that we are indeed all populating one global socioeconomic-environmental ecosystem, and that we must learn to perceive ourselves as part of an interconnected whole.

On the other hand, we have the increasingly strident counter-intellectual drift towards retribalization, the push for religious fundamentalist theocracies, and the legitimization of indigenous nations—the breakup of the nation-state. One needs only to look at post-Soviet Russia, post-communist Eastern Europe, and postcolonial Africa. This counter-intellectual retribalizing movement is examined in Chapter 17.

In addition to these four examples, illustrated in Figure 3, let's look briefly at just five other fields where the two conflicting strands of post-intellectualism become obvious: political philosophy, religion, urbanization, personal identity, and media. In each of these categories we can trace both a hyper–intellectual and a counter-intellectual movement.

Figure 3
Comparison of Hyper-Intellectualism and Counter-Intellectualism

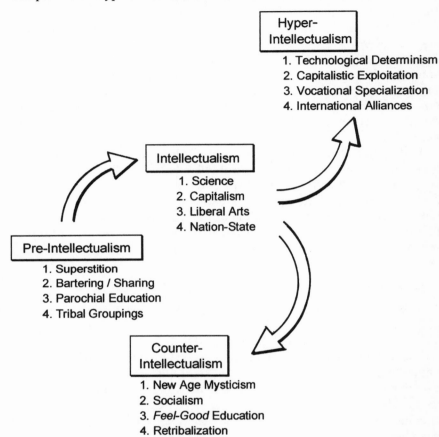

Political Philosophy

Even on the domestic political scene we can see these two opposing strands of post-intellectualism (to the extent that one can discern any meaningful difference between the two major political parties any more). The Republicans theoretically represent the hyper–intellectual approach. Push capitalism to the extreme. *Encourage competition and unrestricted free enterprise; eliminate welfare; reward the capitalists; people must assume responsibility for their own destinies.* The hyper–intellectual script would call for an intensification of the democratic process—even trying to force democracy into existence where Third World countries are not ready to handle it.

The Democrats, on the other hand, represent more of a counter-intellectual approach. *Since society has gotten too complicated and chaotic for meaningful citizen participation, the state must assume responsibility for centralized governance: welfare programs, environmental protection, corporate regulation, affirmative action legislation, and other social programs.* We individual citizens no longer can handle collective decision-making; we no longer can manage an intellectual political system. We must now rely on the technocrats and bureaucrats to run things for us. This counter-intellectual political mindset turns away from democracy to embrace various authoritarian alternatives—from tribal chiefs to religious states, from military dictatorships to soviet Marxism. We recognize the folly of self-government and try to find a way to return to some form of pre-intellectual political governance.

Religion

Humanism, Deism, and various liberal Protestant sects were all manifestations of the modern intellectual turn from authoritarian theistic religious thinking. The hyper–intellectual extension of this modern trend is the continued secularization of society. While polls consistently show that most Americans profess a belief in some sort of Higher Being, it is also true that religion plays an increasingly minor role in the conduct of the affairs of most men and women. *Churches are fine, raising children to believe in God is nice. But don't let religion interfere with the daily affairs of commerce, politics, education, personal moral freedom, science, and industry.* In his exhaustive study of the collapse of the American community, Robert Putnam writes, "In sum, over the last three to four decades Americans have become about 10 percent less likely to claim church membership, while our actual attendance and involvement in religious activities has fallen by roughly 25 to 50 percent."[12] The trend toward the "new morality" (replacing traditional standards of cultural behavior with pluralistic value systems) is part of this hyper–intellectual secular trend.

Simultaneously, we see a counter-intellectual movement in the growth of evangelistic and charismatic religions. Membership in the three largest Pentecostal churches more than doubled in the twenty-year period from 1970 to 1990. Putnam sums up the trend, "Over the last forty years mainline denominations (Methodist, Presbyterian, Episcopal, Lutheran, Congregational, American Baptist, and so on) have heavily lost 'market share,' while evangelical and fundamentalist groups (Southern Baptist, Pentecostal, Holiness, Assemblies of God, and Church of God in Christ, as well as Jehovah's Witnesses, Mormons, and independent congregations) have continued to grow."[13] These trends—along with the rise in Islamic fundamentalism in the Middle East—reflect a counter-intellectual, noncognitive approach to religion. Such authoritarian religions provide a safe haven for those seeking security and comfort in their lives. They provide some structure and order. They don't require any independent thinking or challenging of authority.

Urbanization

Urbanization was a modern, intellectual phenomenon. Modern technologies and industry promoted the rise of the large city. The urban center was needed for commerce, centralized governance, manufacturing growth, communication advances, and cultural opportunities. The hyper-intellectual extension of this trend is *hyper-urbanization*—urban sprawl beyond control (discussed in Chapter 16). The rise of the megalopolis—with the increasing numbers of urban dwellers and the resulting congestion, crime, pollution, and poverty—is a clear example of a modern/intellectual idea carried to the extreme. Expansion without restraint.

The counter-intellectual trend (in the United States at least) is the return to the countryside, rural living, an escape to the mountains, a cabin in the woods, a cottage by the lakeside. This romantic yearning—although seldom achieved by the common urban denizen—remains a clear idyllic counter-intellectual vision. We also witness a counter-intellectual intuitive ecological awareness—the "tree-huggers" and more extreme eco-terrorists who would halt all urbanizing encroachment and environmental despoliation by any means possible.

Personal Identity

In a premodern state, persons were viewed not as individuals but as components of a larger whole—the tribe. With the coming of the modern era, two conflicting intellectual concepts replaced this traditional tribal view. On one hand, individual identity, personal independence, and competition were fostered. *All persons should be allowed to compete freely and rise as far as their talents and abilities will carry them.* This sense of heightened individualism and competition easily morphs into to a hyper–intellectual self-centeredness that leads to a breakdown of family and community ties. *Do your own thing.* Others be damned; it's up to each individual to look out for himself or herself. *If it feels good, do it.*

But on the other hand, there evolved also with the modern era a commitment to equality under the law—egalitarianism. *All persons should be considered equal and should be treated the same.* This leads to a counter-intellectual backlash. If we allow unchecked individualism and personal competition to flourish, many persons will be hurt—due to socioeconomic deprivation, lower intelligence, physical handicaps, racial prejudice, gender discrimination, lack of academic motivation, inadequate financial resources, or other factors. Therefore, for the best of humanitarian reasons, we ask the state to guarantee equal opportunities and equal pay. We pass civil rights laws and establish affirmative action quotas to attain some degree of equal treatment in schools, jobs, and housing. And in so doing, our personal identity is sacrificed for the counter-intellectual security of tribal support and collective identity.

Media

In the premodern tribal world we relied upon oral communication, limiting our ability to think symbolically and abstractly. This pre-intellectual oral culture may be considered basically as a *yin* society—an intuitive, conservative, cooperative, passive culture. The brain is wired so that oral and pictorial communication—emphasizing feelings, intuition, and a holistic grasp of reality—can be considered more right-hemisphere oriented. This right-hemisphere mindset is typically associated with Poets, Artists, and Musicians—we'll call it the PAM mentality.

Modern culture brought us the written word and the printing press. Writing represented an intellectual cognitive society, with an emphasis on analysis and linear processing of information. Neil Postman explains, "To engage the written word means to follow a line of thought, which requires considerable powers of classifying, inference-making and reasoning. . . . In a culture dominated by print, public discourse tends to be characterized by a coherent, orderly arrangement of facts and ideas."[14] This was more of a *yang* orientation—analytic, expansive, aggressive, competitive, active. And it was more left-hemisphere centered, emphasizing logic and abstract reasoning. This left-hemisphere orientation reflects the mentality of Bureaucrats, Engineers, and Number-crunchers—call it the BEN culture.

Traditionally, yin has been considered more feminine and yang has more of a masculine identity. Thus, the oral tradition may be considered more of a right-hemisphere feminine means of communication—a means of connecting with others through feelings and emotion rather than through analysis and critical thinking. Writing, in contrast, is more of a left-hemisphere masculine medium. In a 1998 article for *Utne Reader*, Leonard Shlain summarizes the differences: "The feminine outlook is holistic, simultaneous, synthetic, and concrete, whereas the masculine view is linear, sequential, reductionist, and abstract."[15]

In post-intellectual terms, the hyper–intellectual *yang* extension of modern communication, print, is based on the computer. Think of computer programmers, technologists, engineers, researchers, lawyers, bureaucrats, and the piles of paperwork that characterize our masculine-dominated hierarchical culture. This is a left-hemisphere emphasis on *cognitive* communication, stressing analysis and sequential manipulation of information; the computer represents hyper-intellectualism.

Opposed to this masculine hyper-intellectualism, the counter-intellectual

aspect of post-intellectual media would be McLuhan's "electric media"—
predominantly radio, television, and the movies—that have returned us
to the non-linear, non-analytic "all-at-onceness" environment characteristic of the oral period. Many media critics have pointed out that with
these *yin*-oriented pictorial media, we moved from an analytic, inquiring,
intellectual means of discourse (our modern printing-press culture) into
a sophisticated form of oral/pictorial exchange. In effect, we have returned
to an oral tradition. This counter-intellectual form of communication is a
noncognitive manipulation of images and passions, motion and sensa-
tions, entertainment and fantasy. The electric media have transported us
into a counter-intellectual *affective* culture—back to the right hemisphere.
Print is masculine; television is feminine. In Chapter 12 we explore further
this genderization of the media.

IT IS THE GIVE AND TAKE OF THESE TWO THRUSTS—the hyper–intellectual
BENs and the counter-intellectual PAMs—that typify the web culture. The
hyper–intellectual would pursue expansion and research, advancing on
many fronts—escalating economic opportunities, building greater technological monuments to human ingenuity, and ultimately creating more
bureaucracy and uncertainty. The counter-intellectual would return to a
more secure and predictable ideational world dominated by tradition and
authority and, in the words of Isaiah Berlin, "a faith incarnated in historically hallowed institutions that reason dare not touch."[16]
    There is a parallel analysis with what has been called the "bi-polar vi-
sions of cyber-utopianism and neo-Luddism."[17] On one side, we want to
push ahead with hyper–intellectual applications of science and technology (cyber-utopianism); and at the same time we yearn for a return to a
less hectic counter-intellectual period of simplicity and tranquility (neo-
Luddism). Fukuyama describes this bipolar ambivalence in terms of our
stumbling trek toward the End of History:

There seem to be two parallel processes at work. In the political and economic
sphere history appears to be progressive and directional, and at the end of the
twentieth century has culminated in liberal democracy as the only viable choice
for technologically advanced societies [hyper-intellectualism]. In the social and
moral sphere, however, history appears to be cyclical, with social order ebbing
and flowing over the course of generations [counter-intellectualism].[18]

    Much of the uncertainty and perplexity of our post-intellectual age is
the juxtaposing of these conflicting tuggings: technopoly versus New Age
mysticism; hyper-capitalism opposed to social welfare programs; specialized education vying with affective "feel good" education; world federalism fighting retribalization; libertarianism versus authoritarianism;
atheism versus God; the city opposed to the countryside; individualism
opposed to community; competition versus affirmative action; print or
pictures. *Try this; no, that. Pull here; no, push there.*

PART II

The Causes: How Things Got Out of Control

Innovation is irresistible. Progress is inevitable. Resistance is futile.
—James Gleick

Before we can talk about the long road to cultural healing, we must begin by understanding the illness.
—Morris Berman

Part I dealt with definitions: trying to understand postmodernism, post-intellectualism, as well as the Progress Paradox. This was part of the exposition of the problem—the first step in the problem-solving pattern (Chapter 3)—defining the status quo. The next step in the Analytic Thinking Pattern (see Figure 1) is to assess how the problem—the situation, the dilemma—got where it is. What are the roots of the problem? What are the factors that led us to where we are today? How did we evolve into a post-intellectual state? This is what Part II is about—the Causes: potential self-contradictions inherent in the concept of intellectualism (Chapter 8); three underlying determinants that have led to the unraveling of our intellectual dream (Chapter 9); the actual erosion of our modern idealism over the better part of two centuries (Chapter 10); the decade of the 1960s, that defining moment when we witnessed the post-intellectual age materializing (Chapter 11); and the role that our media technologies have played in this transition (Chapter 12).

CHAPTER 8

Inherent Contradictions of Intellectualism

One of the perplexing dilemmas of the intellectual enterprise is that there are numerous instances where one inherent precept of our modern philosophy conflicts with other modern tenets. Maybe the idea of establishing an intellectual civilization involves too many incompatibilities. Francis Fukuyama asks, "is liberal democracy prey to serious internal contradictions, contradictions so serious that they will eventually undermine it as a political system?"[1] Certainly this possibility must be considered when looking for causes of our postmodern disarray; perhaps the theory of mass intellectualism is inherently self-contradictory.

Some examples: The modern idea of egalitarianism works against the modern idea of economic competition. The modern idea of individualism just doesn't fit well with the Enlightenment ideal of rational order and structure. Loyalty to the modern nation-state comes into conflict with individualism. Modern rational debate often works against tolerance. We try to embrace the search for absolute Truth while we simultaneously encourage respect for multicultural diversity. These and other inherent contradictions tend to undermine the viability of the intellectual ideal. It just may be that the age of modernity carried within its idealistic premise the roots of its own ultimate decline.

LIMITATIONS OF HUMAN RATIONALITY

We start this inquiry, however reluctantly, by questioning the essential premise of the Enlightenment—that human beings are clearheaded and responsible enough to govern their own affairs. Our visionary forefathers burst forth from the Enlightenment galvanized by the ideals of Bacon, Milton, Voltaire, and Locke. They plunged into the American and French revolutions to prove that common citizens could control their own destinies. We deluded ourselves with the newly articulated modern philosophy that human reason would be able to overcome all the irrational and illogical forces of mankind's base nature.

But realistically we find ourselves still driven by our basic passions and animal instincts. We are motivated by our short-term cravings for immediate profits, sensual satisfactions, and lust for power. Technologically we may be able to send rockets to the stars and dissect our own genetic code, but our Paleolithic DNA is still programmed for a life of hunting and gathering.

Herbert Spencer observed over a hundred years ago that "The Republican [i.e., representative] form of government is the highest form of government: but because of this it requires the highest type of human nature—a type nowhere at present existing."[2] If we humans are to prevail on a higher level, we have to deliberately and purposefully rise above our passions and instincts; we must act with intentional reason and a conscious commitment to responsible behavior. First of all, we must accept that we are personally accountable for the outcomes of our actions. If we want to be independent individuals, we must be responsible for the decisions we make individually and collectively. To maintain an intellectual culture we must work for the greatest good for all of humanity; we must be responsible for making decisions that benefit all of society. We cannot think only of our own immediate well-being or of our extended family. And we must be responsible for making decisions for the long-term good of society. We cannot think only of short-terms profits and immediate gratifications.

Daniel Quinn points out that our cultural system would work if only we could improve the nature of *Homo sapiens:* "We just need to be made kinder, gentler, sweeter, more loving, less selfish, more far-sighted, and so on, then everything will be fine."[3] Rather than improving the nature of the human species, however, we are becoming uncomfortably aware that we may actually be nurturing the proliferation of individuals who are less capable of handling the responsibilities demanded by an increasingly complex intellectual environment.[4]

UNRESTRAINED CAPITALISM

Capitalism is good. Capitalism, responsibly implemented, results in the greatest good for the greatest number of people. As Adam Smith so painstakingly spelled out for us, it's hard to beat the profit motive for motivation. Everyone wins from open competition. We all get better-quality products and services at lower prices. End of the free-market sermon.

Our concern is the debilitating impact of hyper-capitalism. The intellectual concept of free enterprise is dependent upon two things. First, the manufacturers and retailers involved in any capitalistic venture shall be responsible and honest in their endeavors—their production, advertising, and marketing operations. Second, the consumers shall be intelligent and discriminating in their purchase of various products and services. Thus, the whole operation is to be carried out on an intellectual level. Contrary to this intellectual ideal, the nature of contemporary commerce today assumes that potential buyers are weak-minded, susceptible to impulse and passion, and easy to manipulate. And consumers all too often corroborate this assumption. As we fail to meet these two assumptions—honest purveyors and analytic consumers—the intellectual foundation of capitalism falls apart. Richard Hofstadter wrote in 1963, "No doubt there is a certain measure of inherent dissonance between business enterprise and intellectual enterprise: being dedicated to different sets of values, they are bound to conflict; and intellect is always potentially threatening to any institutional apparatus or to fixed centers of power." [5]

We can trace the demise of capitalism as an intellectual enterprise simply by looking at the degeneration of advertising messages over the past hundred years or so—from the written word to the pictorial image, from coherent arguments to truncated slogans, from rational assertions to emotional appeals, from exposition to blaring exaggerations, from straightforward claims to subliminal manipulation. Advertising has become an anti-intellectual activity. It is, in fact, designed to make sure the consumer does *not* think. Jerry Mander, a former advertising executive, proclaimed, "If you accept the existence of advertising, you accept a system designed to persuade and to dominate minds by interfering in people's thinking patterns." [6]

Another problem with our modern economic structures may be that our bureaucracies and economic institutions have basically gotten too large for the self-correcting mechanisms of the free marketplace to work. Fast-paced technological leaps and innovative marketing schemes are not compatible with centralized bureaucracies—the banking systems, the regulatory mechanisms, the legislative inertia, the international trade restrictions. Unfettered capitalism no longer is unfettered—but the fettering mechanisms are hopelessly burdened and antiquated. The complexities of modern economic structures and operations are simply too convoluted for governmental bureaucracies to handle.

Greed and Materialism

One self-defeating feature of capitalism is that traditional free-marketplace economics results in greed becoming an end in itself. Materialism and ostentatious consumption become our primary universal cultural goals. This is a clear instance of rationalism (how to make a fast buck most efficiently) running counter to responsibility (the need for a degree of self-restraint). Steve Allen points out the underlying danger of unbridled capitalism: "What is involved is nothing more than the anything-for-a-buck mindset that even Adam Smith, who was, after all, a moral philosopher, recognized as the central problem of free-enterprise capitalism. Its ability to produce profits and a high standard of living has never been in doubt; the question is, can it do so without corrupting its practitioners and the societies in which they function?"[7] We must consider also the dangerous side effects of the concentration of power and wealth—the political corruption, the business deceptions, voter disillusionment with corporate control of government, and the international reaction to American hegemony.

Not only does greed tend to muddle our cultural narrative, it undermines other priorities of a just and equitable society. By promoting competition and economic conflict—while proclaiming *greed is good*—the free-marketplace enterprise actually tends to destroy traditional values such as security, loyalty, and compassion. On one hand we are asked to grind our competitors into the dust; and on the other hand we are supposed to demonstrate sympathy and a sense of fair play to those less fortunate than we. One has trouble serving both the marketplace and transcendent moral purposes—yet traditional capitalist theory sees no contradiction between these values. This confusion of cultural values is examined in Chapter 14.

One undeniable outcome of unrestrained capitalistic competition is the reality that people do get hurt. Unless restrained by government fiat, corporate practices have exploited labor at every opportunity. In Chapter 1, we mentioned the widening income gap between the richest and poorest Americans. The poorest 20 percent of Americans saw their after-tax income (in real dollars) drop 16 percent from 1977 to 1994; during the same time period, the richest one percent saw their after-tax income increase by 72 percent.[8] Tax cuts for the affluent only accentuate the growing chasm between higher levels of management and the disenchanted working class. The rich get richer and the poor get assured they are receiving a good deal. But the gap is real; and it is getting larger. This is not the formula for an intellectually based responsible culture. Rousseau wrote 240 years ago, "If the object is to give the State consistency, bring the two extremes [the affluent and the poor] as near to each other as possible; allow neither rich men nor beggars."[9]

UNIVERSAL EDUCATION AND MASS MEDIOCRITY

Universal education is a good thing. It is mandatory if we are to achieve an intellectual, participatory society. In order to vote responsibly and to communicate coherently with elected officials, all citizens must be liberally educated in all aspects of our cultural affairs. End of the why-we-must-have-universal-public-education sermon.

The ironic reality is that if universal education is to accommodate the masses, it inevitably results in a deterioration of academic standards—lowering scholarly expectations so that the greater populace can be included in the system. Starting with the wave of European immigrants in the 1890s, schools have become de facto welfare institutions—stressing remedial English, health education, home economics, and vocational instruction. And then we added driver education, sex education, drug awareness education, and family education. Year after year our intellectual aspirations withered. Then during the turbulent 1960s we gave up on any intellectual pretensions at all. It was more important to stress relevance than academic challenge; we were to emphasize getting along rather than getting ahead. Schools were to concentrate on the counter-intellectual goals of self-realization, multicultural pluralism, sensitivity, and self-esteem—rather than scholastic pursuits. These may all be valid and worthwhile goals, but they are not intellectual goals. Additionally, we then ask our schools to assume more and more non-academic responsibilities—as surrogate parents, medical clinics, counseling offices, welfare kitchens, law enforcement agencies, and sensitivity-training centers.

Our Anti-Intellectual Bias

Even more disturbing is the overt anti-intellectualism that pervades our contemporary culture. This is one of the great ironies of America. We were founded on intellectual principles; but today we shun intellectual achievement as somehow un-American. Academic success is perceived as being inherently anti-democratic. In *The Culture of Narcissism: American Life in an Age of Diminishing Expectations*, Christopher Lasch writes, "The whole problem of American education comes down to this: in American society, almost everyone identifies intellectual excellence with elitism. This attitude not only guarantees the monopolization of educational advantages by the few; it lowers the quality of elite education itself and threatens to bring about a reign of universal ignorance."[10] Students get the message that, in the spirit of democratic egalitarianism, they should not aspire to rise above the average; it is somehow unfair to achieve a position of intellectual competence. It's just not cool to stand out academically. Our intellectual infrastructure continues to unravel. George Will adds, "Indeed many teachers now consider the traditional idea of teaching to be intellectually suspect and morally offensive because it is tainted by the authoritarian idea that there are defensible standards and by the inegalitarian idea that some people do things better than others."[11]

Society glorifies the macho hero and the sex goddess, while belittling those who are concerned with affairs of the mind. We reward our entertainment celebrities, sports luminaries, and top corporate executives with extravagant incomes, while our nation's school teachers, poets, philosophers, writers, and other intellectual toilers subsist barely a notch above the official poverty line. Alumni of outstanding institutions of higher learning such as the University of Michigan, UCLA, Duke University, and Notre Dame identify more with their football and basketball teams than they do with their research labs or Nobel Prize winners.

The Contradiction of Tolerance and Skepticism

Skepticism is an intellectual quality. To be rational and scientific, one must be skeptical. *Ask questions. Challenge authority. Accept nothing at face value.* But tolerance is also an intellectual virtue—all persons are to be treated equally; we are to respect the personal opinions and philosophies of others. *Don't belittle anybody. Be careful when asking questions.* Our pluralistic educational philosophy stresses that we are to be tolerant and accepting of differing values and viewpoints; consequently we tend to become less skeptical. Our passion for seeking truth becomes watered down. After all, *since we all are to be treated equally, there really are no objective standards or truths. Your truth is as good as my truth.*

Uncritical tolerance is a post-intellectual offshoot of our educational system; *we will embrace a compassionate open-mindedness in which we accept everyone and every belief.* Every theory, every value system, is to receive equal treatment—theism and atheism, capitalism and Marxism, creationism and evolution. We easily confuse an open mind with an empty mind. We use the label of tolerance to avoid the effort of engaging in analysis and critical thinking.

DEMOCRACY AND MASSES PARTICIPATION

Participatory government is an intellectual concept. But, like universal education, once you get too many people involved the process becomes watered down, less intellectual. A democratic system cannot maintain the same level of intellectual debate among the masses that it enjoyed when only the elites were debating. Mass participation (if it can be achieved) lowers the level of those participating in the process. Therefore we find that sound bites, simplistic slogans, balloons, and buffoonery become the norm in contemporary politics. We become more concerned with images than issues, personalities than policies. And we drift further and further into a post-intellectual political arena.

The masses do not want to be intellectually convinced by analytic arguments; they want to be comforted and reassured by folksy nonintellectual images. Neil Postman reminds us, "We are not permitted to know who is best at being President or Governor or Senator, but whose image is best in touching and soothing the deep reaches of our discontent."[12] After the convincing defeats of the intellectual Adlai Stevenson in 1952 and 1956, presidential candidates have been careful not to appear too intellectual. John Kennedy surrounded himself with intellectual advisors, but his election was due primarily to his own image and charisma. And Richard Nixon later won two elections partially because of the more analytic and intellectual tone of his opponents (Hubert Humphrey and George McGovern). The qualities that have been most successful in postmodern elections are the nonintellectual earthiness of Lyndon Johnson, the informality of Jimmy (not James) Carter, and the folksy humor of Ronald Reagan. Michael Dukakis was too formal and intellectual in 1988. Four years later the contest was between the down-home Arkansas saxophone player (not the Rhodes scholar) and the good ol' boy who calls Texas home (not the Yale-educated eastern elitist). And in 2000 the race went to the charismatic tenderfoot rather than to the experienced intellectual.

The electorate today cannot confidently wade through the intricate issues and contortions of the technological culture it is presented with. Specialization in the workplace has contributed to a citizenry that cannot handle the complexities of its own government. Adam Smith foresaw this 225 years ago. Writing about the decline of the intellectual capabilities of the average worker, he warned, "The man whose whole life is spent in performing a few simple operations . . . has no occasion to exert his understanding or to exercise his invention in finding out expedients for removing difficulties which never occur. He naturally loses, therefore, the habit of such exertion, and generally becomes as stupid and ignorant as it is possible for a human creature to become."[13] Here we have the great champion of capitalism warning that the ordinary citizen in that system will not be qualified to participate in the running of the system.

Therefore we turn to the experts, the specialists, and technocrats. The citizens no longer are capable of participating in collective decision-making. We are slipping further and further from that intellectual goal we once set for ourselves. It may well be that democracy is an oxymoron—a self-contradiction in one word. This topic of the paradox of democracy is taken up in more depth in Chapter 18.

ONE UNDERLYING THEME raised in this chapter is this: As more and more people participate in any kind of cultural institution, the enterprise gets more and more muddled and watered down. Standards have to be lowered in order to accommodate the masses. In effect, anything that tries to appeal to and involve the masses becomes less intellectual—television programming, popular music, literature, religion, advertising, schooling, or government. These are the disturbing inherent contradictions of our intellectual undertaking.

Perhaps there never was an Age of Intellectualism. Social philosophers and political leaders just deluded themselves into believing that humans were capable of thinking clearly and dispassionately, that we could conduct our affairs intelligently and responsibly. Perhaps all we ever experienced was a post-Enlightenment Age of Euphoria. New Zealand attorney Al Koning writes,

The era of Enlightenment was an era of enlightenment of the elite. The masses were just as ignorant and as irrational and irresponsible as they are today; they never were free. So, I would argue that the difference between the intellectual and post-intellectual era is not that there are fewer intellectuals but that the masses are allowed to participate in the political process and this is the real cause of the rise of post-intellectualism.[14]

The intellectual ideal says *involve the people*. The attempt is made to include all the citizens—many of whom are not intellectually inclined. Thus, in order to accommodate the masses (in commerce, schooling, and democracy) the intellectual bar must be lowered. We do not then have a citizenry that can behave consistently in a rational and responsible intellectual manner. Perhaps the concept of an intellectual community is too artificial and fragile for a mass society to maintain. Based upon an unwarranted faith in the rationality of mankind, it simply cannot long be sustained. Intellectual pursuits are inherently elitist. Only the brightest and most intellectual tend to willingly get involved in affairs of state, art, education, and culture. With this disconsolate prognosis in mind, we shall continue to examine the modern ideal of an intellectual society.

CHAPTER 9

Three Underlying Determinants

How did postmodernism—specifically, post-intellectualism—come about? It won't do merely to refer to changing lifestyles, artistic revolutions, post–World War II culture shock, rebellious youth, or Vietnam schizophrenia. We need to understand why these dynamics came into play. An examination of our post-intellectual transition reveals three underlying determinants: (1) exhaustion of the policy of *linear growth and expansion;* (2) the phenomenon of *information overload;* and (3) our surrender to *technological determinism.* These are the three factors that have most directly triggered our post-intellectual disarray.

FAILURE OF LINEAR GROWTH TO SUSTAIN US

Out of the Enlightenment came an intellectual commitment to progress, to growth and development. This was our linear culture. We would continue to move forward in a clear, straight line. This was most evident in economics and capitalism. Based on geographic exploration and engineering technology, we were to push onward with an unswerving faith in perpetual economic growth. In his classic *Wealth of Nations,* Adam Smith set down in concrete the definition of modern, free enterprise capitalism based upon unending growth and expansion—ever increasing demands for goods and labor.

Every social enterprise, every financial scheme, every political plan has been based on the ideology that there would always be more—more territory to explore and conquer, more resources to mine and exploit, more trees to cut down, more land to plow, more products to manufacture and sell, more customers, more taxpayers, more babies, more schools, more room to throw away our trash and pollution—year after year after year. Thus have our economic structures been built for centuries on the assumption that our planetary resources are inexhaustible. Political leaders, urban planners, and economists delude themselves with the promise of unending physical growth and development.

Economic and Ecological Realities

This illusory assumption of continual linear expansion had to end at some point. We have to accept that there are ecological limits on how much of the Earth can be plowed, drilled, and paved. The simple physical fact is that we cannot continue to expand until the whole planet is solid city. Fritjof Capra writes that "Smith himself predicted that economic progress would eventually come to an end when the wealth of nations had been pushed to the natural limits of soil and climate, but unfortunately he thought this point was so far in the future that it was irrelevant to his theories."[1] Today, it is no longer irrelevant. That future has arrived. During the twentieth century, this linear expansionistic culture bumped into the ecological and economic realities of a world that has physical limits and finite resources. But we are still trying to function with an institutional infrastructure (our schools, corporations, political parties, cities) designed for the Age of Linear Growth; we don't know how to make these institutions work in an age of dwindling resources and the reality of a finite planet. This fallacy of infinite economic growth is explored in Chapter 16.

Many of our troubles mentioned in the Progress Paradox (Chapter 1) are triggered directly by the failure of linear growth to sustain us indefinitely. Problems of the unemployed and the homeless, the deteriorating inner cities, widespread poverty, our debilitating welfare system, crime in the streets, the punctured Wall Street bubble: these are all due to the fact that economic development and employment opportunities eventually reach a finite limit. The economy stops expanding; the promise of eternal progress falls short. And millions find themselves without jobs, without a stable home, without a secure environment, without a clear understanding of where the future is headed. The exploitation of our natural resources, the resulting global pollution, and our spiraling worldwide population pressures all are evidence of our addiction to continued linear growth and expansion—with little consideration of our responsibility for future generations. Then, too, we have to deal with the economic disparity between the developed societies that have benefited from our centuries-long economic exploitation and the Third World peoples who have fallen further behind. The economic inequities of the postmodern age become more apparent.

As outlined in Chapter 7, post-intellectualism has two faces. The *counter-intellectuals* are those who cry out that growth must stop; they include the neo-Luddites who would have us return to an earlier day of less industrialization. The *hyper-intellectuals* are those adherents of a growth-as-usual policy who insist that we can continue to keep the material economy expanding indefinitely. The truth lies somewhere in between. We cannot return to halcyon days of bucolic pastures and cottage industries—although we may be able to take some steps in that direction. Neither can we continue to expand indefinitely. That reality must be accepted. Tax cuts cannot stimulate unending growth. The economic cornucopia has stopped flowing. We cannot grow to infinity; that is a physical certainty. This shattering of the fantasy of unending growth is the first of our three underlying determinants of post-intellectualism.

INFORMATION OVERLOAD

The modern intellectual mind has an innate drive to explore; we are destined to seek, to invent, to search for the novel, to uncover new information. Hence, the intellectual is always generating new data—leading inevitably to information overload.

A conservative estimate is that the world's storehouse of information doubles every five years (others say every four years, or even less). At the exponential rate of one doubling every five years, the total amount of information in the world increases a thousand-fold every fifty years. Thus, you are trying to cope with a global information environment that is about a thousand times more complex than what your grandparents were facing at your age. You must constantly learn to cope with new information about genetic manipulation, new tax revisions, cell phone updates, nanotechnology, Middle Eastern politics, high-definition TV, the inner city homeless, religious cults, famine in Africa, the Greenhouse Effect, wi-fi developments, domestic terrorism, contradictory nutritional research, new Internet sites, experimental cancer treatments, electric automobiles, corporate debacles, updating your personal web site, political sex scandals, a missing child in San Diego, and your neighbor's suspicious friends. It was stuff your grandparents didn't have to worry much about. James Gleick writes, "The dream of perfect ceaseless information flow can slip so easily into a nightmare of perfect perpetual distraction."[2]

Our increasingly complicated and legalistic society demands more and more information—to comply with a maze of legislative and bureaucratic procedures. When Washington Mutual Bank bought out Home Savings of America several years back, an IRA account of mine was switched from one institution to the other. It took two letters and three booklets, totaling 146 pages, to inform me of the switch. The one outcome I needed to be concerned about was that our account number had been changed. No action was needed on my part. But 146 pages of legalese and financial sophistry were generated in order to effect the transition. There might have been some obscure federal regulation or legal fine point that I needed to comprehend. I don't know. I confess I didn't read all 146 pages.

Information Incoherence

The media have engulfed the American citizen in a profusion of facts and data, structured and unstructured, significant and trivial: from TV commercials, newspaper headlines, and political sound bites to billboards, magazine ads, and storefront posters.[3] As we try to watch the TV news summaries, we are treated to a numbing array of running headlines, pictorial inserts, captions crawling along the screen, news digests, stock market reports, weather forecasts, and sports scores—all layered upon each other, littering our sensory input. Our computers add to the information clutter: WWW sites, e-mail messages, chat rooms, interactive games, crawling headlines, search results, weblogs (*blogs*), and hundreds of non-requested links—banner ads, pop-up ads, pop-under screens, and scads of spam. We have entered into what Neil Postman calls a *peek-a-boo* world, "where now this event, now that, pops into view for a moment, then vanishes again. It is a world without much coherence or sense."[4]

We are exposed to over 3,000 advertising messages a day. More than 50,000 scientific articles are written every week. Over 75,000 new books are published in the United States each year. Over ten years ago, a Bell Labs report stated that in a single day's edition of *The New York Times* there is more information than an individual man or woman would have had access to in his or her entire life in the sixteenth century.[5] The Library of Congress, with close to 130 million items in its holdings, is adding about 10,000 new items to be catalogued every day. There are hundreds of millions of web sites readily accessible, with billions of individual web pages for your perusal; and they are growing at the rate of at least 400 million pages per year. That's on the *visible* web. There may be well over 500 billion documents available on the *invisible* web (or the *deep* web).

The value of any commodity is lessened the more of it there is. This applies not only to physical goods—oil, wheat, gold, housing—but to information wares as well: academic research, TV talk shows, Internet web sites, and terrorism warnings. We simply cannot place a high value on anything that exists in abundance. The more information that is thrust at us, the less we can pay attention to each individual item or datum. Information overload leads to information desensitization. Richard Saul Wurman, in *Information Anxiety*, writes,

The glut [of data] has begun to obscure the radical distinctions between data and information, between facts and knowledge. . . . The more time we spend with reports of separate events, the less time we have to understand the "whys and wherefores" behind them, to see the patterns and relationships between them, and to understand the present in the context of history. Instead, we are lulled by a stream of surface facts, made numb, passive, and unreceptive by a surfeit of data that we lack the time and resources needed to turn into valuable information.[6]

The incongruity is that the availability of information and the capacity for reflective thinking do not go hand in hand. Information is needed for successful problem-solving and critical thinking, but too much information can overload the reasoning process (this phenomenon is examined in Chapter 15). Information does not inevitably support thinking; too often it replaces it.

Information Control

We cannot possibly comprehend (acquire, catalog, organize, retrieve, understand, and evaluate) everything that is available to us. Therefore we rely on others to do the editing and explaining for us. We must ask, however, *Who controls our information?* The family, schools, churches and temples, political operatives, business corporations, military units, government bureaus, medical systems, advertising agencies, courts, libraries, PR firms and the media all are concerned with processing information on our behalf. Each information-control agency filters and interprets information for us—as each institution perceives our needs—and tries to shield us from other information. These agencies, in an increasingly information-saturated environment, assume authority whether we want them to or not. We have less and less influence over those agencies that control our information channels.

Of equal concern is that, as the total information load becomes heavier than these institutions can handle, the information-processing agencies themselves break down. The schools, government bureaus, research labs, law enforcement and judicial systems begin to crack under the information load. They no longer can funnel the appropriate information to us, nor each other. Witness the inability of the FBI and CIA and other intelligence agencies to analyze their own field information, their own internal reports, and "connect the dots," let alone share key information among other bureaus.

In our postmodern culture, where do we turn for coherence? For knowledge? In the cyclical culture, we found knowledge by listening to our elders. In the linear culture, we found knowledge by scientific analysis, observation, experimentation, and logical thinking. In the post-intellectual web culture, we are not sure where to turn for knowledge. The blip culture offers us no coherence.[7] We no longer trust science, or religion, our political leaders, our corporate heads, the police, what we read in the papers, see on the tube, or find on the Web. In our postmodern state, we no longer know how to determine truth; we no longer know how to know. Overwhelmed by the magnitude of the information overload, it may be that we ordinary citizens cannot command the knowledge needed to participate in the decision-making process. In which case we are no longer taking part in a participatory democracy.

TECHNOLOGICAL DETERMINISM

The guidebook to Chicago's 1933 World's Fair grandly proclaimed, "Science discovers, industry applies, and *man adapts himself to or is molded by new things. . . .* Individuals, groups, entire races of men, *fall into step with Science and Industry* (italics added)."[8] What sounded like a glowing prelude to a promising age of innovation has turned into a frightening prediction of machines run amuck. This has led to what is generally defined today as technological determinism—our technologies have taken on an existence and purpose of their own. They determine their own sense of direction. As mentioned in Chapter 6, this is what Neil Postman defined as Technopoly; Jerry Mander called it Megatechnology. Technological determinism is the phenomenon of allowing research and bureaucracy and software programs to determine for us where society is headed—establishing their own patterns and priorities without deliberate human intervention. This is hyper-intellectualism. As summed up by Gleick, "Innovation is irresistible. Progress is inevitable. Resistance is futile."[9]

Technology encompasses more than just science apparatus and equipment. It is both the hardware and human resources used in a methodical and systematic manner to achieve certain specific practical objectives. Technology is, in effect, a systems approach to problem-solving—using brains as well as hardware, intellectual constructs as well as science labs, bureaucratic institutions as well as machines. The alphabet is a technology. So is the calendar, a legal contract, the jury system, the city zoning commission. Thus, technological determinism refers not just to machines run amuck, but also to overwhelming bureaucracy, institutionalism, endless paperwork.

Progress feeds upon itself. Every technological advance opens the door to subsequent leaps of progress. Sir William Armstrong made this observation in the 1860s: "The tendency of progress is to quicken progress, because every acquisition in science is so much vantage ground for fresh attainment. We may expect, therefore, to increase our speed as we struggle forward."[10] Technological progress creates an environment of change; technological breakthroughs begin to increase exponentially. The multiplying branches of science and social engineering develop a thrust of their own; our engineering and legalistic infrastructures take on their own sense of authority and destiny.

Every technology from the wheel onward has brought cataclysmic change; we have had to mold our culture—and ourselves—to fit every scientific advancement. Agriculture is a technology that foreordained that the city (another technology) would have to follow. The technology of the printing press created the nation-state, invented privacy, promoted individualism, demanded that schools be established, and undermined the authority of the church. The automobile created suburbia, interstate commerce, air pollution, fast-food chains, shopping malls, and new courtship patterns. Similarly with the elevator, the airplane, air conditioning, the splitting of the atom, television, the satellite, the transistor, the computer, e-commerce, and deferred stock options. Wherever we turn today we confront the mind-boggling and incomprehensible avalanche of new technological promises and bureaucratic developments hurled at us in every conceivable field—from computers and nanotechnology to automated highway systems and genetic engineering. Every technological advance rearranges all of our social, leisure, economic, political, and informational patterns. Thus it is that "individuals, groups, entire races of men, fall into step with Science and Industry." This is not a new concern, of course. In Chapter 1, we quoted Henry David Thoreau's observation that "men have become the tools of their tools."

Computers and Digital Advances

Today's computer advances outpace the wildest science-fiction fabrications. We are researching or already developing optical computers that use laser beams instead of wires, carbon nanotubes to replace conventional silicon chips, X-ray lasers that could shrink electronic circuits to one-thousandth of their present size, logic circuits that have molecule-sized components, and quantum processors that could conceivably solve a problem in three seconds that would take today's supercomputers one billion years. Science writer George Johnson describes the ultimate machine: "The end is not in sight. By some estimates, the shrinking will continue over coming decades until each component is the size of a single atom, registering a bit of information by the position of an orbiting electron."[11] Nanotechnology promises everything from self-cleaning window glass to, in the words of Michael Crichton, "a mass of tiny computers, smaller than specks of dust, programmed to travel in a cloud over a country like Iraq and send back pictures."[12]

With expanded wireless networks, you'll be permanently ethereally connected wherever you roam. Virtual reality and simulated experiences will become more attractive than reality. Intelligence agents on the Internet will handle all your personal shopping chores—deciding what to buy for you. Your alarm clock will check your PDA schedule for the next day, cross-reference relevant Web sites, monitor early morning traffic reports, and decide for you what time you should be awakened. Even more alarming technological scenarios involve cyber-terrorism. Imagine the mayhem when a crazed Ted Kaczynski (the *Unabomber*) utilizes advanced technologies to attack the establishment—instead of merely throwing low-tech bombs at the technology. It is possible today to download from the Internet the genetic blueprint for a synthetic deadly virus and then use mail-order materials to assemble the new deadly bug.

Microchip sensors implanted in your forearm will automatically adjust both light and temperature controls in intelligent buildings. Some scientists see the day when keyboards and monitors (and possibly even the CPU) will be replaced by tiny chips and telephones implanted in one's head. We have already devised a "tooth phone," a low-frequency receiver that can be embedded in one's molar. We have chip implants in inner ears, vision chips that can crudely replace the retina, and brain implants to help reduce the tremors of Parkinson's disease. Going one step further, engineering professor Bart Kosko predicts that "The distant but inevitable step is not just to back up the brain but to replace it outright. Then the music of the mind will play on a digital instrument with almost godlike powers."[13]

Artificial intelligence and "thinking computers" will be self-generating and self-replicating. And self-improving—following what has been termed *evolutionary computation*. They will learn from their own mistakes and shortcomings and design their offspring to perform even better—spawning thousands of new generations every second. Science writer Brad Lemley speculates, "If computer systems can evolve and adapt, it does become harder and harder to say there is some fundamental difference between biological life and machines. This technology is moving from science fiction to reality. . . . Given that such cyber–beings will grow exponentially smarter and stronger with each and every passing hour, they could quickly become as intellectually superior to human beings as we are to bacteria."[14]

The Promise of Genetic Manipulation

Genetic progress races forward in numerous areas: stem cell research, parthenogenesis (cloning), xenotransplantation (harvesting body parts from genetically altered pigs), neurogenesis (brain cell regeneration), fabrication of synthetic body parts, growing new body parts, and other scenarios beyond our imagination at this point. The promise for doing good is incalculable. The potential for saving lives and ridding society of numerous disabling diseases is a reality. The temptation to play God is overwhelming.

We are on the frontier of *volitional evolution*—the ability to direct our own evolution by genetic manipulation. Close to a thousand children have been born using the process of *pre-implantation genetic diagnosis* to screen eggs or embryos for the presence of disease-causing genes, and then selecting only those embryos that are free of defects to develop. Once we start down that slippery slope toward designer babies, where do we stop? What about enhancing mathematical ability? Increasing hand-eye coordination for embryonic athletics? What if musical parents want their offspring to have perfect pitch? How about eliminating tendencies toward violence? Homosexuality? Columnist Charles Krauthammer warns, "Huxley was right; Orwell was wrong. The future is not a boot stamping on a human face. It is a factory for producing human variants: sub- and super-, hybrids and clones, parts and pieces of the human organism."[15] Some genetic scientists foresee the day when we will be able to create completely new life forms.[16]

On the other hand, human improvement through genetic engineering might be the only answer to keep pace with continued computer advances. The triumph of technological determinism could well be the merging of genetic and computer technologies. In a late 2001 interview, Stephen Hawking stated that if humans hope to compete with the rising tide of artificial intelligence, they'll have to improve through genetic engineering. He claimed that human beings would have to "improve" their own genetic makeup: "We should follow this road if we want biological systems to remain superior to electronic ones." It becomes mandatory that we develop cyber-genetic hybrids, plugging computer components into the human brain: "We must develop as quickly as possible technologies that make possible a direct connection between brain and computer, so that artificial brains contribute to human intelligence rather than opposing it."[17] The only other alternative would be to halt the advances in computer development; deliberately stop improving computer performance. Now, *what are the chances of that happening?*

These then are our three underlying determinants: the failure of infinite growth to sustain us, information overload, and technological determinism. These determinants have inexorably contributed to a post-intellectual culture characterized by uncertainty, chaos, and loss of control. The future literally is beyond our imagination and, many fear, beyond our control.

No one knows where our postmodern thrust is leading us. Science has provided us with an exhilarating technological joyride; our scientific and engineering miracles have provided the engine for a thrilling excursion. But we lack a clear idea of where we are headed. We have no road map. The armored motor home we entered in Chapter 1 keeps gaining speed, as if the accelerator were stuck to the floor. We race along, cocooned inside this amazing vehicle, but with an escalating sense of loss of control. At the same time—through some amazing feat of quantum reality—we find ourselves outside the vehicle staring at this spectacle, so transfixed by the dazzle of today's technology that, like the deer frozen in the sudden glare of oncoming headlights, we don't know in what direction to run. Eric Drexler, one of the leading proponents of nanotechnology, writes, "There are many people, including myself, who are quite queasy about the consequences of this technology for the future. We are talking about changing so many things that the risk of society handling it poorly through lack of preparation is very large."[18]

CHAPTER 10

The Transition to Post-Intellectualism

The Enlightenment triggered a cultural revolution. But from the beginning there were numerous counter-revolutionary factors at work. Isaiah Berlin writes, "Opposition to the central ideas of the French Enlightenment, and of its allies and disciples in other European countries, is as old as the movement itself."[1] Best and Kellner elaborate, "Beginning with [Edmund] Burke's celebrated *Reflections on the French Revolution* [sic], written just one year after the 1789 French Revolution, the institutions and values of modernity—Enlightenment, secular rationality, criticism, individualism, capitalism, and revolution—were sharply contested from various quarters."[2] Conservatives such as Burke wanted to preserve the status quo—perhaps with a few token nods towards reform. They "ridiculed the Enlightenment notion that individuals can be governed by reason, and they stigmatized the 'masses' as being ruled by base desires and appetites. . . . They believed that social stability could only be maintained through time-honored wisdom of tradition and the rule of the church and nobility."[3] Their thinking was not far from Plato's admonition that the "tempers and tastes of the motley multitude . . . will oblige [the artist, poet, and public servant] to produce whatever they [the masses] want."[4]

NINETEENTH-CENTURY QUESTIONINGS

There were many other philosophical and religious arguments put forth in opposition to the idea of modern rationalism and scientific empiricism. These include romanticism, existentialism, transcendentalism, and Marxism—as well as voices raised in opposition to industrialization and urbanization. The irony is that post-intellectualism was inadvertently triggered by men of deep intellectual prowess—theorists, artists, and thinkers such as Hobbes, Rousseau, Burke, Marx, Darwin, and Freud (to name just a few). They contributed—either directly or indirectly—to a climate that discouraged the rational, humanist, individualistic, and democratic movement defined as intellectualism. They all played a role in the transition to post-intellectualism.

Romanticism

It was Rousseau who perhaps best exemplified the transition from the modern to the romantic. E. O. Wilson elaborates:

Rousseau, while often listed as an Enlightenment *philosophe*, was really instead the founder and most extreme visionary of the Romantic philosophical movement. For him learning and social order are the enemies of humanity. . . . His utopia is a minimalist state in which people abandon books and other accouterments of intellect in order to cultivate enjoyment of the senses and good health. Humanity, Rousseau claimed, was originally a race of noble savages in a peaceful state of nature, who were later corrupted by civilization—and by scholarship. Religion, marriage, law, and government are deceptions created by the powerful for their own selfish ends.[5]

Romanticism flourished throughout all of Europe. The early movement was characterized by Johann Gottfried von Herder's declaration, "I am not here to think, but to be, feel, live!"[6] Herder's early writings influenced other young German romantics such as Johann von Goethe and Johann Schiller. Three English romantics typify the movement. William Blake was concerned with the struggle of the soul to free itself from what he termed the "mind-forged manacles" of reason, law, and organized religion. Much of his poetry lashed out against the symbols of the industrial revolution— the mills, forges, and furnaces. William Wordsworth was perhaps the most philosophical of the romantic poets. Much of his poetry was concerned with "moralizing, protesting that urban man—by which he means modern man—by cutting himself off from nature has cut himself off from the roots of his own Being."[7] Samuel Taylor Coleridge in his later years probed introspectively into the state of the artist who has lost his creative impulse because he has been alienated from nature. In this intensely personal reflection, he foreshadowed the anxiety and estrangement of the coming existentialist movement.

Existentialism

Men and women began to perceive in the nineteenth century that the universe was not governed by a perfectly functioning set of cosmic laws.

Just the opposite—life is absurd, fickle, and perilous. It is characterized by anxiety and futility, by alienation and estrangement. Kierkegaard, the founder of modern existentialism (see Chapter 4), felt that it was up to each individual therefore to find some way to make sense out of it all. He opposed the unquestioned acceptance of the logical positivism and scientific rationalism of the Enlightenment. Truth does not exist as the result or proof of some logical abstraction—that is, science. It is a personal revelation defined by each individual. Truth is arrived at by living and experiencing it, not by rational analysis. Logic is not the ultimate arbitrator—although your existential truth may be science. It may also be religion, or materialism, or any other value system that you can embrace utterly without reservation, without need for any justification. You must ultimately build your personal philosophy on some foundational principle in which you place absolute faith. Thus, existentialism is a clear precursor to postmodern rejection of absolute truth.

Later existentialists built upon Kierkegaard's groundwork. Nietzsche, when he proclaimed *God is dead*, was arguing that our *belief* in God was dead—that modern civilization had lost its ideational faith in God and therefore had lost the foundation of all truth and morality. He promoted secular humanism and declared that each individual must work to develop his or her full potential, independent of any outside authority. Martin Heidegger, Jean-Paul Sartre, and Albert Camus all probed the absurdity of life and the awareness of death. They all contributed to the breakdown of a neatly structured rational universe. Although existentialism generally supported the Enlightenment push towards individualism, it also promoted anti-science passion, a worldview stressing disorder and absurdity, and a postmodern concept of relative truth.

Transcendentalism

The American transcendental movement was headed up most notably by Ralph Waldo Emerson and Henry David Thoreau—even though many others wrote and lectured in the pre–Civil War period of transcendental influence. Transcendentalism emphasized intuition and spiritualism over empiricism. Some truths transcend science and reason. Although their greatest emphasis was on personal insight and individual growth, many transcendentalists were also active in political movements and social reform—temperance, peace, universal suffrage, and the abolition of slavery.

The transcendentalists shared with the existentialists a celebration of deep-seated individualism. They rejected sensate materialism, extolling the spiritual existence of the individual who would rise above the petty concerns of the material world. As the source of human inspiration and meaning, intuition would supersede the "cold intellectualism" (Emerson's term) of Enlightenment rationalists. The transcending ideas that guide us through life come not by way of the five senses or by the powers of reasoning but by religious revelation or divine inspiration. The true seat of human existence is not the brain, but the oversoul or, to use the Quaker term, *the inner light*.

Marxism

Borrowing from Georg Wilhelm Friedrich Hegel and his system of *dialectical analysis*, Marx developed his version of *dialectical materialism*. This critical approach provides a theoretical explanation of how cultures establish themselves (*the thesis*), how an opposing force comes into play (*the antithesis*), and how a new system replaces the old (*the synthesis*). This new synthesis, in replacing the old, then becomes the thesis; and the process repeats itself unendingly. In Marxist theory, the modern capitalist society (the thesis) is overthrown by the oppressed working classes (the antithesis) and the egalitarian classless communist society (the synthesis) is created. "Materialism" in Marx's analysis refers not to economic consumption, but rather to a concern with the sensate and material world. Marxism is both a theoretical analysis of the nature of history and a form of literary analysis.[8] It is both a theory of what will inevitably come to pass and a prescription for what must be done to make it come to pass. It is a penetrating critique of the character of capitalism and also a blueprint for a socialistic system that promises an egalitarian order.

Marxist theorists are often identified as intellectuals. Indeed, some Marxist purists would see themselves as extending the ideals of the Enlightenment. However, the end result of Marxist thinking—Soviet communism—is far from an intellectual state. Not only is capitalism swept aside, but democracy is eradicated, personal liberties are curtailed, privacy disappears, individualism is replaced by collectivism, science is perverted to meet the needs of the state, and the concept of civil rights evaporates. The modern intellectual culture is abolished. The result is a post-intellectual authoritarian state.

Thus, the conservatives, the romantics, the existentialists, the transcendentalists, and the Marxists—each in their own way—added to the outline of a counter-Enlightenment movement. Each of these philosophies contributed to our postmodern angst and apprehension.

Industrialization and Urbanization

Fueled initially with steam power, then with the miracle of electricity, the Industrial Revolution resulted in a rapid social dislocation that was without precedent in human history. It was an inescapable manifestation of technological determinism. Enlightenment musings had not prepared the populace for this kind of cultural disruption. Industrialists and capitalists formed a new social class and triggered a nationwide source of resentment. Labor unions and child labor laws were created in response to widespread exploitation and economic inequities. These were counter-intellectual responses to the excesses of hyper-intellectual progress.

Increased industrialization, concentrations of capital, labor opportunities, electrification, modern water systems and sewer lines all contributed to the rapid urbanization of the nation. Big cities came to dominate the cultural landscape (to be continued in Chapter 16). The resulting squalor, congestion, and depersonalization were overwhelming. The Enlightenment ideal held that individuals would be able to intellectually comprehend and control their environments. Rapid industrialization and excessive urbanization both worked against this ideal. By the twentieth century, average citizens understood less and less about their industrialized urban environments, and they felt less and less in control of their lives.

TWENTIETH CENTURY DISILLUSIONMENTS

The twentieth century dawned churning with modern confidence and optimism. Science, technology, and the promise of social reform were to fulfill the intellectual dream. Then the shock of World War I eroded the confident rationalism of modernity—rattling the foundations of Western culture. William Barrett asserts bluntly, "August 1914 is the axial date in modern Western history, and once past it we are directly confronted with the present-day world. The sense of power over the material universe with which modern man emerged, as we have seen, from the Middle Ages, changed on that date into its opposite: a sense of weakness and dereliction before the whirlwind that man is able to unleash but not to control."[9] The war shattered mankind's faith in its ability to live rationally in a modern state. This was to be the war that would "make the world safe for democracy." The disheartening reality turned out to be that it was the war that gave rise to Bolshevism, fascism, and Nazism. Even in the Middle East, idealist hopes for a modern revival were soon dashed. Fareed Zakaria writes, "After World War I, a new liberal age flickered briefly in the Arab world, as ideas about opening up politics and society gained currency in places like Egypt, Lebanon, Iraq, and Syria. But since they were part of a world of kings and aristocrats, these ideas died with the old regimes."[10]

Scientific Uncertainties

It started in the nineteenth century—that disquieting feeling that maybe Newton didn't quite have it all worked out so definitively. As spelled out in Chapter 4, modern science slowly gave way to postmodern ambiguities.

Most obviously, Darwin undermined faith in the biblical tale of God's handiwork. This heresy could not be accepted into mainstream theological dogma. However, the Church no longer had the authority that it had when dealing with Copernicus or Galileo. Bishop John Shelby Spong observes, "The Christian church resisted Darwin with vigor, but the ecclesiastical power of antiquity had already been broken, and the Church's ability to threaten Darwin with execution as a heretic no longer existed."[11] Therefore, science and the Church were cast into a postmodern conflict that continues to this day. Then, with Freud's examination of the roles played by our basic animal instincts, both neurotic and erotic, our Enlightenment faith in human rationality was further challenged. We were recast as a bundle of conflicting emotional drives and irrational passions. Our ability to understand and govern our personal instincts was called into question—let alone the larger obligation of handling democratic self-government.[12]

In the early twentieth century, much of the physical sciences also began to reflect uncertainties and misgivings. Entropy, relativity, chaos theory, the uncertainty principle, fractal geometry, cosmic string theory, and quantum weirdness all had their impacts on the ability of the average citizen to comprehend what was going on. Science became less accessible to the layman. The world became a much more foreboding and disturbing place. Postmodern science becomes increasingly relativistic and chaotic.

Mystery and wonder are fine; but if we ordinary citizens are to actually participate in democratic decision-making, we need to have some understanding as to what science is all about. With the confusion and uncertainties that abound, how are we to make intelligent, informed collective decisions about funding for space exploration, missile defense systems, medical research, alternative energy sources, fusion research, and genetic technologies? Creationism and astrology make about as much sense to many people as do biotechnology and holography.[13]

Failure of Humanism

David Ehrenfeld in his 1978 *The Arrogance of Humanism* defined humanism in terms of several assumptions: human civilization will survive; Truth will always prevail; humans are inherently rational and capable of altruism and perfection; all problems are solvable—by humans; and most of these problems are solvable with technology.[14] These assumptions are drawn directly from John Locke and the philosophes. We would continually evolve and improve our condition. This was Francis Fukuyama's recounting of the End of History—the ultimate triumph of liberal democracy. But following World War I, intellectuals in both Europe and America re-examined their humanistic ideals and found them wanting.

First came the hedonistic excesses of the exuberant 1920s—challenging the assumption that men and women could conduct themselves with reason and restraint, with minimal intrusion from a central government. Then came the Depression years of the 1930s—questioning the essential soundness of a laissez-faire economy based on unrestrained capitalism. Many thoughtful persons debated the merits of adopting a technocratic state; since modern culture had gotten too complex for the average citizen to comprehend, we would have to turn government decision-making over to the technocrats and bureaucrats. Others became infatuated with the promise of the new communism that had arisen in Russia, assuring equality and prosperity based upon collective sharing of resources. Both technocracy and communism reflected disillusionment with the promise of humanism and libertarianism. Both were steps in the direction of post-intellectualism—the first, technocracy, was a hyper-intellectual move towards a scientific technopoly; the second, communism, was a counter-intellectual return to a form of authoritarian tribal security.

We were jolted out of the Great Depression by the convulsion of World War II. For half a decade Americans pulled together with the intensity and unity of purpose that has seldom, if ever, been equaled. We understood clearly what we were doing. We ended the war not only victorious, but with a vision and sense of resolve that promised a renewed faith in American destiny. We created the United Nations and infused it with a stability that would compensate for what we threw away in the short-lived League of Nations. Our wartime generals became peacetime visionaries. Douglas MacArthur gave us the framework for a reformed and Westernized Japan. George Marshall gave us a Plan that would rebuild a strong democratic Europe. Dwight Eisenhower gave us eight years of domestic prosperity and growth. And we enjoyed a mid-century revival of technological prowess that outshone the beginning of the century: television, the transistor, xerography, magnetic recording, satellites, supersonic flight, miracle drugs, plastics, and air conditioning. What more could we ask for?

But this period of euphoria was all too brief. First we got bogged down in the "police action" in Korea. Then we lost faith in our democratic crusade in the quagmire of Vietnam. The assassinations and cultural revolutions of the 1960s sent us reeling. We lost faith in our politicians, our business practices, our schools, and the nuclear family. We escaped reality by turning to hallucinogenic television and psychedelic drugs. We became entangled in the web culture—not knowing which way to spin. Our bedrock of modern destiny was slowly eroded by the three determinants of post-intellectualism: the failure of economic growth and development to sustain us, the information overload, and megatechnology. Chaos and uncertainty gradually replaced structure and order in our cultural narrative. The apparition of postmodernism steadily began to creep into our consciousness.

Surrendering a measure of individualism and independence, we turned increasingly to big government, faceless institutions, and a maze of entitlement programs: the New Deal, Fair Deal, New Frontier, and Great Society. Our Enlightenment-inspired intellectual orientation gradually faded. Then we tried to return to our libertarian roots by moving in the direction of less government control. We deregulated crucial industries—banking, trucking, telecommunications, airlines, electrical power, the savings-and-loan industry—generally with disastrous results for the consumer. The ideal of the self-regulating practices of the free marketplace was demolished. We lost our feeling of self-sufficiency, our assurance of self-determination.

The Revival of Fundamentalism

Concurrent with this dismantling of modern, humanist structure has been a rising tide of religious fundamentalism. Men and women need something to believe in—a cultural narrative. People instinctively will turn to some promise of stability and order. If it isn't to be found in science or reason, then *back to the Bible!* Fundamentalism is a counter-intellectual response to the breakdown of modernity and humanism.

The most alarming illustration of the turn to religious extremism in the twentieth century is the radical element of Islamic fundamentalism. Muslim extremists cannot tolerate the West's tolerance. It is hard to accept that we accept those who are different, those who have diverse beliefs. This basic foundation of American liberalism is anathema to the creed of "true believers." What's more, America's lack of fanatical religiosity is an indication of moral depravity. This gives rise to the image of the *Great Satan.* Religion professor Lamin Sanneh explains, "By separating church and state, the West—and America in particular—has effectively privatized belief, making religion a matter of individual faith. This is an affront to the certainty of fundamentalist Muslims, who are confident that they possess the infallible truth."[15] Thus, we are the targets of the fundamentalists' wrath both because we are big and dominating and because we are not religious enough.

THESE WERE THE FACTORS that contributed to our swing from modernity to postmodernism: a longing for the stability and security of conservatism; the passion and spontaneity of romanticism, existentialism and transcendentalism; the promise of Marxism; the upheavals of industrialization and urbanization; the transition from scientific exactitude to evolution, relativity, uncertainty, and chaos; the disillusionment of two world wars; the breakdown of humanistic modern order; and the revival of fundamentalism. These were what moved us from intellectual idealism to post-

intellectual reality. John Ralston Saul underscores the disillusionment of
the past century:

We see ourselves as victims of the disorder which inevitably follows upon the
breakdown of religious and social order. In such a vacuum the collective Western
consciousness couldn't help but splinter. It follows that the succession of great,
all-encompassing ages—Reason, Enlightenment, Romanticism—had to end with
an explosion. The resulting shards inevitably produced a confused age in which
innumerable ideologies fought it out for control of our minds and our bodies.[16]

John Lukacs, who wrote his *Outgrowing Democracy* in 1984, gives us one
of the more depressing assessments: "Yet we, near the end of the twentieth
century, ought to recognize that the ideology of the so-called Enlightenment has proven largely outdated, that it has little to teach us. Much of
the mechanical and of the educational philosophy, many of the institutions
of the eighteenth century are now hopelessly antiquated, which is why so
many of the institutions of the United States have become arterioscle-
rotic."[17] Whatever it is we wound up with, it surely wasn't what John
Locke and Thomas Jefferson had in mind.

CHAPTER 11

The Real Story of the Sixties

Post-intellectualism is as much a state of mind as it is an historical time period. It is a diminishing of intellectual commitment. However, having said that, I find it helpful to identify the 1960s as a pivotal two-decade span in the evolution of our post-intellectual experience.[1] The 1960s were the period when postmodernism boomed its way into our consciousness. This was the Age of Aquarius, the rebellion against Jim Crow laws and sexism, the launching of the environmental movement, the cynicism born of the Vietnam debacle and prominent political assassinations, the glorification of drugs and profanity, and the extraordinary spectacle of a disgraced president being forced to resign. Why did so much of our social stability seem to fall apart during that extended decade? From Vietnam to Watergate, what caused the Sixties?

From D-Day to Camelot

Dwight Eisenhower's World War II military victory was a triumph of modern democracy over premodern despotism. Humanism and justice had prevailed. But Ike's eight years as President marked the beginning of the end of our intellectual linear culture. Eisenhower's presidency epitomized intellectual/capitalist dedication to sustained expansion and growth. His administration gave us nuclear energy and the interstate freeway system—two technological monuments to development and progress. This was followed by John Kennedy's initiation of the space program—another manifestation of continued linear progress and technological prowess. But no subsequent president has achieved any domestic material accomplishments comparable to the development of nuclear energy, the interstate system, or the space program. Never again would we witness national programs based on such distinct linear technological progress and growth. Major programs of following administrations, from the Great Society to Medicare, would be post-intellectual welfare and entitlement efforts—not triumphs of linear exploitation and development. Programs to shore up education, Social Security, civil rights, military defense, environmental protection, agricultural subsidies, international peacekeeping, Medicaid, election reform, housing programs, and homeland defense are all simply post-intellectual housekeeping necessities. They do not move civilization ahead; they are not indicative of modern capitalistic growth and technological progress. Major federal programs from the late 1960s on have been little more than patchwork attempts to hold the system together.

Eisenhower's administration also saw an uneasy standoff in Korea and the beginnings of our Vietnam involvement. No longer was the world easily defined in terms of right and wrong. We no longer clearly understood what we were supposed to be doing. During Ike's administration we began to witness social critics questioning our intellectual directions.[2] This was the beginning of our postmodern political and cultural disorientation. Eisenhower himself, at the end of his second term, foreshadowed the enveloping web culture with his warning of the growing hegemony of the military-industrial complex.[3] We had moved from the linear culture into the muddled web culture.

President Kennedy ushered in an era of post-intellectual charisma and uncertainty: the Bay of Pigs fiasco, the Cuban missile crisis, Vietnam, race riots. We became embroiled in chaotic situations over which we had little control. On the literary front we had Rachel Carson's *Silent Spring* (1962) and Betty Friedan's *Feminine Mystique* (1963)—both challenging our conventional perspectives. Nothing seemed to be holding together. The Age of the Enlightenment expired around 1960 (*Camelot* was, after all, a preintellectual medieval culture). As the 1960s extended into the 1970s, continued governmental deception and public cynicism escalated—culminating with Richard Nixon's resignation. To the established order, it was a time of values run amuck, a loss of societal direction. Modernity itself was falling apart.

THE ANXIETY OF INFORMATION

What happened in the Sixties was Information. We were overcome not by drugs, nudity, and social anarchy—but by a whirling disorientation triggered by the angst and alienation of a stupefying torrent of new data and revolutionary ideas. This is one of the most stunning dynamics of the late twentieth century—the crushing information explosion that suddenly overpowered us. Raw bits and pieces of data are added to the world's information storehouse at such an incomprehensible pace that no single library, think tank, government agency, or supercomputer can grasp the totality of what's going on.

Tom Brokaw in his 1998 book, *The Greatest Generation*, argues that the World War II cohort was "a generation birthmarked for greatness, a generation of Americans that would take its place in American history with the generations that had converted the North American wilderness into the United States."[4] Why? What made them special? Certainly they were patriotic, self-sacrificing, and courageous. But why them? Were not their offspring—the rebels of the 1960s—made of the same genetic material? Why were the warriors of the 1940s made of such great stuff, while succeeding generations (Beatniks, Hippies, Yuppies, Baby Boomers, Generation Xers, the Y Generation) have failed to impress anyone with their greatness? If it's not the genes, then it must have something to do with the times in which they grew up. And *the times, they have a-changed*. The revolution of the Sixties was the Information Revolution.

The information tsunami appeared on the horizon in the 1950s—with the rapid spread of television, the impact of the transistor, the videotape recorder, the commercial jet, the office photocopier, the launching of the first satellite, and the introduction of a huge computing machine called UNIVAC. This tidal wave of stuff and substance swept ashore in the 1960s with the invention of the microchip, the laser, the first communications satellites, the audio cassette, the rapid spread of the office computer, color TV, fiber optics, the first flight of the supersonic jet, and the introduction of ARPANET (the precursor of the Internet). These two decades were the crest of the Information Age. Census data show that white collar workers outnumbered blue collar workers for the first time in the 1950s. This is what futurist Alvin Toffler identified as the Third Wave (the Agricultural and Industrial Revolutions being the first two.)[5] The Information Genie was out of the bottle. We were now swallowed up in the blur of the Information Era—the insecurities and uncertainties of postmodernism. Postmodern times call not for greatness and heroes, but for cynicism and survivors.

The Increasing Pace of Change

The overwhelming information onslaught has resulted in an acceleration of the rate of change. James Gleick writes in 1999, "We are in a rush. We are making haste. A compression of time characterizes the life of the century now closing. . . . The wave patterns of all these facts and choices flow and crash about us at a heightened frequency. We live in the buzz."[6] We adopt multitasking technologies so that we can get more done in a shorter time frame. Linton Weeks describes a real Franciscan monk,

Brother Sebastian: "While on hold he watches TV news, checks his pager and faxes letters to friends. Pretty much all at the same time, he also prays for families pictured on his prayer board."[7] Even reading to children comes under pressure. We now have *One-Minute Bedtime Stories* for harried parents who must condense familiar bedtime tales so that they can get back to their lap tops and PDAs.[8] Better yet, AOL has introduced a program to have your computer read the bedtime stories to your kids.

The more information we have, the more that our information environment changes. The more that our information environment changes, the more we must adapt to the new world we find ourselves in. We adapt by developing fresh technologies, by discovering new stuff. In short, we add more information to the cultural mix. But then our information environment has changed again. So we must continue to adapt—by getting new information. Then our information environment has changed again. And on and on. We keep spinning faster and faster in this never-ending cycle. As explained by E. O. Wilson: "The more knowledge people acquire, the more they are able to increase their numbers and to alter the environment, whereupon the more they need new knowledge just to stay alive."[9] This is the escalating feedback loop that has dominated our information culture since the 1960s.

We are relentless in our pursuit of up-to-date input. During the political season, we follow the fortunes of candidates by watching the polls and surveys cranked out on a daily basis. Pollsters track audience responses to political speeches while the speech is in progress—feedback can be instantaneously delivered to the speaker so that he or she can adapt to unseen audience smiles and smirks. Some school districts are providing parents with feedback in the form of hourly progress reports on their children. Day traders follow Wall Street ups and downs on a minute-by-minute basis. We are reminded of the TV series *Max Headroom* where the board members of a fictitious future TV network make instantaneous programming decisions based on second-by-second program ratings. We continually accelerate the rate at which we must receive feedback.

Our response to change and complexity is always to generate more levels of bureaucracy and hierarchical control—add more information processors and problem-solvers to the mix. What we wind up with is an unending spiral of increasing density and corresponding turmoil. The more new situations we have to cope with, the more complicated our decision-making becomes. And therefore the more difficult it becomes to engage in successful problem-solving. The Progress Paradox continues to escalate.

Educated citizens used to take time to read great works of literature and philosophy. Not today. We are guided by Nike's advertising slogan, "Just Do It!" Just act without thinking. This is postmodernism. Don't take time to think, to analyze, to reflect. Just respond intuitively. React. Make a decision. Even more to the point is Nextel's slogan: "Think fast. Communicate faster." Quick. After not thinking things through, communicate your gut reactions right away. Throw together a *PowerPoint* presentation; use your wireless connections; hit the *Reply* button; create your own *blog* and spread your ersatz thoughts through the Internet. Thus we add to the jumble of impulsive suggestions and unstructured schemes that characterize the web culture. We are denied the luxury of having enough time to contemplate, to analyze, to meditate, or to proceed in an orderly fashion.

THE GENERATION OVERLAP

The 1960s ushered in the robe-and-sandal-clad flower children. Where did these hippies come from, these sons and daughters of The Greatest Generation? This counter-culture multitude sprang from a solid intellectual heritage—social criticism, fervent individualism, and a dedication to equality and human rights. But how are we to account for the erosion of morality and the denunciation of capitalism? Why were young people coming of age in the 1960s so out of sync with their preceding generations?

Transition to Adulthood

Rebellion is a normal part of growing up. Young people have to struggle against the restraints of their elders—parents, teachers, clergy—questioning, challenging, mutinying against authority. This is a natural part of the process of maturing—breaking out of the chrysalis to emerge as an adult. Then after young people break free of their childhood restrictions, they are ready to move into adult society. And guess what! Throughout history they have always eased right back into the same society they had been rebelling against. They wound up going back to church or temple, they joined the establishment workforce, they got married and had children, they supported the school system, and they assumed the mantle of citizenship. This is because that was the only society available to them. No matter how defiant adolescents may have been, there was always the certainty that when they grew up they would be living in the same world that their parents had come to terms with. There were no other options.

Until the 1960s. The information explosion had altered Western culture to the extent that the younger generation then coming of age would not inherit the same world their parents had known. That old world, fabricated from outdated information, no longer existed. The orderly ages-old transition to adulthood was suddenly disrupted. New information and new insights demanded that new social patterns be set in motion. The youth of the Sixties turned to their elders and declared, *We won't accept your hypocrisy and lies about our involvement in Vietnam. We won't tolerate your racist Jim Crow laws any longer. We refuse to accept the sexism and ho-mophobia that have discriminated against women and gays throughout history. We want to protect our environment against the capitalistic abuses that you have inflicted on our natural ecosystems for the past two centuries.* And to an amaz-ing degree, many of the older adults looked at them and said, *I dunno, maybe they're right.* The information environment had shifted under the feet of young and old alike.

The Estranged Generation

Then the youth—infatuated with their new-found sense of perception and independence—proclaimed, *What's more, we reject all the rest of your outmoded values. Under the banner of free speech, we reserve the right to stand on the front steps of the Establishment and yell, "Fuck you!" Also, we think that public nudity and free sex are okay. We refuse to be bound to your old-fashioned concepts of marriage and the nuclear family. (Make love, not war!) And, by the way, we think that drugs are a fine way to gain spiritual insight and personal freedom.* And so we validated postmodern tolerance and pluralism. No longer would a single standard of morality prevail throughout the king-dom. No longer was it clear in what linear direction we should all be headed. Groups as diverse as the Black Panthers, the Gay and Lesbian Alliance, La Raza, Greenpeace, the NAACP, the National Organization for Women, and the Gray Panthers were varied in their structure, policies, and tactics—yet they were tacitly united in opposition to the established hierarchy that had prevailed for most of the modern era. Thus were we ushered into the post-intellectual web culture.

The 1960s were a counter-intellectual rebellion against sensate truth, against scientific empiricism and materialism, against rationalism. We be-gan to lose our faith in *things*. Technology, economic growth, and scientific progress all began to lose the bloom of modernity. Sensitivity training, astrology, love-beads, incense, communal living, and self-awareness all represented a groping toward new insights, a new synthesis.

This gave rise to the "feel-good" era of public schooling—the elevation of self-esteem above all other considerations. All students would get gold stars for showing up in class and not spitting on their teacher on any given day. But with this distortion of self-esteem, recognition loses all signifi-cance. If everyone gets a gold star, then gold stars become meaningless. Add this quandary to our growing list of inherent contradictions of an intellectual society: we crave recognition, but universal and undeserved recognition lessens everyone's stature. The counter-intellectual would have us all embracing each other for simply being human and taking time to smell the roses. The hyper-intellectual would have us competing and pushing everyone else out of our path on our way to the top of the ladder of recognition. *Whatever!*

The Obliteration of Childhood

Another outgrowth of the Sixties was the disintegration of childhood. Prior to the sixteenth century, the concept of childhood simply did not exist.[10] Up through the Renaissance, children entered society as diminutive men and women, ready to live in the adult world, assume economic responsibilities, and participate in adult pastimes. There was no training period for adulthood because there was nothing to train for. Adults had no specialized occupational skills. Adults had no responsible civic duties. Most significantly, adults could not read; literacy in the working class was virtually nonexistent. It required no intellectual skills to move into adulthood.

Childhood was an inevitable consequence of the printing press. With movable type came books; and with books came the need for schools. We needed to train adolescents both for specialized occupations that emerged with the industrial age as well as for the civic responsibilities of a libertarian society.

In the last fifty years, however, we have witnessed a gradual erosion of childhood. Neil Postman points out that one of the main reasons for this disappearance of childhood has been the information revolution "which has made it impossible to keep secrets from the young—sexual secrets, political secrets, social secrets, historical secrets, medical secrets; that is to say, the full content of adult life, which must be kept at least partially hidden from the young if there is to be a category of life known as childhood."[11] If children have access to adult content of the real world—if the parent and the child have been watching the same TV programs, going to the same R-rated movies, playing the same video games, and surfing the same Internet sites (including pornography)—what does the adult have to pass on to the child? Youngsters watched with adults the same live pictures of the World Trade Center collapsing. They experienced the same immediate reactions of horror, confusion, fear, incomprehension, and nightmares. There was no filter to protect them from the adult world. Childhood has been obliterated.

One cannot ignore the correlation between the social upheavals of the 1960s and the coming-of-age of the first television generation. We are returning to an oral and pictorial tradition (more of this in Chapter 12). We have entered a nonliterate age. Television, radio, the movies, audio recordings, computer games, icon-driven computer programs, and virtual reality experiences all are nonlinguistic. Young children often beat their grandparents at computer games because the youngsters are deciphering the pictorial icons and reacting intuitively while the old folks are still reading words and trying to follow written cues.

We experience also the democratizing inclusion of youth in our cultural forums. Literacy and intellectual maturity are no longer prerequisites for participation in today's society. Students determine what is relevant in school. Young people decide on their own systems of morality. Kids generally are increasingly in control of their environments—their clothes, their music, their diet, their fads, their social life. At the same time, adults seek a more impulsive childlike existence. Prime-time TV series feature childish adults, and cartoon series are devised for adults. At the movies, adults flock to flicks that feature comic-book plots and Star Wars special effects. Adults play children's video games and wear blue jeans and sneakers to the office. The generational line continues to blur

We used to speak of the *generation gap*. But such a gap no longer exists. What we have today is the Generation Overlap. The child and adult have morphed into a kind of adult–adolescent. We have a new generation of semi-literate young adults who have a diminished sense of responsibility, a limited commitment to lasting relationships, little faith in the future, and no substantial grasp of long-term consequences. This is the postmodern child-citizen.

It is as if we went through a cultural sonic boom in the 1960s. As you speed along in subsonic flight, you are buffeted by familiar sounds and experiences; you understand where you are and what is happening to you. Even as you approach the speed of sound you are still in familiar territory; you know what you are doing. This was America up through the 1950s. Once you reach the speed of sound, however, you are enmeshed in a horrific experience. The sound waves pile up in a frightening crescendo—a shock wave of suddenly compressed air. Every sound wave you generate stays with you, building on each preceding sound wave, resulting in a thunder of unimaginable intensity. This was America in the 1960s—experiencing an incomprehensible cultural sonic boom. Then, once you are flung beyond that barrier into supersonic speed, you find yourself in an eerie new environment—frighteningly unfamiliar, incomprehensible, unsettling. We are soaring faster and faster through a strange uncharted environment without a clear reference point.

This cultural sonic boom consisted of several phenomena that came together in the 1960s: the information juggernaut, the acceleration of change, the generation overlap and obliteration of childhood. We were staggered by the cumulative impact of cascading voices, opinions, arguments, incidents, perceptions, injustices, technologies, and multicultural values—all magnified and disseminated by the expanding web of media outlets. No reasoned patterns could any longer be discerned. The information overload stunned us to the point of incoherence. We lost our orientation as we became ensnared in the web culture. We were hurled into a post-intellectual society—a chaotic cultural landscape. That is what happened in the Sixties.

CHAPTER 12

Living in a Mediated Reality

The electric media have played a substantial role in the creation of our post-intellectual culture. Many critics attack the content of these media as causes of our social discontent—with their sexual exploitation, violence, racial stereotypes, and obscenities. But actually it is the intrinsic nature of these media themselves, not the content of the media, that we need to be primarily concerned with. The electric media are inherently anti-intellectual—not because of their shallow and salacious content, but because they deal in pictures, sounds, and the spoken word.

We experience the mediums themselves—regardless of their specific content. We watch *television*. We go to *the movies*. We listen to the *radio*. We bond with our *iPods*. It is the actual mediums that we attend to; the particular messages being transmitted are secondary. This is what Marshall McLuhan was referring to with his popular catchphrase, *the medium is the message*.[1] What is significant is that you schedule your evening around the tube. It doesn't matter if you are watching *Monday Night Football*, *Masterpiece Theater*, *Jeopardy*, or *Law and Order*. What matters is that you have turned over a portion of your life to *the medium*. Logging on to the Internet for an hour or two every day is the cultural experience—not the specific web sites you happen to visit. Playing video games is the social deed—whether you are competing at *Beach Spikers* or creating a persona in *Sims Online*. This is, in effect, technological determinism as it applies to the media. The media themselves, the technologies—not their content—fashion our culture.

RETURNING TO THE ORAL AND PICTORIAL TRADITION

Imagine Western civilization without the telephone, radio, movies, television, or the computer. These media are the determinants that have molded the twentieth century. McLuhan and Fiore pointed out that "Societies have always been shaped more by the nature of the media by which men communicate than by the content of the communication. . . . It is impossible to understand social and cultural changes without a knowledge of the workings of media."[2] Premodern cultures were shaped in the pre-intellectual oral tradition. Print technologies created the intellectual modern linear world. The electric media have immersed us in a postmodern, nonintellectual oral and pictorial culture of feelings and experiences. We have returned to the pictograph and the spoken word (albeit with some pretty dazzling visual effects and some overpowering sound systems).

Picturization and Hemisphericity

A major distinction between print technologies and the oral-pictorial electric media can be explained by brain hemisphericity. Physiologists and psychologists have long noted the differences between the way we perceive pictures and sounds as opposed to the way we perceive and interpret printed symbols. The right hemisphere is concerned with pictures, sounds, feelings, and intuition; it perceives the world in terms of a holistic, emotional grasp of the big picture. The left hemisphere is concerned with linear analysis and sequential processing of abstract print and mathematical symbols; it is well suited for reading and writing and computation. Reading a book leaves you with different set of memories than does listening to an audio book; reading a newspaper story leaves you with a different impression than hearing the same story on the radio.

In Chapter 7, we introduced the idea that right-hemisphere-oriented individuals would more likely be the Poets, Artists, and Musicians (PAMs). And left-hemisphere persons are typified by the Bureaucrats, Engineers, and Number crunchers (BENs). A culture dominated by PAMs would be more empathetic and passionate—less competitive, less driven by technology—than a BEN-oriented culture. However, for better or worse, what we did some three hundred years ago was to adopt the BEN culture as our modern paradigm. We could create business contracts, we could build cities and nation-states—all based on the left hemisphere. If we are to deal with rational constructs and scientific analysis, understand cause-and-effect relationships, evaluate evidence and arguments, then we must be able to handle the printed word and the mathematical symbol. Premodern or postmodern PAMs cannot easily manage a modern BEN-designed civilization. But that is what we are trying to do today. As we are increasingly unable or uncomfortable dealing with the printed word, we have trouble handling abstract concepts; we fail to demonstrate the reason and responsibility needed to maintain freedom and democratic institutions.

I mentioned earlier that the oral/pictorial electric media represent more of a feminine sensitivity than the more rational, linear print media. This viewpoint is summarized by Leonard Shlain who writes that "certain masculine characteristics began to characterize a society after a critical mass of its people had learned to read and write. What triggered this profound shift was literacy's reliance on the analytic thought processes linked to the brain's left hemisphere. Meanwhile, the feminine traits associated with the right hemisphere were systematically devalued."[3] The modern era of the printing press, with the ensuing emphasis on analysis and reasoning, was a masculine period. The evolution to a postmodern era, with the electric media leading the way, returned us to a more intuitive feminine mode of perception and thinking. The 1960s represented the surfacing of our culture's feminine side—think love beads, peace signs, racial equality, sensitivity training, environmental awareness, and mellowing out. Much of the confusion and chaos of the web culture results from the bipolar way we interact with our cultural environment: reason versus passion, analytic versus intuitive, linear versus holistic, competitive versus compassionate, yang versus yin.

The Transition to Illiteracy

As we have turned to the radio, movies, television, graphics, and PowerPoint presentations, we have subtly abandoned the capacity for critical reasoning that has provided the underpinnings of Western civilization. Media scholar Walter Ong explained twenty years ago, "Analysis requires disengagement, distance—both real and psychological. By distancing the reader strategically both from his material and from those who are speaking to him about it, reading fosters analytic management of knowledge, 'objectivity,' as oral communication alone cannot."[4] In returning to an oral-pictorial culture, we have actually altered our perception and thinking patterns and capabilities.

The brain, like any other part of the body, improves with use and exercise. As either hemisphere is repeatedly energized, it creates more and more synaptic connections between neurons or brain cells. It becomes stronger. And as either hemisphere is underutilized, it tends to wither and atrophy. With practice comes facility; this is true whether playing the piano, learning French, shooting hoops, driving a car, or reading and thinking. Thus, as we exercise the left hemisphere—reading, computing, analyzing, evaluating, thinking—we become better at it. And as we use the right hemisphere—looking at pictures, listening, imagining, emoting—we improve that half of the brain. Over a period of a couple decades, individuals who receive most of their input through pictures and sounds are less practiced in handling printed symbols; they are less capable of processing the written word. They have conditioned themselves—both through habit and through real biological changes—to become less literate. Right-hemisphere people literally, physically, have fewer neural axons and dendrites to carry out rational processing of symbolic input. Thus we witness a steady decline in the ability of the populace as a whole to handle the print and mathematical infrastructure of their society. What we have is an increasingly divisive split between the counter-intellectual PAMs and the hyper-intellectual BENs. This is the post-intellectual chasm we are concerned with.

We are conditioning ourselves year by year to handle the written word less and less. A flood of national reports, federal research projects, and independent studies over the past quarter century has revealed that 60 million Americans (about one-third of the adult population) are totally or functionally illiterate—that is, they cannot read a newspaper article, write a letter, understand simple written directions, use the phone directory, or read the instructions on a bottle of medicine. About fifteen percent of recent urban high school graduates read at less than the sixth-grade level; young adults (between the ages of eighteen and twenty-three) on the average, read at the level of a ninth-grader. The printed word has receded into the background. The written report is something to be condensed and transformed into a color-filled visual presentation. Textbooks are dumbed down with colorful charts and irrelevant photographs. Even the pulpit is augmented with audio-visual presentations and colorful sideshows.

Some forecasters predict that print as we know it could well disappear. With our computers, we have evolved from print-based text (DOS) operations to pictorial icon-based intuitive operations. Keyboard literacy has been replaced by graphical interfaces, windows and icons, pull-down menus, mouses, touch-screen technologies, and voice commands. "User friendly" means *designed for the semi-literate and unfocused.* "Intuitive" software means *you don't have to read anything before using it.* Computer denizens, racing their mouses around their colorful pads, depend more upon right-hemisphere hand-eye spatial coordination than they do on left-hemisphere linear skills utilizing the written word. William Crossman, writing in *The Futurist,* sees this transformation as a technological godsend:

The voice-in/voice-out (VIVO) computer will be the last nail in written language's coffin. By enabling us to access stored information orally-aurally, talking computers will finally make it possible for us to replace all written language with spoken language. We will be able to store and retrieve information simply by talking, listening, and looking at graphics, not at text. With this giant step forward into the past, we're about to re-create oral culture on a more efficient and reliable technological foundation.[5]

This is a truly scary scenario. Print literacy is indispensable to careful analytic thinking. One cannot assemble or analyze a precisely articulated premise, a detailed explanation of causes and effects, a consideration of desired outcomes, and a variety of possible solutions by *listening* to the points of an argument. One must be able to compare what was presented in a given sentence with what was set down three paragraphs earlier; one must be able to reread and contemplate the contents of the previous section; one must be able to weigh a particular set of arguments with another set presented by another researcher; one must be able to sift and dissect conflicting pieces of evidence by comparison and contrast. This kind of meditative analysis simply cannot be done through an ephemeral oral and/or pictorial presentation. Oral and pictorial presentations may be effective for good entertainment, rabble-rousing, persuasive advertising, soul-grabbing preaching, sexual seduction, superficial political propaganda, or simple commands. But it simply will not do for detailed thoughtful analysis of a complex subject.

THE REALITY OF THE ELECTRIC MEDIA

In addition to the effects of brain hemisphericity, there are several other impacts we need to consider—the influence of virtual reality, advertising practices, and violence in the media, along with the pacing of the electric media. We suffer from stimulus addiction. The media have destroyed our ability to concentrate and now they must rely on sensory bombardment to hold our attention—fast-paced action, quick-cut editing, continual camera movement, special effects, flashy colors, pounding music, and any other means to intensify the visual and aural excitement. MTV videos. Five-second sound bites. Fifteen-second commercials. Three-second promos during station breaks. Rapid-fire rap records. The frenetic pace of *Sesame Street*. Truncated political debates. The critically acclaimed TV series *24* frequently displayed concurrent action in three or four different locales with inserts and split-screens. In TV commercials, dramatic action sequences, and music videos, rapid transitions (cuts, swish pans, wipes, and fast zooms) occur at the rate of about one per second.

Perceiving the world through flashing pictures and short sound bites diminishes our ability to think logically, sequentially, and abstractly. There is little opportunity for intellectual reflection and literate analysis. We are to react. Quick! Now! The faster we respond, the more likely our responses are to be impulsive. And the more impulsive we are, the more easily we can be manipulated—to the delight of politicians and marketers. Faber, the ancient professor in Ray Bradbury's *Fahrenheit 451*, explains the power of the advanced four-walled television system: "The televisor is 'real.' It is immediate, it has dimension. It tells you what to think and blasts it in. It *must* be right. It *seems* so right. It rushes you on so quickly to its own conclusions your mind hasn't time to protest."[6] The more time you spend with the electric media, including computers, the less time you have to reflect on the meaning of it all. The more you are saturated with others' images and sounds, the less you can remain an independent person. The fire captain in *Fahrenheit 451* explains, "Whirl man's mind around about so fast under the pumping hands of publishers, exploiters, broadcasters that the centrifuge flings off all unnecessary, time-wasting thought."[7]

The Impact of Virtual Reality

What we see and hear and touch and smell and taste is what is real to us. And if what we see and hear are moving pictures and recorded sounds, then these mediated images become our reality. We perceive the world by looking at a two-dimensional flickering picture framed in a 25-inch box. And we add to our picture of reality by surfing a labyrinth of Internet sites on a 17-inch computer monitor. Thus is defined what is real. Neil Postman comments, "Television is our culture's principal mode of knowing about itself. Therefore—and this is the critical point—how television stages the world becomes the model for how the world is properly to be staged."[8] Thus, while we watched live the horrific pictures of jetliners crashing into the World Trade Center, we heard accounts over and over again exclaiming, *It was just like a movie!* The world becomes one pervasive special-effects show.

We play in computer simulations and virtual-reality worlds. We live in a cyberspace habitat—with our cell phone, our laptop, our PDA, and our WiFi handheld. Home is where our Internet address is. We don't live and work and play in physical surroundings; we live in information systems. We exist in virtual environments. Post-intellectual media have constructed their own reality, their own substance. Futurist Edward Cornish predicts that increasingly "Many people may largely abandon the 'real world' in the future, preferring to live in the fictitious worlds created by the entertainment industry." He continues, "So, in the years ahead, we will live increasingly in fictions: We will turn on our virtual-reality systems and lie back, experiencing heavenly pleasures of sight and sound in a snug electronic nest. The real world will be almost totally blotted out from our experience."[9]

Advertising and Consumerism

Commercial mass media demand that we are, first and foremost, consumers. We must buy things. It is only as demand for products and services can be generated by the media purveyors (owners, publishers, advertisers) and paid for by the receivers (readers, viewers, consumers) that the system can continue. Therefore, we must respond to the advertisers' messages. Do not think about the commercials; do not analyze what is being said about the product or service; do not ask questions; do not look for reason in the advertising appeals. Clarity of argument is not needed—volume, repetition, simplicity, and dazzle will carry the message. Just purchase stuff. Unthinkingly, unquestioningly, unhesitatingly, just react emotionally to the pretty pictures, sexy models, pulsating sound track, and flashing images. Advertising, as much as any other postmodern phenomenon, illustrates how the intellectual ideals of Enlightenment thinkers have been distorted into a hyper-intellectual obsession with materialistic values.

Consumerism demands the creation of false wants. We must buy quantities of things we really do not need. How are we to define ourselves except by our material possessions? How are we to impress our colleagues and neighbors unless we have the latest and biggest? In order to succeed, the overall culture of the mass entertainment/information industry has to remain essentially anti-intellectual. Thinkers do not make good consumers. So it is to the advantage of the mass media industries to make sure that you do not cultivate habits of analysis and critical thinking. Intermittent forays into intellectual topics may be tolerated—the occasional news analysis talk show, a few educational cable channels, the cathartic value of PBS, a few Hollywood films that actually raise issues. But be careful not to give the media consumer too much of the above; it raises the dangerous specter of a thinking citizenry. And a consumer society must remain a nonintellectual society.

Desensitization and Alienation

Many critics are concerned with violence in the media. And sex. And blasphemy, drugs, sexism, racism, and every other social ill they can point a finger at. Sporadic outbursts of high-school shootings or serial killings trigger an outpouring of anti-media wrath, much of it deserved. The media certainly contribute their share of vulgarity and ugliness to the cultural landscape. But those who blame the media for all our societal disintegration are groping for easy scapegoats and simplified answers.[10] The serious consequences of media vulgarization come not from copycat crimes; the danger is not that specific individuals may suddenly go berserk and commit mayhem as the result of one particular vicious media incident.

Rather, the danger comes from long-term cumulative impact—the desensitizing experience of regular exposure to a mediated world of violence and vulgarity, greed and brutality. Media critic Michael Medved stresses that it is this desensitizing influence we need to focus on, not the role-modeling function of the media: "The most profound problem with the popular culture isn't its immediate impact on a few vulnerable and explosive individuals, but its long-term effect on all the rest of us."[11] The media do not turn us individually into criminals and social misfits, but they do desensitize us to much of the violence and ugliness that is perpetuated by the criminals and social misfits. We begin to accept the computer-generated carnage of *Grand Theft Auto 3* as acceptable entertainment.

Our reality is that which is portrayed in the mass media: the distorted values we get from television drama, the racism and anarchy preached in rap recordings, and the frenzied and violent havoc of interactive computer games. The media and the computer games are "shaping the norm." As a result of this daily diet of injustice and mayhem paraded before us, we begin to assume that the world is falling apart. This is the reality we build for ourselves: all strangers are potential threats, slaughter on our streets is to be expected, thousands are being killed in civil wars everywhere, tens of thousands are starving to death every day, terrorists are poised for another attack tomorrow. The media—in both news reports and dramatic fiction—contribute to the numbing of America. The media present a picture of a society that is collapsing all around us. We then turn to the media to confirm our fears; we ask the media to corroborate our perceptions that society is falling apart. We seek out the news reports and the dramas that verify our cultural disintegration. We become increasingly convinced that our "mean world" is growing ever more hostile.[12]

TELEVISION, RADIO, THE MOVIES, audio recordings, and even the computer, are returning society to a pre-literate oral and pictorial culture. We are encouraged to express ourselves spontaneously, to trust our intuition, and to enjoy the renewal of passion. These are not bad traits to cultivate. But in the process we are also lessening our ability to think and form independent judgments. And without this ability to analyze, weigh evidence, compare and evaluate, we citizens are woefully incapable of participating in any form of self-government. Crossman's "giant step forward into the past" also promises a giant retreat from the complex job of participatory democracy—a society where individual citizens must be able to understand complicated issues, debate courses of action, and decide in what direction their government should proceed. Geoffrey Meredith explains that "our collective thought processes will move from being linear and single and sequential to simultaneous and multilayered and holistic. Society will become less 'left-brained' and analytical and more 'right-brained' and intuitive. The more we think nonlinearly the less we will communicate with text, which will cause even more nonlinear thinking, which will lead to less text, and so forth in a continuously self-reinforcing cycle."[13]

Abstract ideas can be adequately handled only by a literate citizenship—ideas such as freedom, representative government, global involvements, economic theories, and civic responsibility. If we are to maintain a functioning democracy, literacy is a basic requisite. An informed electorate is a necessity—not an option. Postman reminds us that the writers of the Constitution "assumed that participation in public life required the capacity to negotiate the printed word. To them, mature citizenship was not conceivable without sophisticated literacy."[14] The alternative? Meredith concludes, "We will have returned to the troubadour, the cave painter, the oral tradition."[15] Back to the good old days of letting the authorities tell us what to do—the bureaucrats and technocrats who understand what's going on. Rely on the specialists. Embrace the establishment. Chill out and enjoy the pretty pictures.

PART III

The Effects: Six Crises of the Twenty-First Century

More than any other time in history, mankind faces a crossroads: One path leads to despair and hopelessness, and the other to total extinction. Let us pray we have the wisdom to choose correctly.

—Woody Allen

The danger from computers is not that they will eventually get as smart as men, but that we will meanwhile agree to meet them halfway.

—Bernard Avishai

In Part I we were concerned with Definition of the Problem. Part II looked at the Causes of the Problem. In this third part of the book, we want to turn specifically to Effects of the Problem—six crises of the twenty-first century. This is not just a cataloguing of specific hot spots, political debates, and current-event debacles. Much has been written about explicit calamities and the imminent collapse of culture as we know it. Rather, this is an attempt to get a handle on six broad underlying phenomena of our post-intellectual world: the demise of individualism (Chapter 13); the abandonment of a unifying moral authority and the subsequent embracing of materialism (Chapter 14); the rejection of reason in the last few decades (Chapter 15); environmental and population issues that have resulted from hyper-intellectualism (Chapter 16); the resurgence of religious fundamentalism and retribalization (Chapter 17); and, finally, the very real threat to democratic self-rule (Chapter 18). These six topics are presented as *effects* of our post-intellectual mindset; but each also can be seen as a *cause* of our further slide into postmodernism.

CHAPTER 13

Discarding Individualism

In a premodern cyclical culture, everyone was defined as part of the tribe. You were simply Sioux, Maori, Bantu, or Uzbek. You had no aspirations, no ambitions, no separate goals or dreams other than those of the tribe. Then out of the Enlightenment came a remarkable insight: the individual exists! Each separate woman and man was to be recognized as a unique human being. This was the rallying cry of the Enlightenment thinker. *Be your own person.* Dare to ask questions, investigate on your own, take a position, think for yourself. In defining individualism, John Stuart Mill sums up the intellectual mind. "He who lets the world, or his own portion of it, choose his plan of life for him, has no need of any other faculty than the ape-like one of imitation. He who chooses his plan for himself, employs all his faculties. He must use observation to see, reasoning and judgment to foresee, activity to gather materials for decision, discrimination to decide, and when he has decided, firmness and self-control to hold to his deliberate decision."[1] Mill concedes that the person who allows others to dictate his or her life "might be guided in some good path, and kept out of harm's way," but, he asks, "What will be his comparative worth as a human being?"[2] One of the most disquieting consequences of post-intellectualism is the loss of identity—that unique assemblage of values, dreams, secrets, distinctive characteristics, and self-esteem that defines each one of us.

LOSS OF IDENTITY

The creed of individualism was most clearly articulated by Howard Roark in Ayn Rand's *The Fountainhead:* "Men have been taught that it is a virtue to swim with the current. But the creator is the man who goes against the current. . . . Independence is the only gauge of human virtue and value. What a man is and makes of himself; not what he has or hasn't done for others. There is no substitute for personal dignity. There is no standard of personal dignity except independence."[3]

The essence of postmodernism, on the other hand, is the eradication of the individual creator—joining in the group effort or the team project. Individual input is deliberately subordinated. Individual identity is sacrificed. Businesses are run by committees and task forces. Politicians rely on surveys, focus groups, and media pollsters. Schools turn to group projects rather than encouraging competition and individual recognition. This is a counter-intellectual return to the collective refuge of tribal security. And in our communal sanctuary, we surrender some of our sense of individual identity.

The Turn to Anonymity

Many computer-based interactive activities are collaborative experiences in which personal input is blended into the group endeavor—with little or no recognition of individual efforts. Groupware applications enable multiple users, located anywhere in the world, to work simultaneously on the same document, technical drawing, or electronic painting. This *desktop video conferencing* is a communal electronic group-think process that undermines individual creativity. The same loss of personal input is seen in "massively multiplayer online role-playing games" in which tens of thousands of players, at distant terminals, join in collective contests such as *EverQuest* or *Counter-Strike*. Individual skill or insight is lost in the greater collective endeavor.

We also embrace anonymity because to stand out might make somebody else feel bad. Individual acknowledgment means that some people will win more gold stars than others. But we don't want to be insensitive; we don't want to make the losers feel unworthy; we want equality. Francis Fukuyama reinforces the opposing modern viewpoint—the importance of competition and individualism: "A civilization devoid of anyone who wanted to be recognized as better than others . . . would have little art or literature, music or intellectual life. It would be incompetently governed, for few people of quality would choose a life of public service. It would not have much in the way of economic dynamism; its crafts and industries would be pedestrian and unchanging, and its technology second-rate."[4] The hyper-intellectual path of unrestrained individualism leads to the degradation of others. And the alternate counter-intellectual path of anonymity leads to self-degradation. These are two of the opposing strands of our post-intellectual web culture.

Bureaucratization and Loss of Self-Sufficiency

Bureaucracy is a technology. Our definition of technology (Chapter 9) was a "systems approach to problem-solving," a structured methodical way of achieving precisely defined objectives. Bureaucracies are set up as solutions—ways to do things that we could not otherwise accomplish. As Western civilization grows ever more convoluted, we fall back on our government agencies, watchdog groups, zoning commissions, oversight committees, PTA boards, homeowners' associations, and independent auditors. It takes big bureaucracies to cope with big problems. And the bigger our bureaucracies and government institutions become, the less self-sufficient the individual becomes. As we call in the specialists—the financial experts and political advisors, the jury consultants, and wedding planners—we are personally diminished. We feel we can't do the job on our own.

Bureaucracy was an intellectual invention. But overpowering invasive bureaucracy creates a post-intellectual mindset. It contributes to technological determinism. Back to Thoreau: *men have become the tools of their tools.* The more we rely on technology and bureaucracy, the less we understand what is going on around us; and the less we understand, the more anxiety we feel. What happens to our sense of identity? Our sense of uniqueness and self-worth? Our personal independence? In a post-intellectual world, we accept that our destiny is no longer in our own hands—our information load has become so overwhelming, our technological environment so intimidating, our economic situation so confounding. We no longer have command over our personal environment because we no longer understand our personal environment. And because we have little idea as to what the specialists are doing—with our finances, our computers, our legal matters, our society—our confusion and alienation escalate.

We want to feel that we can still control our technologies. For example, you can get specific information you need from the Web. But then you are dependent upon Google or Yahoo (or some other search engine) to sort things out. How much independence do you pretend to have as you sit captive to your browsers and imbedded programs? Links and screens pop up whether you want them or not. You can choose what programs to download from the Internet (of course it was some computer program that told you what to download). But in downloading any new software application or upgrade from the Internet, how much control do you actually have? We trust Microsoft, McAfee, Adobe, Netscape, Acrobat, and Norton to scan thousands of our existing files, determine what we need, where to place each new file (C:\WINDOWS\PROGRAM FILES\ ACCESSORIES\GOBBLEDEGOOK\ *click "Next"*), and sit amazed, powerless, watching icons dance around our screen, assuring us that hundreds of new files and upgraded programs are being installed and configured correctly. *There now, everything is under control.*

LOSS OF PRIVACY

In a premodern tribal culture, there was no privacy—just as there was no individual identity. Everyone stood naked in front of the tribe. There was nothing to hide. There was no *place* to hide. The concept of privacy did not exist. Privacy is the invention of an intellectual culture. The printing press gave us books to read in private; modern architecture gave us private spaces. But today—in our counter-intellectual return to a pre-literate culture—we have discarded our commitment to privacy. Thus we have our postmodern sensitivity training programs and therapy groups where we willingly choose to strip ourselves emotionally and stand naked again in front of the tribe.

The electric media provide the window for our voluntary exhibitionism. People from all walks of life eagerly surrender their privacy to appear on salacious talk shows, manipulative courtroom simulations, exploitative reality shows, and voyeuristic Web sites to expose themselves in front of millions of onlookers. It is a willing surrender of our privacy. Nudity in the public media reflects our return to tribal nakedness. Thus, we find it easier to accept public and corporate intrusions into our private lives.

The more information that is known about you, the less your individuality can be protected. As Marshall McLuhan observed over thirty years ago, "The more the data banks record about each one of us, the less we exist."[5] More and more people have access to billions of individual government records and even our genetic information. We see increased sharing of our Social Security numbers. We authorize the merging of financial institutions (banks, insurance companies, and brokerage houses) into corporate monoliths that share our personal financial and medical data. We accept workplace telephone and keyboard monitoring. We accelerate the adoption of smart cards that can be used to record our every transaction and track our every movement.

We are reminded daily of dozens of new high-tech threats to our personal privacy: miniaturized spy gear; surveillance cameras in commercial and public buildings and highways (smack your kid in the Wal-Mart parking lot and wind up on national TV); sophisticated surveillance devices that can see through walls and eavesdrop on conversations from hundreds of feet away; and high-resolution satellite cameras that identify cars in driveways.

Many of these privacy incursions are voluntary and self-inflicted. We adopt personal tracking systems (anti-hijacking devices in vehicles, wristband transmitters to keep track of our youngsters). We consider embedded personal identification devices (surgically implanted microchips, a bar-code ID number etched on every citizen). We welcome increasing use of surveillance cameras at nursery schools and day-care centers and in school classrooms—so that parents and administrators can check up on their children (and their teachers) on the Internet. And we facilitate privacy intrusion with our personal family surveillance gear (home spy cameras, pagers, nursery monitors, household bugging devices, the ubiquitous camcorder). The list is exhaustive—and scary.

Commercial Intelligence-Gathering

Corporate intelligence-gathering has existed for years—adding information to your permanent marketing profile every time you make a purchase through an Internet site or a cable channel, order from a mail-order catalog, phone certain 800 and 900 numbers, respond to a magazine or telephone poll, or donate to a worthy cause. Today we are moving into *retail ethnography* or *observational research*. That means *We're looking directly at you while you shop and make retail decisions.* Using hidden surveillance cameras, concealed microphones, and two-way mirrors, retailers are finding ways to zoom in on you and watch you as you reach for that can of hair spray or study that clothing label. They want to observe you as you make your purchasing decisions.

"Sniffer" software can be placed on your PC without your knowing it is there—as part of a bundled package when you buy the computer or as you inadvertently download it as part of some other software application. Spy software and *parasites*—which will trace and keep a log of every single keystroke you make, including all of your passwords, credit-card entries, and security codes—can be so thoroughly imbedded in your system that no anti-virus program can detect their existence. In many of its software packages, Microsoft has implanted unique identifiers that place a hidden electronic marker in every document you create. All of your Internet clicks and transactions are subject to on-line profiling. Omnipresent cookies are placed on your hard drive by many of the web sites you visit; and psychographic profiles can be built from your web-surfing *click-stream*. Advertising-placement companies such as DoubleClick, Inc., then place web page banner ads on your computer screen, targeted specifically to your marketing profile. Television commercials designed specifically for you will soon be appearing on your TV set.

Scanning and merchandizing technologies such as RFID (radio-frequency identification) transponders (*Speedpass, E/ZPass*) and "smart shopping carts" (with onboard computers) probe deeper into your marketing psyche. Privacy invasion evolves into manipulation. When you lose control over information known about you, you lose control over your own decision-making. The marketers, the psychological profilers, and the political manipulators subtly take over control of every option offered to you. They pull you ever so steadily in their desired direction—even as you think you are making your own choices. In an intellectual society you make your own decisions. In a post-intellectual world, others make your decisions for you—whether you realize it or not.

Government Surveillance

With visions of terrorist attacks implanted in our consciousness, we willingly surrender personal privacy to increase our security. The USA Patriot Act gave federal agencies increased surveillance and information-gathering authority—with much less congressional oversight or judicial supervision. Roving wiretaps (which are OK'd secretly) can be authorized to allow federal agents to intercept a person's telephone conversations from any cell phone or wired telephone number. The FBI *Carnivore* program was beefed up to require Internet service providers to make their services more wiretap friendly, allowing the Bureau effectively to pick up any e-mail message it desires.[6] The National Security Agency has the capability to monitor globally up to two million phone calls, e-mail messages, and faxes every hour. Other increased surveillance undertakings focus on bank transactions, library records, the use of discount cards at grocery stores, and the contents of your hard drive—even all those obscene contributions to your favorite chat room and those loathsome e-mail notes you thought you deleted without sending. After the Pentagon announced its Terrorism Information Awareness Office to sift through thousands of government and commercial databases in a search for anything suspicious, it next proposed its LifeLog *cyberdiary* to create a "voluntary" national memory bank that would collect every data entry from your personal computer.[7]

Following IRA bombings in London in the early 1990s, England quickly embraced heightened video surveillance. There are now an estimated 2.5 million surveillance cameras in Britain (that are acknowledged). They are located ubiquitously throughout every public spot—from airports and taxi stands to nursery schools and hospital nurseries, and even inside buses and elevators. One estimate is that the average Briton may be photographed by 300 separate cameras in a single day. Privacy scholar Jeffrey Rosen writes that the cameras "were hailed as the people's technology, a friendly eye in the sky, not Big Brother at all but a kindly and watchful uncle or aunt."[8] Rosen goes on to observe, "The cameras are designed not to produce arrests but to make people feel that they are being watched at all times. . . . And rather than thwarting serious crime, the cameras are being used to enforce social conformity in ways that Americans may prefer to avoid."[9]

New computerized video surveillance systems use *faceprinting* technologies to identify individuals by scanning a number of crucial facial landmarks and digitizing the data into a numerical code. Such a technology poses an ominous potential for public surveillance. Step outside—into the range of the ubiquitous surveillance cameras—and you can be immediately identified and tracked. Once every citizen is required to have his or her faceprint recorded, you can be assured that whenever you show up at your bank, that rock concert, that political demonstration, the airport terminal, that student protest, or a house of ill repute, you indeed will be recognized. Not maybe. Not sometimes. But definitely, every time. All in the name of domestic security. Needed, perhaps. Maybe even inevitable. But certainly not consistent with an intellectual climate based on individualism and privacy. However, one must be careful with such anti-patriotic protestations. In December 2001, Attorney General John Ashcroft told Congress, "those who scare peace-loving people with phantoms of lost liberty . . . only aid terrorists."[10] *It's not patriotic to defend your privacy.*

Finally, Rosen adds one other chilling insight: "the Supreme Court has held that constitutional protections against unreasonable searches depend on whether citizens have subjective expectations of privacy that society is prepared to accept as reasonable."[11] Wow! In a splendid bit of circular reasoning, it is now established that as electronic surveillance becomes ever more invasive, we have less reason to assume that our privacy is protected; and so—because our expectations are lowered—the electronic snooping is not unreasonable! Thus, the erosion of privacy can be accelerated because in our postmodern culture it is no longer unexpected. The more privacy we lose, the less unreasonable it is to lose our privacy. Therefore, the Fourth Amendment (guarding against "*unreasonable* searches and seizures") becomes less and less relevant.

OUR PERSONAL FREEDOMS ARE DIMINISHED as we surrender our individualism—as we forfeit our identity and our privacy. If you cannot buy a product without your smart card knowing about it, if you are not able to have a private conversation with a friend, if you are unable to travel to the corner coffee shop without being on camera, if you can't check out a book or a video without the police finding out about it, then you have lost some of your personal independence. Freedom—like individualism and privacy—is an intellectual idea. Security, peace, and equality are non-intellectual needs. (More about this in Chapter 18.)

If you want your individualism and self-reliance, it means you will have less security, less of a guarantee that you will come out okay. You are on your own—to succeed or fail. The more security you demand, then the more you must be willing to sacrifice your freedom and individualism, your privacy and self-sufficiency. You cannot expect total independence if you want other people or bureaucracies to take care of you—whether you are relying on family members or police protection, corporate pension plans or government welfare programs. You cannot expect Big Brother to take care of you unless you allow Big Brother to become very intrusive.

In our post-9/11 apprehension, we must be concerned with national security. And we are willing to sacrifice a measure of personal freedom and convenience. But we must be mindful that such a calculated sacrifice also accelerates the unraveling of our intellectual fabric. Larry Ellison, founder and C.E.O. of Oracle Corporation, has proposed that—with Oracle's help—all government databases be combined into one single comprehensive data file that includes everything about everybody: "The single thing we could do to make life tougher for terrorists would be to ensure that all the information in myriad government databases was integrated into a single national file."[12] Rosen responds: "But when the same software applications are used by the government to track, classify, profile and monitor American citizens, they become not technologies of liberty but technologies of state surveillance and discrimination. They threaten the ability of Americans to define their identity in the future."[13] When Rosen asked Ellison if he thought such a global database was actually going to be set up in the future, Ellison replied, "I do think it will exist, . . . And we're going to track everything."[14]

We are creating a climate of intrusion tolerance. Consider the present cohort of high-school students. We are conditioning an entire generation of American teenagers to accept locker searches, see-through backpacks, and random drug testing—all as normal. In the future these same persons, as adults, will consent to a much more invasive social environment—and demand that the next generation be even more compliant in accepting security requirements.

We add to our feelings of alienation and anxiety. We don't know which way to turn. Bill Joy quoted Woody Allen as saying, "More than any other time in history, mankind faces a crossroads: One path leads to despair and hopelessness, and the other to total extinction. Let us pray we have the wisdom to choose correctly."[15] This sardonic observation serves to underscore the futility felt by many. Our challenge, in this postmodern period of uncertainty and disorder, is to hold on to as much of the intellectual vision as we can.

CHAPTER 14

Swapping Materialism for Morality

Middle Eastern terrorists want to stamp out Western modernism for two reasons. First, the morality issue: Islamic fundamentalists cry out, *The American infidels represent all that is decadent and depraved*—secularism, feminism, carnal pleasures, abortion, homosexuality, nudity, the American Civil Liberties Union, and People for the American Way. (Okay, the last two were thrown in by Pat Robertson and Jerry Falwell.) Tolerance is a moral wrong in the eyes of those who are intolerant. Additionally, our popular trappings—from blue jeans and baseball caps to Coke and Pepsi, from rock and rap to McDonalds and KFC—have blanketed the globe with our brand of cultural hegemony.

Second, America is reviled because it has succeeded rather spectacularly as the most powerful economic engine on the planet. Fareed Zakaria comments simply, "We are rich and they envy us. We are strong and they resent this."[1] Western power represents postcolonial imperialism, resources control, and human exploitation. As both the Great Satan and as the Yankee Imperialist, America represents that which is resented and despised by many nationals and extremists throughout the globe. This chapter is concerned with the interplay of these two factors—decreasing morality and increasing materialism.

ERADICATION OF MORAL BOUNDARIES

Something has happened to our moral standards in the last half-century—something more than the usual intergenerational lamentations about the younger generation falling apart. Columnist William Raspberry cites a 1999 nationwide poll "that found two-thirds of American adults [are] convinced that we are becoming more morally lax. . . . We have, say the respondents, less respect for authority, less respect for one another, less commitment to marriage, less personal responsibility and good citizenship, less belief in the work ethic, in God, and in religion."[2] He goes on to report, "82 percent [of the respondents] believe young people don't have as strong a sense of right and wrong as their counterparts of 50 years ago." What may be even more notable is that those surveyed "also ranked their own standards as weaker than their parents." That is quite an admission: *My kids aren't living up to my standards. And my standards are lower than my parents' were.*

In the 1960s we discarded the cultural narrative of our forefathers. As we demonstrated against racism, sexism, gay bashing, environmental exploitation, and a bogus war, we also—just for good measure—tossed out prohibitions against casual sex, drug usage, and obscenities in language and the media. In effect, we declared traditional morality null and void. We now exist in a state of ethical anarchy and noncritical tolerance of all sorts of deviant beliefs and behaviors—what Steve Allen refers to as a period of *moral numbing:* "a growing, blind, and even stupid insensitivity in which many have lost their awareness of evil to such an extent that we no longer give much of a damn about questions of right and wrong."[3]

The Coarsening of America

Civilization tempered violence and vulgarity; but as civilization wanes, violence and vulgarity escalate. Critic Godfrey Cheshire gives us this perspective:

Imagine reviving John and Abigail Adams, H. D. Thoreau, Ralph Waldo Emerson, and Henry James, and giving them a tour of the current culturescape, with its Howard Sterns and Jerry Springers, its pierced belly buttons and vapid shopping malls, its cult of the ugly, the vulgar, and the trivial. Would they not gape in shame? What would Martin Luther King Jr. say to rap's crude ethos of misogyny and greed? What blessing do you suppose Jesus would bestow on a nation hooked on fat cars, brainless celebrities and Internet porn?[4]

There are numerous examples of our cultural coarsening. Broken families are one result of 1960s rootlessness, and demographers are now predicting that more than half of all children born in the 1990s will spend part of their childhood in a single-parent household; the broken family in turn is a cause of delinquency, vandalism, and further social collapse. Media vulgarity is the effect of lowered moral standards (the argument is that media are only reflecting what goes on in society); but this media obscenity is then a cause of further desensitization and crudeness.[5] How about substance abuse? Although figures for specific drugs fluctuate from year to year, the overall trend is one of steadily increasing experimentation and addiction. How about sex? Roman Martinez writes that we "have grown up in a world where divorce is prevalent, where promiscuity is rampant, and where roughly one-third of all children are born out of wedlock. . . . For us, casual sex is just another way of getting some exercise and having a good time—kind of like bowling, but without the shoes."[6]

The Irony of Tolerance

Tolerance is a concept that was bundled with modern civilization. Accepting the cultures and idiosyncrasies of those who are different from one's own tribe is a rational, reasonable thing to do—to be tolerant of someone who looks, talks, dresses, dances, prays, and eats differently. Thus we no longer support the idea that my tribe is better than your tribe (and therefore I am justified in trying to beat up your tribe). The modern concept of human rights and civil liberties holds that all tribes should treat each other with respect.

Today, however, the liberal idea of civil tolerance has been distorted into a hyper-intellectual mutation that says we should tolerate and accept everything. The postmodernist proclaims there is no truth other than what exists for each of us individually. There is no value system except as you create it for yourself. Therefore, there is no universal ethical code. Since all cultures are to be accepted as equally valid, there is no unanimous set of values. What does your tribe believe in? Polygamy? Free sex? Atheism? Polytheism? Slavery? Cannibalism? Buying your term paper from an Internet source? *Whatever! If it works for you, it should be accepted by all of us as being valid.* Thus, we promote tolerance for anything and everything— outrageous religious practices, quack medical claims, and bogus scientific theories. A liberal tolerance of people's differences metamorphoses into an unquestioning acceptance of all things bizarre and, ultimately, results in a complete breakdown of standards and values.

Noncritical tolerance reflects the hyper-intellectual attitude: accept and respect all value systems. At the opposite extreme, of course, we have the counter-intellectual position, as exemplified by religious fundamentalists and other closed-minded zealots: tolerate nothing except those uncontested truths that my tribe has embraced. All other value systems are to be rejected or destroyed.

Religion in a Post-Intellectual Web Culture

Religion plays an ambiguous role in our post-intellectual society. Generally today we see a trend away from mainstream religion. This is a hyper-intellectual result of postmodern secularism. From Copernicus to

NASA, we have incrementally crowded God out of the sky. Bishop John Shelby Spong traces the demise of our premodern theistic belief system: "The understanding of God as a theistic supernatural parent figure in the sky was finally rendered no longer operative. God was simply drained out of existence as a working premise in our society. Rewards and punishments, either in this life or in the life to come, ceased to be the primary motivators of our behavior."[7]

This is not to say that religion plays no role in today's culture. Obviously it does. We go to church; we recite the creeds; we say our prayers; we baptize, marry, and bury in the church; we bracket our public ceremonies with invocations and benedictions. But these residual trappings mask a hollow cultural commitment; we are simply going through the ceremonial motions. Theistic faith no longer dominates our moral and cultural undertakings; the fear of God no longer governs our daily activities. We have evolved into a postmodern culture of relativistic religious convenience. This is the hyper-intellectual strand of the web culture, pulling us away from organized religion.

At the same time, as noted in Chapter 7, counter-intellectual threads of the web culture pull us back towards a charismatic, nonintellectual premodern religious experience. The last three decades have seen a rise in evangelistic and fundamental religions (even while mainstream sects are declining in membership)—which, ironically, signals a decline of personal responsibility. Whereas the modern humanistic belief proclaimed that individuals were accountable for their own lives, the return to a premodern acceptance of the omnipotence of God or Allah or the high priests absolves the individual of considerable personal accountability. *I am but a poor sinner.* Thus, in our disoriented web culture, we are experiencing a hyper-intellectual trend away from religion as a dominant force in the lives of most individuals; and we are simultaneously witnessing a counter-intellectual revival of fundamentalism that dominates the lives of true believers. And in both cases, the result is a lessening of personal responsibility.

The Failure of Responsibility

As mentioned in Chapter 3, we can hold on to freedom only so long as we honor the intellectual compact to behave with responsibility. This has to include moral responsibility. Perhaps the most significant cause of our moral meltdown is, very simply, the failure of personal accountability—one of our two pillars of intellectualism. No system of morality can be imposed by outside authority. It must come from within. Society can demand adherence to rules and restrictions—people can be coerced into compliance. But society cannot legislate belief in values. If the only reason you conform to a set of standards is fear of punishment—whether from civil law enforcement or from a vengeful God—then the system of values is inherently bankrupt. Individuals must *believe* in the rules—not merely obey the rules. You will stop at a red light because it is a rational and responsible thing to do, not because you want to avoid getting a ticket. You will treat persons of different skin color with respect because they are human beings, not because some civil rights legislation demands equal treatment.

Thus, an intellectual society rejects the idea of censorship. If a people need to be censored, then something has failed in their value system. Any kind of censorship, whether from the church or from the state, reflects a lack of self-confidence by the society. *We can't trust ourselves to do the right thing; some higher authority must tell us what to do and what not to do. We are not intelligent enough, responsible enough, nor moral enough to govern ourselves.* Censorship is the hallmark of an authoritarian regime. Either you exhibit personal responsibility or you accept that someone else will tell you what to do. If you want to avoid censorship, if you want to be free of any form of external restraint (government censorship, the voice from the pulpit, condominium restrictions, or the black-shirted enforcers of a totalitarian regime), then you must exercise internal restraint. You must show some moral responsibility.

MATERIALISM AND GREED

Ever since Copernicus and Galileo weakened the moral dominance of the church, we have been searching for an alternative source of ethical authority. Neil Postman remarks that "science undermined the whole edifice of belief in sacred stories and ultimately swept away with it the source to which most humans had looked for *moral* authority. It is not too much to say, I think, that the desacralized world has been searching for an alternative source of moral authority ever since."[8] We pay lip service to religious principles; but the church no longer plays a central role. We turned to science as we moved from Sorokin's ideational culture to a sensate culture; but today science no longer is our guiding narrative. Humanism looked promising; but we couldn't sustain the commitment to reason and responsibility. Marxism was tried; and it fell spectacularly short. We continue to support the shell of democracy; but we grow increasingly cynical about the role of government. In short, at the beginning of the twenty-first century Western civilization has no universally recognized moral center, no common cultural narrative, no unifying belief system.

Except for one thing. Materialism.

What we have today in the West is unanimous acceptance of, and universal commitment to, materialistic success as our common cultural touchstone. This is what we believe in today—wealth, instant gratification, sensual and carnal pleasures. And as much of it as possible. Right now. Even such an exemplary capitalist as currency speculator George Soros says, "Unsure of what they stand for, people increasingly rely on money as the criterion of value. . . . The cult of success has replaced a belief in principles. Society has lost its anchor."[9]

All goods and services must be commodified—labeled with a price tag, analyzed on a cost-benefit basis. Morris Berman writes that we have become a culture "in which corporate profit and its associated mentality have begun to dictate everything. After all, why read (let alone memorize) Robert Browning when the *cash* value of things is the only value of things?"[10] Even if one wants to enjoy a Brahms symphony or a walk in the woods, there should be some way to cost it out in terms of mental health or emotional balance. All activities must be justified on a profit-loss sheet. Everything becomes a commodity. Sports stadiums are named for their commercial sponsors; and major athletic contests are labeled with their corporate backers. George Will (no quiet voice when it comes to defending free enterprise) facetiously wonders where it all will end: "What about the General Motors White House? . . . Ford could counter with the Lincoln-Mercury Lincoln Memorial. Naming the Nike Capitol Building could be done tastefully: a single dignified white swoosh on the dome. That would not be an eyesore to people across the street at the Microsoft Supreme Court Building."[11]

Greed and Corruption

If materialism is instituted as our cultural goal, then greed becomes the means for attaining that goal. As uttered by the character Gordon Gekko in the film *Wall Street*, "Greed, for lack of a better word, is good. Greed is right. Greed works."[12] This hyper-intellectual interpretation of Adam Smith is used to justify any and all excesses of predatory capitalism. It results in what Enron's own bankruptcy report labeled "a culture that appears to have encouraged pushing the limits."[13]

One result of insatiable greed is outright corruption. If the chief goal in life is acquisition of material wealth, then that value outweighs all other values—including honesty, compassion, loyalty, and fair play. When the pursuit of worldly riches dominates all sectors of society, then men and women will find ways to justify using any means to get there. Truth doesn't matter. Integrity doesn't carry any weight. Getting money is all that counts. No matter how you do it. We find it easier and easier to rationalize questionable and fraudulent tactics. The pursuit of wealth overrules all other ethical considerations—leading inevitably to corruption. *New York Times* financial columnist Paul Krugman writes that "The Enron debacle is not just the story of a company that failed; it is the story of a system that failed. And the system didn't fail through carelessness or laziness; it was corrupt."[14] Enron executives walked out with more than a billion dollars in their collective pockets while tens of thousands of employees and shareholders were left holding the empty portfolios of more than 3,000 subsidiaries and faux partnerships that were set up solely to deceive. Krugman adds, "And nobody I know in the financial community thinks Enron was an isolated case."[15]

The overriding transgression is not what these executives got away with when their empires collapsed; it is what they got away with when their houses of cards were still standing. The questionable accounting practices, obscene executive perks, and phony numbers had been generally accepted throughout all of Corporate America. A 1998 survey of 180 chief financial officers of America's top companies revealed that two-thirds of them had been asked to rework their accounting practices to show a more favorable corporate picture—and twelve percent admitted having done so. A 2001 study by the Financial Executives International found more than 450 instances where companies had altered their books between 1998 and 2000; this was as many cases as in the period from 1977 to 1997.[16] All because getting as much money as possible is the only goal—regardless of what you have to do to get it. The ultimate answer to corporate corruption is not more rigorous oversight, a beefed-up Securities and Exchange Commission, or closer congressional scrutiny. It must come down to personal integrity. As Warren Buffet writes, "To clean up their act on these fronts, CEOs don't need 'independent' directors, oversight committees or auditors absolutely free of conflicts of interest. They simply need to do what's right."[17]

Many of these questionable practices are generated in an attempt to manufacture paper gains without actually producing anything of value. Smith defined a capitalistic system based on manufacturing goods and providing services. He did not envision an illusory world of off-book partnerships, off-shore tax dodges, hyped earnings, no-cost executive loans, short selling, deferred stock options, futures contracts, insider trading, phantom subsidiaries, dishonest accounting practices, global hedges, deceptive stock analyses, manipulative IPOs, derivative contracts, global arbitrage, and consultants masquerading as auditors. All of these fiscal fictions and fabrications contribute nothing to the economy, produce nothing of substance for the consumer, and result in nothing but quick profits for the financiers and speculators. This is blatant hyper-capitalism, without any responsibility.

Even without such blatant corruption, rapacious capitalism must be challenged purely on moral grounds. Capitalistic excesses lead to exploitation of the less fortunate—child laborers, illegal domestics, slaves, and sweatshop workers. We also have corporate violence—conglomerate takeovers, widespread layoffs, mom-and-pop operations forced under by discount chains, business decisions made solely on the basis of profit-and-loss sheets—with no consideration of social consequences, community impact, or consumer justice. And greed for short-term profits leads to environmental despoliation. Cut down the forests; suck up all the oil. All that matters is that we make a buck as quickly as possible.

AMERICANS USED TO GO TO THE STORE to buy what they needed. Now they go to the mall to see what it is that they should want. Our economy flourishes not because it satisfies the needs of consumers, but because it creates the lust for products that consumers don't really need. The fictitious newscaster from the movie *Network*, Howard (*I'm-as-mad-as-hell*) Beale, also proclaimed, "We are now a corporate society, a corporate world, a corporate universe, . . . and this whole endless, eternal, ultimate cosmology is expressly designed for the production and consumption of useless things."[18] As discussed in Chapter 12, you have value only as you fulfill your dehumanized role as a consuming cog in the gears of the corporate establishment. Your essential obligation is to buy stuff. You have no identity other than your Visa or MasterCard number. You know not how to define yourself except by that which you purchase—how you outfit your house, how you transport yourself about, how you decorate your body, how you entertain yourself. One result of this materialistic obsession is the overwhelming consumer debt that we have hung around our necks. One report points out that more people declared bankruptcy in 1999 than graduated from college that year.[19] *We are turning out more bankrupt individuals annually than college graduates.*

With no single unifying moral touchstone, we have adopted material success as our universal standard. Wealth and worldly goods become the ultimate goal. We confuse possession with identity; we substitute consumption for freedom. However, as noted by the philosopher Bertrand Russell, "It is preoccupation with possession, more than anything else, that prevents men from living freely and nobly."[20]

In premodern times we were controlled by political and religious authorities—tribal chiefs, dictators, and priests. Today in our postmodern times we are controlled by materialistic authorities—corporate chiefs, marketing dictators, and the creative priests of advertising agencies. Douglas Rushkoff observes, "In a sense nothing has changed: the same kinds of techniques that have been used for centuries by emperors, kings, popes and priests, are now being used in service of the corporation. Where it's different is that we have technologies in place that make these coercive techniques automatic."[21] Postmodern communication technologies are fond of claiming that they empower the individual. However, closer consideration reveals that most of these empowered individuals begin to look a lot like old-fashioned consumers. The choices we are given are simply questions about which brand to buy, which new electronic toy we want next, what new self-image do we want to purchase, how do we want to express ourselves materialistically.

CHAPTER 15

Rejecting Reason

In most of our social and political endeavors, we (our government offi-cials, corporate boards, educational leaders) simply are not succeeding in following an analytic, objective process in our collective decision-making efforts. We are not making good decisions; we are not effectively solving our myriad societal problems. We are wallowing in *dumbth*—the post-intellectual breakdown of reason. This is what underlies the Progress Paradox.

As outlined in the four steps of the Analytic Thinking Pattern (Chapter 3), the practice of rational deliberation involves a logical, sequential pro-cessing of information in order to decide on a course of action—whether in business, science, medicine, law, education, or politics. In one format or another, we must *define the problem* (documenting the effects and prob-ing the causes), *establish our criteria or objectives* we want the solution to accomplish, *consider and select a solution* (keep an open mind at this point—this is where both the reactionary fundamentalist and the knee-jerk leftist abandon the process), and engage in honest *evaluation* of our efforts. In any academic or professional arena, these four steps define the rational problem-solving mindset. This is the *cognitive* pillar of intellectualism.

But we must also consider the *affective* pillar of intellectualism—respon-sibility. One must have the *will* to be reasonable. It does little good to understand the ATP model (or the scientific method or instructional de-sign principles) if you don't *want* to go about decision-making in a rational manner. This, to a great extent, is what postmodernism is all about—the abandonment of rationality, either unintentionally or deliberately. Unin-tentionally we may give in to the anarchy and insecurities of our chaotic culture. We give up on logical problem-solving. We can't handle it. Or we may choose deliberately to shun rational decision-making. We may opt for the passion and intuition of the romantics. Or the faith and commitment of true believers. Obviously, terrorists do not choose to tackle their grievances with reason; they don't have the commitment to be rational. In any case, the failure of the *will to reason* is a crucial factor in the decline of critical thinking.

There are a number of specific causes for our failure to live up to our intellectual commitment. Here is my subjective listing of fourteen obstacles to clear thinking—six factors dealing with the postmodern loss of the will to reason, and eight difficulties with the actual problem-solving process—the failure of reason.

WHERE REASON FAILS: SIX DIFFICULTIES WITH THE WILL TO REASON

Rather than engage in the arduous process of rational deliberation, we can let tradition, greed, complacency, and cronyism replace intellectual rigor. We can accept predigested dogma as a substitute for original thought. We can welcome the security of authority; turn the decision-making over to others (the emperor, the pope, our union organizer). We might decide to conform; *we'll try the same thing they did next door.* We can resort to prejudice and ideology; *we already know what the answers are, so there's no need to bother with reconsideration and analysis.* We might engage in ethnocentric bickering; *my tribe (racial faction, religious tract, national group) deserves the best deal.* We also can try intuition and guesswork; *if it feels good, do it.*[1] In each case, we willingly discard some degree of responsibility. We turn away from our greater intellectual obligation (to think about the future, to place the greater social good above our own selfish interests).

The Burden of Thinking

In Chapter 8, we considered the argument that humans are not entirely rational animals. We are governed by our passions and prejudices, our lusts and our longings. Collective decision-making is demanding. Freedom is hard work. And we will by nature slide into the lazy pattern of letting others handle the tricky job of thinking—the specialists, the business agents, and help-line staffers. Columnist G. D. Gearino writes, "Humans are naturally prone to intellectual laziness, . . . In fact, most of us are happy to let someone else do the thinking. After all, it can be hard work. If other people are willing to think, God bless them."[2] This is a major factor in the attraction of religious fundamentalism. All the answers are laid out for you. There's no need to think on your own.

Mental Rigidity

In a rational society, all participants would come to the forum with an open mind—ready to present their arguments, listen to others, weigh the evidence, and arrive at a reasonable conclusion. They agree ahead of time that they will reach an agreement. This is how we engage in collective problem-solving. Today, however, antagonists come to the negotiation table with minds firmly encased in concrete. The closed mind will reject facts and evidence that do not support preformed ideas. Indeed, when opposing viewpoints clash in contemporary society (Republicans and Democrats, theists and atheists, pro-lifers and pro-choicers, Arabs and Jews, Yankee fans and Mets fans), it is a given that there will be no good-faith resolution of the issues involved. Participants in such encounters—whether in legislative halls, the corner tavern, or at the breakfast table—enter the encounter with minds stubbornly positioned and leave the fray with minds even more firmly entrenched. No rational discourse has taken place. No resolution has been achieved.

The Influence of Electric Media

Critical thinking is not possible without print literacy. Relying solely on oral-pictorial communication, one cannot adequately understand the scope of a problem, investigate its causes, analyze its effects, construct a careful set of desired outcomes, consider all possible solutions, compare each of these alternatives to the criteria or objectives, select the best combination of proposed solutions, and structure an evaluation plan. Walter Ong observed twenty years ago that as our verbal style is changed by television—becoming looser and less structured—so, too, is our thinking: "Electronic verbalization, particularly through radio and even more through television, is affecting our present speaking and writing and printing styles, and thus *our modes of thought* [italics added]."[3] Careful rational analysis simply cannot be done relying solely on the ephemeral spoken word and colorful pictorial presentations.

Postmodern Distrust of Reason

Stephen Toulmin writes that "the critique of Modernity has broadened into a critique of Rationality itself."[4] We are told that just as every culture is entitled to its own system of values and morality, so too is every culture entitled to determine its own system of epistemology and rationality. In addition to moral relativism, we now are faced with reasoning relativism. Divine revelation, metaphysical insight, and transcendental epiphanies all claim to be valid means of decision-making and problem-solving. Besides, if we trust the engineers and technocrats to handle our problems, they often will use rational technologies to work against the best interests of society. Engineering expertise does not necessarily guarantee pursuit of the best societal goals.[5] Science can be used for evil purposes. Therefore we distrust the rationalists and scientists.

Analysis Paralysis

You must have adequate information to make a reasonable decision. If you are traveling down a highway and come to a fork in the road, you can go left or right; but if you have no information about where each fork leads or the nature of each road, you are not able to make an intelligent decision. However, too much information is equally debilitating. Information overload results in *analysis paralysis*. With too many incoming data flooding our cerebral input circuits, we are numbed into inaction.

Take the example of the fork in the road. Suppose you had access to all the following information about each alternate road: mileage to your destination; width of the road; number of lanes; width of shoulders; condition of shoulders; average grade; steepest grade; percentage of road that is gravel, oil-sealed, asphalt and concrete; number and severity of curves; speed limits; extent of police patrolling; population density (rural, suburban, urban); general terrain (wooded, bushy, desert, wild, cultivated farmland); scenic highlights; roadside attractions; places to eat; service stations; availability of water; number of rest areas; cleanliness of restrooms; number and depth of potholes; overall need for maintenance; frequency of repair crews; length of road under repair; number of detours; traffic density; number of intersections, stop signs and traffic signals; use by truckers, motorcyclists, farm equipment, and bicyclists—and every other datum you can think of. Now, with all this information available, would you be able to analyze thoroughly all possible combinations of factors and make the best possible decision? To the contrary, overwhelmed by the task of sorting out the trivial from the significant, you would experience a state of dysfunctional bewilderment. An abundance of information simply results in decision-making paralysis.

Technology Undermining the Will to Reason

When we use technology—the assembly line, the computer, the bureaucratic commission—to solve a problem, we also diminish the human spirit. In turning our decision-making over to technology, we sacrifice some of our own self-reliance. In discussing the impact of existentialism, William Barrett explains that "the essence of the existential protest is that rationalism can pervade a whole civilization, to the point where the individuals in that civilization do less and less thinking, and perhaps wind up doing none at all."[6] The more we rely on technology and bureaucracy, the less we feel we need to think for ourselves. As Bernard Avishai puts it, "The danger from computers is not that they will eventually get as smart as men, but that we will meanwhile agree to meet them halfway."[7] Our technologies make us less accountable for our own decision-making.

WHERE REASON FAILS: EIGHT DIFFICULTIES WITH THE REASONING PROCESS

Once we move beyond difficulties with the *will to reason*, we get into shortcomings with the actual problem-solving process—working with the ATP model. We fail in defining and researching the problem thoroughly, or coming up with the right objectives, or considering all appropriate solutions. There are numerous ways to catalog the difficulties we have with critical thinking. Let me group some of them under eight arbitrary headings.

Information Chaos

We are overwhelmed with so many conflicting and irrelevant bits and pieces that we are unable to filter out the substantial from the trivial, the valid from the vacuous. Every half-baked opinion is defined as evidence; every bit of nonsense on the Web is accepted as legitimate.[8] A tragic example of information chaos (data overload) was the failure to recognize and act on terrorist threats prior to September 11. Despite all the Congressional investigations and media speculations about "what the White House knew and when," the simple fact is that there were so many suspicious activities and vague warnings, that it was virtually impossible for top-level authorities to digest all the reports coming in from field agents and "connect the dots." It is ironic that the FBI and other intelligence-gathering agencies feel the need to collect more information (through wireless wiretaps, interception of e-mail messages, and asking utility meter readers and UPS delivery men to report any neighborhood anomalies) when they cannot process and connect the information that they are collecting now.

Superficial Problem Analysis

Frequently we look only at the obvious surface signs of a problem—the blisters, the fever, the pus—and treat those symptoms. If we would probe deeply enough to find the actual roots of the problem, it would be much easier to solve the immediate crisis. That's because what we usually need to do is eliminate causes of the problem. In many foreign entanglements, for example, we look at terrorist bombings, border squabbles, civil uprisings, and refugee troubles; and we react to those immediate sore spots— initiating a peace-keeping force or mounting a humanitarian relief project.

These, however, deal just with the superficial symptoms of the deeper problems. We may catch a few of the bad guys and punish them; we may throw money at the situation and prolong the lives of a few starving babies. But we have done nothing to solve the problem—the long-term underlying issues of economic disparities, religious and philosophical conflicts, repressive dictatorial regimes, clashes between tribalism and modernism, and global population pressures. We spend considerable time and energy furiously bailing out our sinking boat with our little tin pails, but nobody takes the time to try to patch the hole in the hull.

Problem Isolation

We often fail to grasp the relationships of parts of the overall problem. We deal with individual symptoms and miss seeing the big picture. Herman Daly wrote a quarter-century ago, "Probably the major disservice that experts provide in confronting the problems of mankind is dividing the problems into little pieces and parceling them out to specialists."[9] These bureaucrats and technocrats have but a tunnel-vision glimpse of the overall human condition; they cannot put the problem in perspective. There are no isolated issues.

Problems with our schools, for example, are actually the result of economic displacement, family breakdowns, racial troubles, poor urban planning, welfare inequities, law enforcement difficulties, immigration policies, drug abuse, population pressures, and curriculum overload. However, no single educational or governmental agency is empowered to deal with these factors in any kind of comprehensive integrated manner. Therefore, the incomplete and shortsighted solutions we come up with lead inevitably to future problems and complications. We have become a leaf-blower society. We tackle our immediate problems and merely blow them out of the way as quickly as possible—shuffling them somewhere else, where some neighbor or other agency will have to deal with them later.

Solutions as Problems

Practically all problems we face are the results of solutions to previous problems. Consider this simplified syllogism: First, *virtually all our problems are caused by human actions*. Every problem is the result of something that humans have done—with the exception of natural disasters and diseases (and even in those two instances, humans contribute greatly to the magnitude of the problems). Every social injustice, every war and urban riot, every economic difficulty, every instance of drug abuse, every traffic jam—each and every instance is caused by some act of men and women.

Second, *all human actions and activities are undertaken as solutions to needs or problems.* Every building, tool, committee, artifact, road, piece of clothing, every institution and bureaucracy—everything human beings have ever done or created—has come about in an attempt to solve some specific problem or in response to some felt need. Every work of art, hot fudge sundae, hula-hoop, and bit of pornography was created to meet some need.

Third, therefore—since all problems are caused by human actions and all human actions are attempts to solve some problem or meet some need—*virtually every problem we have is a consequence of a solution to some previous problem!* Stated conversely, anything we do to solve a problem today is likely to compound problems tomorrow. The automobile was created as a solution to transportation problems; it in turn led to problems with smog, urban sprawl, and traffic congestion. Drugs were invented to combat the problems of various diseases; their abuse has led to addiction and death, intensified crime, and other economic and social devastation. Pesticides were invented to wipe out nasty bugs; their use has contributed to environmental contamination and human illnesses. This is the essence of the Progress Paradox: every solution or bit of progress we make in tackling technological and material problems leads to future problems. Theodore Roszak explains that "Every mature technology brings a minimal immediate gain followed by enormous long-term liabilities."[10] This is why it is so necessary to examine thoroughly the underlying factors involved in every problem.

Hazy Needs and Objectives

Criteria are those things that you want your solution to achieve—your objectives, your targets. In a formal problem-solving process, these objectives would have to be quantified—stated in concrete measurable terms that can be attained within a given time frame. For example, a general criterion such as "Society should adequately educate its youth" could be stated as "Within ten years, 95 percent of all nineteen-year-olds should have completed high school and passed such-and-such standardized tests." Only with such precisely worded targets can we ever determine whether or not objectives have been reached. And we must be able to precisely measure the success of our efforts by a given date—or we will never know if we have achieved anything, if we have ever solved the problem. Statements such as "no child shall go to bed hungry" or "all racial intolerance shall be eliminated" make for fine political rhetoric; they might help to rally a crowd. But they certainly do not state realistic objectives that could ever be attained.

Opposing and Negative Criteria

In compiling your criteria or objectives, you cannot ignore opposing viewpoints. You may want to protect wilderness areas from any and all development; but if you completely ignore the property rights of land-owners you are not going to come up with a workable compromise. You may believe strongly in freedom of speech; but you must also respect the rights and sensibilities of those who want to protect children from expo-sure to pornographic web sites. If Palestinians want to achieve a peaceful self-governing state (their primary objective), they have to accept that Is-rael also must be guaranteed a secure continued existence (the opposing criterion). No solution is going to work unless it addresses the concerns of those who are opposed to your primary objectives. I may disagree with the pope on the issue of birth control (and I do), but I must consider the position and sensitivities of the Catholic Church in addressing global population problems.

One must also consider negative criteria—those unwanted side effects that you want not to happen. Think of all the possible harmful outcomes that you want to make sure any good solution will avoid—people being hurt, the economy melting down, the environment being trampled, future border squabbles—and state explicitly in your list of criteria that those things should not happen.

Unintended Consequences

We find that frequently the source of the problem we are encountering is the unintended consequence of an ill-conceived solution to a previous problem.[11] Often the unintended consequence is the result of not incor-porating the appropriate negative criteria when setting up our objectives. When we were developing the technologies to replace the horse with the internal combustion engine, for example, the automobile looked like a great idea. As a solution to our transportation problems, it would meet most of the criteria we might have considered over a century ago—relative affordability, personal flexibility, convenience, safety, cleaner streets, and so forth. But no one thought to include *the avoidance of air pollution* as a negative criterion. Related to unintended consequences is *end-product anal-ysis* or *full-cost accounting*. Frequently we fail to take into consideration what the total tab will be when projecting the costs of any particular so-lution or project.[12]

Incomplete Search for Solutions

You have the obligation to consider all possible options and feasible solutions. Do not assume that any opinion or idea is not worthy of deliberation. During the early stages of examining solutions, do not limit your considerations by tradition, budgets, conventional thinking, or your bosses' wishes. Brainstorm. Keep all options open. Many possibilities will be discounted when you weigh them against your criteria; but do not exclude them from consideration at this stage.

Nowhere has this need to consider all options been more eloquently penned than in John Stuart Mill's essay *On Liberty*. He gives four reasons why all possible alternatives *must* be considered. One, any conceivable solution just *might* turn out to be the best decision. Two, any proposal—even if it is not the best alternative when considered in its entirety—may contain elements of truth; it may contribute to the final solution. Three, no solution can be agreed upon until it has been rigorously measured against all other proposed solutions. Four, a given solution may have been the best answer at some point in the past, but unless it is periodically revisited we cannot assume it is still the most efficacious path to follow.[13] Therefore, force yourself to think expansively and creatively. Intellectually, you cannot afford not to consider all possibilities.

ONE MORE HANDICAP should be added to this catalog of difficulties we have with the process of collective decision-making—*the acceleration of problem-making*. The more technology we use, the more it breeds a technological state of mind. We are thrust into a labyrinth of self-generated technological leaps without time for adequate planning and deliberation. Technological advances in all fields enable us to devise solutions faster and faster. But since each solution tends to generate more problems (the Progress Paradox), we are simply creating additional problems faster and faster. In turn then we must rely on technology to solve the new problems. But in so doing, we are digging ourselves deeper and deeper into a technological hole—counting on promised technologies that will be delivered tomorrow. We see no way out of our immediate dilemma but to continue borrowing against the future in this way—thus compounding tomorrow's problems. We will worry about straightening out the long-term problems later.

In Chapter 11, we explored the acceleration of change, the challenge of trying to keep up with what is happening in our information environment. Orrin Klapp relates this accelerated pace with decision-making: "Better information-processing can speed the flow of data but is of little help in reading the printout, deciding what to do about it, or finding a higher meaning. Meaning requires time-consuming thought, and the pace of modern life works against affording us the time to think."[14] Thus, instead of taking time to think, we rush faster and faster into the next set of technology-generated complexities and problems. The challenge of handling our cultural problems with reason and clarity becomes increasingly complicated with each passing innovation.

CHAPTER 16

Courting Ecological Disaster

Western civilization was founded on the modern idea of growth and development. Francis Bacon exhorted us to develop our scientific tools and methods so that we might exploit nature for our own purposes. Early explorers and capitalists pushed onward to establish our linear culture—building upon the biblical injunction to "Be fruitful, and multiply, and replenish the earth, and subdue it: and have dominion over . . . every living thing that moveth upon the earth,"[1] However, we may have gone too far in our commitment to growth and progress. Over a quarter-century ago Aleksandr Solzhenitsyn warned of the dangers of worshipping progress: "Society must cease to look upon 'progress' as something desirable. 'Eternal progress' is a nonsensical myth."[2] And it is a dangerous myth. Our environmental despoliation is clearly the result of progress and our hyper-intellectual hubris.[3]

THE PURSUIT OF ECONOMIC GROWTH

All economic theories are based on the promise of continued growth—infinite expansion and development. For all eternity. Every year we must have more industry, consumers, and taxpayers. And we will produce more of everything—more housing, vehicles, factories, pharmaceuticals, and wireless Internet devices. And of course we will consume more—more food, water, clean air, fuels, more minerals, metals and building materials. This is what keeps the economy humming. Our dedication to perpetual growth and progress has become an addiction—a narcotic dependence on continued expansion and escalation. It is easy to project continued growth if one doesn't take into consideration the depletion of natural forests, the mineral ores mined, topsoil erosion, global warming, the outlay for pollution clean-up, increased medical complications, and the psychological costs of congestion. Eventually these *end-product costs* must be reckoned with; we must look at the total price tag for modern development.

The pursuit of unending progress and development fails to acknowledge one basic reality: *perpetual physical growth is not possible*. We live on a finite planet with limited resources. We are running out of arable land and potable water; we are running out of places to dump our trash; we are running out of places to put people. Kenneth Boulding, former president of the American Economic Association, once observed that "Only madmen and economists believe in perpetual exponential growth."[4]

We hold on to the enduring political myth that somehow we can cut taxes, increase government spending, and pay for it all tomorrow with increased economic activity—that is, growth. But we cannot do that indefinitely. Such self-delusion is intellectually irresponsible. The borrow-and-spend-and-pay-tomorrow mentality is a deceit. John Gray sums up the argument: "And the idea of indefinite progress is easily associated with the notion that social dilemmas are soluble by the generation of ever more resources through economic growth. This association is not a necessary or inevitable one, as we can see from the example of John Stuart Mill, who insisted that a stationary state need not be one in which human improvement has come to a halt."[5] We shall look further at the observations of Mill in Chapter 22—where we explore the possibility of devising a viable economic model based upon a stable population.

Growth proponents repeatedly recite the mantra: *We can achieve perpetual growth because technology has always saved us in the past*. To gamble mankind's future on the conjecture that we can continue to pull technological miracles out of the hat is risky business indeed. Such an argument overlooks the reality of the Progress Paradox. Even as we make technological strides, we create more complex problems. Also, no amount of technology-dependent progress can change the fact that we are inevitably running out of nonrenewable resources. And, most importantly, we are running out of space where we can humanely stuff additional billions of human beings.

GLOBAL POPULATION GROWTH

Forget about world wars, computer advances, and genetic miracles, the single most overwhelming fact of the twentieth century is this: *the global population has increased about four-fold since 1900!* That is the most significant fact of the last hundred years (see Figure 4). And the population continues to swell—expecting to triple in the 48 poorest countries of the world in the next fifty years.[5] In 1972 the President's Commission on Population Growth and the American Future stated, "There is hardly any social problem confronting this nation whose solution would be easier if our population were larger."[6] What was true for our country thirty years ago is even more true for the entire planet today. On a global scale, we face no greater crisis than overpopulation. As we crowd more and more people into our fragile biosphere, we intensify every one of our environmental and social woes. To quote Pogo, *We have met the enemy and he is us*—more than six billion of us.

One result of increased population density is decreased privacy and personal freedom. The larger the population of any community—whether we look at the city, nation, or planet—the more we have to accept government intrusion and bureaucracy; the more we have to substitute interdependence for independence. Increased population pressures cannot help but result in more rules and regulations, more forms and formalities, law enforcement activities, government snooping, data-tracking, public surveillance, and traffic signals.

Starving on the Edge

One incontestable biological truth is that every species—bacteria, butterflies, lemmings, dandelions, and coyotes—will multiply and grow as long as there is enough food and room for nourishment. This is the way nature guarantees perpetuation of the species: propagate as aggressively as you can. Humans are not exempt from this law. Every single gain we make in increased food production (better fertilizers, super pesticides, drought-resistant hybrids, the Green Revolution, aquaculture, genetically altered plants and livestock) is matched by a corresponding expansion of human population to consume that increased output. We can no more alleviate human suffering by improving agricultural methods than we can reduce the number of cars on the road by widening freeways. The more growth we facilitate, the more growth we will have. *If we grow it, they will come.*

Population will always expand to consume the available food. And then expand a little more than the food supply can handle. It follows that when the food supply runs low—when enough butterflies or lemmings or people are starving—the population will begin to shrink. But there are always those living at the border where survival meets famine—trying to subsist on the edge where the food supply is dwindling. Ecologist David Pimentel of Cornell University estimates that more than half of the world's population suffers from malnutrition.[7] There will always be millions of humans living on the brink of starvation—regardless of how much more food our technology produces. We really want to end global suffering. Honestly! It pains us to see so many people in misery. But such a quixotic pursuit is

Figure 4
World Population Estimates (in Millions)

6   *(2000)* **6,000**

5   *(1990)* **5,000**

                                                           (1980) **4,470**

4
                                                           (1970) **3,600**

3   *(1960)* **3,000**

                                                           (1950) **2,500**

                                                           (1940) **2,250**
2   *(1930)* **2,000**
                                                           (1920) **1,800**
                                                           (1900) **1,600**

                                                       (1850) **1,100**
1
                                                    (1800) **910**
                                                    (1750) **710**
                                                    (1700) **625**
                                                  (1650) **520**
                                                       300

              10 million   **30**   **100**

| 6000 B.C. | 5000 B.C. | 4000 B.C. | 3000 B.C. | 2000 B.C. | 1000 B.C. | 1 A.D. | 1000 A.D. | 2000 A.D |

Note: Years indicated in italics

doomed to failure. We can never keep up with the burgeoning population crunch by producing more food. Humanitarian aid, ironically, only intensifies the problem by keeping people alive long enough to have more babies. Controversial biologist Garrett Hardin writes,

The world hunger problem is really a population problem. In the simplest words: Every bit of food given to a hungry nation that has grown beyond the carrying capacity of its environment adversely affects the future of that nation. . . . if a population is so malnourished that its physiological ability to produce children is reduced, the first effect of improving a people's nutrition is to increase their fertility. This means that saving lives with external aid this year will make the task of feeding the population next year even more difficult.[8]

This blunt reasoning has been termed *Lifeboat Ethics*—if we try to get everybody into the lifeboat, the greater the chances are that we all will sink. It's not an easy argument to make—or to agree with. But the reasoning is unassailable.

We would do well to heed the warnings of Thomas Robert Malthus, who in 1798 published his *First Essay on Population*, in which he articulated what has come to be known as the Malthusian Principle—*population grows faster than the means to support it*. If we are not able to suppress our insatiable appetite for growth and expansion, our population will be contained by three factors: warfare, pestilence, and famine.[9] Ideally, we should be able to find some better way of dealing with our population pressures than by killing each other, spreading disease, and starving others to death. We should be able to act rationally to slow down our runaway population expansion—in a way that butterflies and coyotes can't. We know what to do. But we don't do it. The Catholic Church refuses to accept that birth control is the most humane thing we can do to relieve global misery. The leadership of the United States refuses even to give birth control information to suffering countries. This is not the way an intellectual culture should be functioning. We are not handling our numbers with reason and responsibility.

Hyper-Urbanization

The city is a modern technology. It evolved as a solution for dealing with the problems and challenges of agriculture: grain storage, money-lending, marketing and commerce—eventually encompassing defense, manufacturing, and the arts. It was a logical manifestation of linear growth and development. Today, however, the city has become a mega-technology—a post-intellectual bedlam of hyper-urbanization.[10] Oswald Spengler, writing about 85 years ago, described where we were headed: "I see, long after A.D. 2000, cities laid out for ten to twenty million inhabitants, spread over enormous areas of countryside, with buildings that will dwarf the biggest of today's and notions of traffic and communications that we should regard as fantastic to the point of madness."[11] We reached that point well before 2000, with more than fifteen of the planet's metropolitan centers exceeding ten million inhabitants. And many critics would concur that such population densities are indeed madness.

The city is not a natural ecosystem. A concrete-glass-and-plastic environment is alien to our animal genes. The city, like the electric media, plunges us into a synthetic environment of manmade images and coded messages. Both the city and the media lead to a desensitization of our natural environment. It all blends together in a manufactured, artificial, virtual reality—Leisure World, television-world, DisneyWorld, WWWWorld, and shopping-mall world.

We have resigned ourselves to the authority of the city. We accept the congestion and cacophony, the urgency and the emotional stress, the grime, crime, and violence. In every urban center, we sense the desperation and confusion, the tumult and frantic acceleration of the pace of life. We are battered by the incessant urban din—reinforcing the dissonance between our inner nature and our technological environment. In a futile flight, we run away to suburbia. But we succeed only in expanding the circle of urban congestion and despair—adding more freeways, shopping malls, industrial complexes, and housing tracts to the sprawl. Technological determinism decrees that we continue to add to this greater urban labyrinth—despite everything in our genes that cries out for a bit of nature and reality. Oh, well, maybe those genes can be modified in DNAworld, and then we'll all fit in.

ENVIRONMENTAL ROULETTE

One result of modern science and our economic commitment to expansion and exploitation has been mounting global environmental damage. Our hyper-intellectual distortion of Bacon's exhortation to use science to master nature has become a frenzied push to exploit nature for our immediate gain. This expand-and-exploit state of mind has dominated American economics and politics since the early nineteenth century, justifying every public and private project from damning the rivers of the west to the Panama Canal to draining the Everglades for housing developments—regardless of the ecological impact.

Dwindling Resources

We are a throwaway society. We throw away everything—including our environment. One indisputable outcome of our relentless exploitation is that we are using up our natural resources—mining, drilling, digging, pumping, and blasting. Some resources will disappear this century; others may last for a few hundred years—but in the end there will be nothing left to dig up or suck out of the earth. Summarizing the year 2000 report of the annual *State of the World* publication of the Worldwatch Institute, Robert Braile writes, "From eroding soil in Kazakhstan to melting glaciers in the Peruvian Andes to depleted fisheries off New England and elsewhere, the world's ecological health at the dawn of the millennium is deteriorating. . . . Species are disappearing, temperatures are rising, reefs are dying, forests are shrinking, storms are raging, water tables are falling: Almost every ecological indicator shows a world on the decline."[12] Half of the world's tropical forests were destroyed during the twentieth century. The ozone layer is slowly disappearing. One quarter of the world's coral reefs have been lost. Topsoil around the globe is being used up and washed away; in the United States every acre of plains farmland annually loses seven tons of topsoil to wind and erosion. Potable water is disappearing. The planet has half the drinkable water per person than we had in 1960; it will be halved again in 25 years.

We use our science and engineering prowess to accelerate the exploitation and exhaustion of our natural resources even faster. We use seafloor seismic imaging to locate deep-sea schools of fish; we use satellite reconnaissance to locate and develop oil reserves. The more we improve our mining and fishing technologies—the more efficient we become—the faster we suck the system dry. This is not an intelligent approach to resources management; this is not an intellectual way to run a planet.

Extinction of plant and animal species proceeds at an ever-increasing pace. We may be losing as many as 30,000 species of flora and fauna a year.[13] Extinction threatens 11 percent of all bird species, 25 percent of all mammal species, and 34 percent of all fish species.[14] All seventeen of the world's major oceanic fishing grounds are being harvested more rapidly than they can be replenished. Due to population pressures throughout the globe, native peoples and poachers have resorted to survival "bush-meat" hunting which leads in turn to the *empty-forest syndrome*.

Bumper-sticker environmentalists and field biologists alike give about four reasons why we should be concerned with maintaining the Earth's biodiversity. First, more than 40 percent of all painkillers, antibiotics, anti-cancer drugs, and numerous other modern medicines were originally derived from plants, animals, fungi, and micro-organisms found in the wild. The extinction of flora and fauna species might deprive us of the next cancer cure or cardiovascular treatment. Second, we need the psychic elbowroom and recreational benefits of the wilderness. We need the vistas and open spaces, the green hillsides and blue waters. We need contact with other creatures. Third, there is the survivalist justification. Jon Turney warns, "if we continue to deplete biodiversity and eradicate ecosystems that do not meet our immediate requirements, we could provoke some kind of total system collapse in the biosphere."[15] We simply don't know how much more we can lose before our own fate is threatened. Fourth, the moralist argument: *Homo sapiens* have no right to wipe out species or to obliterate natural ecosystems that can never be recovered. Do we really want to carry Genesis 1:28 that far? Turney argues that "we have some duty of stewardship to the web of life from which we emerged."[16]

Increasing Pollution

As we look at global pollution, there are innumerable areas of concern: smog and acid rain, fouled waterways, overflowing landfills, massive oil spills, pesticides, agricultural runoff, carcinogenic contaminants, nitrogen buildup, nuclear wastes, global warming, and—according to NASA— more than 100,000 pieces of space junk orbiting the Earth. Many of these problems occurred simply because we were not sufficiently informed as to the nature of our long-term environmental tinkering. No one could have anticipated smog or the residual toxins when we first introduced the internal combustion engine or DDT into our lifestyles. For almost fifty years chlorofluorocarbons (CFCs) were used as the perfect chemical for refrigeration—until it was discovered in the 1970s that CFCs were eating away the atmosphere's protective ozone layer. Other effects are due purely to the fact that we chose not to think about the long-term consequences; we eagerly embraced nuclear energy in the 1950s as a cheap and pollution-free source of energy—although we had no idea how we were going to dispose of the radioactive residue.

We are continually increasing the risk of genetic pollution: the likelihood grows that genetic hybrids will intermingle in the field or in the lab and wipe out pure strains that are needed for biodiversity. No one can foresee the kinds of genetic accidents waiting to happen: hybrid crops that cross-pollinate to produce superweeds that are resistant to all known pesticides; oil-eating microbes that could escape from the ocean and find their way into our gas tanks; a fungus-cocoa hybrid that produces a delicious chocolate substitute, but results in delayed disruption of one's insulin balance. No one can anticipate the unintended consequences of all our genetic tinkering. One example: Bt corn—which is genetically modified to produce its own pesticide—not only kills the European corn borer, but it also has resulted in the massive killing of monarch butterflies. Approximately 20 percent of the American corn crop is planted in Bt corn. Again, we have little idea what we are doing in the long run.

IT HAS TAKEN NATURE A COUPLE BILLION YEARS to work out the balance of plants, animals, rocks, and water that the planet needs. We humans can do nothing to improve upon nature's trial-and-error process. Humans can only screw things up with zoning plans and dam projects, reforestation schemes and computer simulations. Fisher and Fisher colorfully explain: "Like a Rube Goldberg contraption designed to create and foster life on Earth, our ecosphere can apparently withstand little tinkering. Bend one little pole the wrong way, and the whole interlocking mechanism goes out of whack."[17] To ignore this reality is to deny our intellectual responsibility for the future of the planet. The bottom line: we simply don't know what we're doing, what ultimate impact we will have.

There are something like one quintillion insects on the globe (that's a million trillion). If all those insects were to disappear from the face of the earth, our terrestrial ecosystem would collapse very quickly. With no bugs or bees left to recycle our wastes, pollinate the plants, and provide fodder for the bottom of the food chain, very little living matter could survive. On the other hand, if the planet's 6.3 billion *Homo sapiens* were to disappear, the earth would do very well, thank you. Air pollution would disappear, landfills would shrink, greenhouse gases would cease, freeways would crumble to dust, streams would eventually clear up, coral reefs would grow again, forests would regenerate, and all Burger Kings would shut down. What does that say about the anthropocentric arrogance of the human species?

Many factors contributed to the election of President Bush in 2000. But undoubtedly one factor was the intellectual tone of Al Gore contrasted with the comforting appeal of George W. Bush. The populace indicated they were not much moved by ecological preaching and intellectualizing. In fact, the election of 2000 is one of the clearest indications of our anti-intellectual tilt. The point is not that Bush is a nonintellectual—but that the post-intellectual electorate chose not to think about long-term ecological responsibilities.[18] The citizenry chose instead the promise of easy fixes and short-term profits.

Dire ecological predictions are easily dismissed by those who contend that all is well. But one haunting question must remain in the back of our minds: *Just what if the environmental doomsayers happen to be right?* How much are we willing to gamble that we can continue to expand and develop, explore-exploit-and-move-on, without catastrophic results? Proceeding as we are, we shall continue to deplete our resources and pollute our ecosystem beyond repair. But onward we proceed in our hyper-intellectual arrogance. Progress. This is not environmental roulette. It is environmental suicide.

CHAPTER 17

Embracing Tribalism and Religious Fundamentalism

Ecological devastation is the result of *hyper-intellectualism*. Religious fundamentalism and retribalization are the results of *counter-intellectual* thinking, a return to a premodern outlook. Retribalization is the merging of a person's individual identity into the larger cultural consciousness of a group identity. Marshall McLuhan states simply, "Tribal cultures cannot entertain the possibility of the individual or of the separate citizen."[1] The ultimate expression of this de-individualized mentality would be the suicide bomber who is willing to throw away his or her life for the cause of the tribe. Individual existence just doesn't matter.

By contrast, Thomas Jefferson described what it means to be intellectually independent, explaining why he would never be considered a member of any political party (or of any other group): "I never submitted the whole system of my opinions to the creed of any party of men whatever in religion, in philosophy, in politics, or in any thing else where I was capable of thinking for myself. Such an addiction is the last degradation of a free and moral agent."[2] This is the hallmark of an intellectual mindset—the refusal to be pigeon-holed by any set of religious beliefs or tribal doctrines, the determination to reason for yourself, to research independently, to maintain an open-minded perspective, to refuse to allow any religion, party or tribe to do your thinking for you.

The resurgence of religious fundamentalism and the fanaticism of tribal intolerance both work to undermine this Western underpinning of individuality and independence. One of the best summaries of the loss of individualism was expressed by philosopher A. A. Bowman: "Of all the forms of wanton self-destruction, there is none more pathetic than

that in which the human individual demands that in the vital relationships of life he be treated not as an individual but as a member of some
organization."[3]

RESURGENCE OF RELIGIOUS
FUNDAMENTALISM

It is a sad irony that religion, which should be the wellspring of spiritual
good will and tolerance, so often is the breeding ground of animosity and
narrow-mindedness. Modernity was supposed to eradicate prejudice and
wipe out intolerance. But it hasn't turned out that way. When confronted
with today's uncertainties and chaos, many who have failed to come to
grips with the modern world turn to their religious heritage or tribe for
security; and they turn against those who are different. Andrew Sullivan
points out how the religious fundamentalists perceive the West to be utterly Godless and sinful, and then goes on to add, "It is not a big step to
argue that such centers of evil should be destroyed or undermined, as bin
Laden does, or to believe that their destruction is somehow a consequence
of their sin, as Jerry Falwell argued."[4]

While lashing out at modern rationalism, religious fundamentalism is
also behind the persecution of subjugated groups within the borders of
states dominated by religious clerics—women and homosexuals, for example. Consider the deaths of fifteen schoolgirls in Mecca who died when
religious police (the Commission for the Promotion of Virtue and Preven-
tion of Vice) locked the doors of their burning school and would not let
the girls escape because they were not properly covered with head veils.
Or the tribal council in Meerwala, Pakistan, ordering the gang rape of an
18-year-old girl because her brother was seen walking unchaperoned with
a girl from a tribe considered above his class.

One problem in dealing with closed-minded fanaticism is that the true
believers are so unshakably sure of themselves. They are loud, demanding, and intimidating. Elie Wiesel describes the mindset of the fanatic:

The fanatic is stubborn, obstinate, dogmatic: Everything for him is black or white,
curse or blessing, friend or foe—and nothing in between. . . . The fanatic simplifies
matters: He is immune to doubt and to hesitation. Intellectual exercise is distaste-
ful, and the art and beauty of dialogue alien to him. Other people's ideas or theories are of no use to him. . . . The fanatic derides and hates tolerance, which he
perceives as weakness, resignation or submission. . . . He doesn't speak, he shouts;
he doesn't listen, he is too busy yelling; he doesn't think, he doesn't want *anyone*
to think.[5]

At the same time, the voices of the intellectuals are muted. The open-
minded liberal does not rant and rave. While the extremists shout, the

intellectuals are wrestling with the issues. To the undecided and impressionable masses, the voices of the level-headed are drowned out by the screams of the fanatics.

The Holy War of Terrorism

It cannot be denied that terrorist attacks on the modern West are religiously inspired. Fareed Zakaria observes simply that "For [bin Laden] and his followers, this is a holy war between Islam and the Western world."[6] Islamic terrorism is not targeted solely at American secularism, of course. It has been a worldwide, decades-long war waged against Christians, Jews, Hindus, and Buddhists everywhere. More than that, it is a culture clash between fundamentalists and liberals of all faiths. Sullivan explains, "This surely is a religious war—but not of Islam versus Christianity and Judaism. Rather, it is a war of fundamentalism against faiths of all kinds that are at peace with freedom and modernity. This war even has far gentler echoes in America's own religious conflicts—between newer, more virulent strands of Christian fundamentalism and mainstream Protestantism and Catholicism. These conflicts have ancient roots, but they seem to be gaining new force as modernity spreads and deepens."[7]

Religious fanaticism lurks on the fundamentalist fringes of all the world's religions. The Mahasabha and Rashtriya Swayamsevak Sangh sects of Hinduism have been stirring up religious hatred since the first half of the twentieth century. It was the Buddhist right-wing cult, the Aum ShinriKyo ("Supreme Truth"), that launched the 1995 poison gas attack in the Tokyo subway. The Jewish American Zionist, Baruch Goldstein, in 1994 massacred 27 Muslims in the Abraham Mosque in Hebron out of religious conviction. Both the Ku Klux Klan and the Aryan Nation claim right-wing Christian origins. The People's Temple (Jim Jones) and the Branch Davidians (David Koresh) attest to the fanatical power that charismatic religious leaders can wield. Abortion-clinic bombings and murders committed by Christian zealots reveal the distorted mentality of the religious terrorists. These, and hundreds of other incidents, all attest to a lack of intellectual tolerance by religious extremists—of whatever denomination. Religious fanaticism is incompatible with modern rationalism.

TRIBAL ASSAULT ON INDIVIDUALISM

Retribalization is a return to the pre-intellectual grouping of the extended family, the clan, the tribe—small, closely knit communal bands who share kinship, community, and ethnic ties. With the inauguration of the modern age, these tribal ties were pulled apart by the printing press, urbanization, industrialization, legal contracts, and the ascendancy of the nation-state. In today's postmodern disorder, men and women seek a way to regain this security of the extended family, a sense of belonging—a way, in Neil Postman's words, "to recover a source of transcendent identity and values."[8] A quarter-century ago, sociologist Harold Isaacs summed up our return to a tribal mindset:

> For about two hundred years, the best and the brightest intellectuals in the Western world believed that with the advance of science, the growth of knowledge, the mastery of nature, reason would win and all earlier forms of human backwardness would just go away. . . . Science advanced, knowledge grew, nature was mastered, but Reason did not conquer and tribalism did not go away. . . . At its worst, our current retribalization signals the end of the illusion.[9]

To embrace tribalism is to submit to authoritarianism. Those who accept, without questioning, the word of the authorities—the tribal chiefs and priests—have no need to think for themselves; they need simply to heed the truth as it is dictated to them. They have embraced the security of a nonintellectual tribal mindset. Your tribal identity is, in effect, your personal narrative—your cultural mythology.

Victimization and Affirmative Action

In an intellectual culture, individuals assume responsibility for their own lives. In a nonintellectual religious or tribal culture, people are covered by the cloak of collective responsibility. In such a climate of individual irresponsibility, we adopt the mantra, *it's not my fault*. The post-intellectual no-fault mentality ultimately leads to an increase in the politics of victimization. This reinforces what candidate George W. Bush referred to as "the soft bigotry of low expectations."[10] If an individual or a group expects little of itself, it will achieve little. It becomes a self-fulfilling prophecy: *I can't succeed, why should I even try?* Failure is thus assured. So when a group—a religious sect, a tribe—relies on cries of victimization to explain its failures, it absolves itself of any need to try to succeed: *It's not my fault; someone else is to blame.*

Cultural critics and bohemian intellectuals of the 1950s have been replaced by tribal representatives and special-interest political victims. Our classrooms, political forums, op-ed pages, and web sites are populated not by open-minded intellectuals debating broad political philosophies, but by narrow-interest ideologues and political activists—civil rights proponents, gay and lesbian advocates, feminist spokeswomen—campaigning for their particular victimized groups.

A capitalistic society built upon libertarian theories promotes economic conflict, financial aggression, and a struggle for success. Carried to hyper-intellectual extremes, such practices result in ruthless manipulation, class abuse, and economic exploitation—even slavery. Out of the post-intellectual turmoil of the 1960s came a concerted push for rectifying some of these past economic inequities. Affirmative Action was established to make up for decades—even centuries—of injustice and discrimination.[11] It evolved into an attempt to legislate racial equality, civil tolerance, and respect for all individuals—ideals that should have been promoted and implemented as an integral part of an intellectual society. By declaring a commitment to affirmative action in restoring the rights of suppressed groups, we instituted a counter-intellectual remedy to hyper-intellectual excesses. The assertion that no group should be exploited was eventually twisted to mean there should be no losers.

Affirmative action promotes a pluralistic diversity that decrees that anything and everything is acceptable and is to be tolerated. So we strive today for equality rather than superiority, sensitivity instead of competition. Thus—to take but one academic example—we have English teachers at all levels who uncritically accept all sorts of spelling and grammatical abuses of the English language because to correct the errant pupil would not only harm the young psyche, but would be critical of the child's cultural or racial background.

Tribalism and Racism

Racism is a product of tribalism and religious intolerance—an anti-intellectual manifestation of fear, insecurity, ignorance, and distrust of those who are different. William Raspberry noted in a speech, "Tribes ensure their survival by resisting outsiders."[12] *It's my clan against your clan.* Counter-intellectual retribalization has thus spawned hate groups throughout the nation—Ku Klux Klan chapters, neo-Nazi cells, reactionary militia units, and assorted religious cults. Although exact numbers are hard to pin down, there are hundreds of such groups throughout the United States.[13]

Affirmative action also encourages a more subtle form of racism. By undermining the intellectual concepts of individual competition and self-determination, affirmative action tends to stigmatize those groups the programs are intended to help. Affirmative action identifies your tribe as a group that cannot make it on its own merits. Back to the "soft bigotry of low expectations." Carried to the extreme, this attitude results in voluntary denial of individualism and reinforcement of a victimization mindset.

Those who take refuge in tribal identification also contribute to a racist mentality in another way. By claiming that the injustices and past prejudices heaped on their tribe define their present position in life, they are saying in effect that race (or gender or religion) is the ultimate determinant of identity. This form of racism argues that tribal identity is the most important factor in establishing who one is. The fact that you are an

African-American, a woman, or a homosexual becomes more significant than the fact that you are a successful mother, a musician, a chess champion, or an engineer. In a tribal state, collective success becomes more important than individual achievement; tribal recognition is more important than individual identity. This is not only anti-intellectual, but—as noted above—it is authoritarian. The authority of the tribe is more important than the independence of the individual. Tribalism then contributes to an acceptance of political authoritarianism and a weakening of democratic principles, helping to erode the concept of the larger political association—the nation-state.

WEAKENING OF THE NATION-STATE

The tribe exists because of its innate ethnic and cultural homogeneity. The modern political state, on the other hand, is an intellectual conglomeration of diverse ethnic and cultural voices. To sustain this deliberate creation, citizens must abide by abstract social, economic, and political contractual relationships rather than rely on close-knit tribal and community bonds. As we enter the twenty-first century, however, we find that the tribal mentality predominates in many areas of the globe. Thomas Friedman quotes one educated Saudi citizen who laments, "The tribal mentality here is very strong, and in the desert, when the tribe is attacked you'd better stick together or you're dead."[14]

The Fading American Dream

Historically, the idea of being an American meant seeing oneself primarily as a free individual—not as a member of some racial or ethnic group. Immigrants at the turn of the twentieth century (Greeks, Italians, Poles, Irish, Germans) were anxious to embrace the "American" identity. They came to the New World to be assimilated. Today, however—rather than being a nation of intellectual citizens of the abstract state—we have become an amalgamation of lobbying groups. Years ago, we forsook the metaphor of the melting pot and began to talk in terms of the mixed salad, wherein each ingredient would retain its own identity while still contributing to the whole plate. Today we have moved beyond that imagery to the smorgasbord where every dish retains its separate identity; you don't mix your Kim Chee and burritos in the same dish.

Citing the work of Peter Salins, columnist Robert Samuelson points out that three things were required for assimilation: "First, immigrant families had to adopt English as the national language. Second, they had 'to take pride in their American identity' and the country's democratic principles. And, finally, they had to embrace the so-called Protestant ethic—'to be self-reliant, hardworking, and morally upright.'"[15] Today we find, first, that major communities—indeed, sub-cities—cling to their native tongues as their primary language. Second, rather than "taking pride in their American identity," we find major segments of the population thinking of themselves not as *Americans*, but as African-Americans, Italian-Americans, Jewish-Americans, Korean-Americans—putting the emphasis on the tribal modifier (*African, Italian, Jewish, Korean*) rather than on the more abstract and intellectual nation-state identity of *American*. Third, the "Protestant ethic" is, to a great extent, synonymous with what we have been discussing as intellectualism—a commitment to individualism, self-reliance, and moral responsibility. We have largely abandoned that ethic today. We fall back on the cult of victimization.

Media also play a major role in weakening the nation-state. The oral and pictorial electric media tend to recreate a preliterate, intuitive oral tradition. They return us to an instinctive tribal tradition of communicating with sounds and images. In describing the Global Village, McLuhan and Quentin Fiore explain this facet of retribalization: "We are back in acoustic space. We have begun again to structure the primordial feeling, the tribal emotions from which a few centuries of literacy divorced us."[16] In his classic *Understanding Media*, McLuhan explains further:

Since literacy had fostered an extreme of individualism, and radio had done just the opposite in reviving the ancient experience of kinship webs of deep tribal involvement, the literate West tried to find some sort of compromise in a larger sense of collective responsibility. . . . The Gutenberg technology had produced a new kind of visual, national entity in the sixteenth century that was gradually meshed with industrial production and expansion. Telegraph and radio neutralized nationalism but evoked archaic tribal ghosts of the most vigorous brand.[17]

The same media we chastised in the 1950s for creating a mass society are seen today as contributing to a de-massified web culture. We are using the electric media to fragment McLuhan's global village into isolated tribes.

In an intellectual nation-state, all citizens would be working together to solve the problems of the state. However, in a splintered multi-tribal state, we are a nation of ethnic special-interest pressure groups. By struggling for cultural identity and separateness, the tribes succeed only in weakening the fabric of the nation. Strand by strand, the unraveling continues.

Reality of the Fragmented Globe

The arbitrary lines and bold colors we draw on maps are an artificial and temporal fabrication. Witness the breakup of the Soviet Union, the redrawing of the Balkan states, and shifting tribal boundaries in Africa.

The globe is constantly being fractured into ever-smaller tribal units. It may be that in the future this neat global grid of nation-states will be replaced by an overlapping jumble of blurry and disputed boundaries, tribal territories, economic unions, hyper-urbanized city-states, military pacts, short-term dictatorships, temporary regional alliances, and corporate spheres of global influence.

When McLuhan first popularized the idea of the global village some forty years ago, he never promised that the rapidly shrinking, increasingly networked planet would be a utopia of harmony and understanding. To the contrary, he predicted that our electronic ties would increase our agitation and frictions—as we became ever more involved in everybody else's business. In their anxieties and insecurities, the disenfranchised tribes and alienated religious clans lash out against the abstract intellectual superstructure and then turn on each other. We have the inner-city gang members fighting to protect their turf, members of the religious jihad striking out against the infidels, native populations waging civil wars against oppressive regimes, international terrorists fighting against imperialist threats, and anarchists waging war against established order. Revolution and terrorism become a way of life. The reality of these tribal hostilities cannot be ignored. The list is long and constantly shifting. Even before September 2001, The Center for Defense Information in Washington had identified 39 wars going on in various parts of the world that year—major conflicts involving at least 1,000 military and civilian casualties.[18] The vast majority of these wars were based, at least in part, on tribal animosities.

Hundreds of millions of other tribal members drift across meaningless national borders or exist more-or-less peacefully as self-contained tribes within the territories designated to be within political nation-states: Native American Indian tribes, Aboriginals in Australia, the Ainu of Japan, Maoris in New Zealand, Inuit peoples up north, the Sami of Scandinavia, Kalahari bushmen, the Imataca and Canaima of Venezuela, and on and on. There are some 3,000 such identifiable native nations in the world today. And about one-third of the globe's population identifies primarily with some tribal nation—rather than with some recognized political state drawn on colorful maps.

AS WE BECOME MORE SUSPICIOUS, confused, and contemptuous of what *they* are doing in the Balkans, or the Middle East, or China, or sub-Saharan Africa, we tend to turn inward. We seek the security of our tribes, our way of doing things, our ancestral values and cultural narratives. We withdraw into our segregated tribal cocoon. Added to this isolation is an overpowering sense of fatalism and futility: *The world is in chaos. It is beyond my ability to comprehend or contribute to a solution. Therefore, I seek refuge in my tribe. I will cooperate and work with those in my immediate clan—*

and everybody else be damned. This is the antithesis of an intellectual mindset.

This is our continuing tragedy: we can see what we should become, but we consistently fail to achieve that vision. Modern intellectual civilization—with its reliance on individualism and collective decision-making—doesn't seem to be working out. We turn to retribalization as an alternative. But there are too many of us, too economically interdependent, too technologically involved, to ever go back to a natural tribal state. Even Daniel Quinn, author of *Ishmael* and crusader for a simpler tribal lifestyle, concedes, like Rousseau 240 years earlier, that we cannot return to an idyllic natural state of non-civilization: "Old-style ethnic tribalism is, for the foreseeable future, utterly out of reach for us."[19] Once we have embarked upon a journey dedicated to progress, growth, science, and technology, we cannot simply turn around in our tracks and undo all that we have built. We cannot return to a primitive hunter-gather culture, nor even to a romantic agricultural narrative. We cannot undo electrification; we cannot put the information genie back in the bottle; we cannot dismantle our transportation and communications networks. Not with more than six billion inhabitants to be housed and fed.

CHAPTER 18

Giving Up on Democracy

These are among the profound questions tormenting the human race: Is there a God? What existed before the Big Bang? Does intelligent life exist outside of our planet? *Are human beings capable of self-government?* Democracy is essentially collective decision-making. But today we are not doing a very good job of political decision-making; we are not solving our social and economic problems—hence, the Progress Paradox. We are stumbling around in a postmodern shadow-box version of representative government. We confuse democracy and freedom with peace and security.

The desire for freedom is innate in the human spirit. As is the yearning for peace and security. But you cannot have both freedom and peace in full measure. De Tocqueville warns, "One of the most ordinary weaknesses of the human intellect is to seek to reconcile contrary principles, and to purchase peace at the expense of logic."[1] You hold on to your freedoms only if you are willing to abandon some guarantee of peace and tranquility. If you want peace, you need only to put yourself under the protection and guidance of the proper authority. Rousseau reminds us, "Tranquility is found . . . in dungeons; but is that enough to make them desirable places to live in?"[2] One of the ironies of the 1960s was the emergence of the oxymoronic Peace and Freedom political party. It sounds like a great slogan, but it is simplistically inconsistent. Maintaining freedom is not a peaceful process.

The same is true of security. You cannot have both complete security and total freedom. The more security you want, the more freedom you must be prepared to surrender. Today, in our quest for a secure existence, we are all too willing to sacrifice individual privacy and personal liberties.

And in our fight against terrorism and our need to beef up post-9/11 homeland security, we willingly agree to give up some of our freedoms and civil rights. But we should keep in mind Ben Franklin's words: "They that can give up essential liberty to obtain a little temporary safety deserve neither liberty nor safety."[3]

Freedom is an uncertain intellectual journey; it is an ongoing adventure on the high seas. Peace and security are both nonintellectual safe harbors. Our country's founders could have enjoyed considerable peace and security under the British crown; but they opted instead for freedom—resulting in considerable conflict and insecurities. In order to hold on to your freedoms, you must work at it. To maintain a democracy, to engage in collective decision-making is hard work. You can enjoy the freedom of the jungle, or the peace and security of the zoo; but you can't have both.

Preconditions for Democracy

Following the end of World War II and then again after the collapse of the communist realm, many newly independent nations rushed to embrace democracy. However, most of these countries—after decades of colonial or communist rule—had little intellectual infrastructure to sustain them through the early phases of democratic independence. Instead, we see tribal rivalries and ethnic passions spreading anarchy throughout the globe. Before any people can establish a system of representative government, they must have the essential underpinnings—the economic and social conditions, as well as the intellectual commitment, that can nourish a nascent democracy. Referring to the oil oligarchies of the Middle East, Fareed Zakaria writes, "Importing foreign stuff—Cadillacs, Gulfstreams, and McDonald's—is easy. Importing the inner stuffings of modern society—a free market, political parties, accountability, and the rule of law—is difficult and dangerous."[4] George Will reminds us that "not every society has the prerequisites—of institutions (political parties, media) and manners (civility, acceptance of pluralism)—of a free society."[5]

There are three intellectual essentials that any people must have before they can hope to sustain a representative government—three modern Western principles, the *inner stuffings of modern society*. First, the people must demonstrate a *respect for individual human rights,* an egalitarian tradition of observing civil liberties for all citizens—regardless of ethnic origin, skin color, shape of facial features, religious beliefs, sexual orientation, or food preferences. All persons must truly respect and be protective of the civil rights of all their fellow citizens. They must *want* to do this.

Second, any aspiring democracy must have a *solid commitment to universal education*—not just a system of vocational training or religious indoctrination, but an unwavering dedication to the nourishment of an enlightened citizenry. This means a liberal-arts curriculum that prepares the open-minded individual for responsible collective decision-making: history, philosophy, rhetoric, arts and literature, comparative cultures, science, math and economics for the consumer, and critical thinking—an education that prepares the citizen for responsible social criticism.

Third, any country that wants to sustain a viable self-government must have a *sound middle-class economy.* No nation can expect to practice true democracy if it maintains a schism between an aristocracy and a peasant class. There may be rich people and poor people, but the system must allow—indeed, encourage—the possibility of movement between the classes. Otherwise there is no incentive for making the system work.

Thanks to our legacy from Mother England, we started the grand American experiment with a strong commitment to these three principles. But one or more of these preconditions are lacking in virtually all developing countries. First, most cultures show little respect for those who are different—those of other tribes or ethnic backgrounds. Second, when many nations talk about education they are talking about either establishment propaganda (nationalistic jingoism or religious indoctrination such as the Islamic *madrassahs*) or specialized professional training—both of which work against the education of the whole person, the enlightened citizen. Third, few developing countries have a true functional middle class—a dedication to free enterprise economics that offers all its citizens a realistic shot at financial security and independence. These three attributes are in short supply throughout the globe. Even more frightening: all three of these prerequisites are eroding today in the United States. Retribalization undermines the idea of respect for all persons. The need for specialized vocational schooling works against the ideal of a broadly educated citizenry. And for millions of disenfranchised illiterates and inner-city hostages, there is little hope for moving into the middle class.

THE DYSFUNCTIONAL ELECTORATE

As our social, economic, and political environments become increasingly complicated and entangled, the average citizen no longer feels capable of participating in the national forum. We are overwhelmed with proposed tax cuts and/or tax increases, corporate disasters, and conflicting research on economic theories, educational reforms, bioterrorism, and nutritional findings. It becomes impossible for an individual to comprehend and respond coherently to all the issues engulfing us. This is the postintellectual web culture: *We no longer are in control.*

Media and the Ill-Informed Citizen

The way we use the postmodern electric media—for entertainment, scandal, gossip, and titillation—we face what I have termed the post-

Figure 5
Media and the Freedom Dilemma

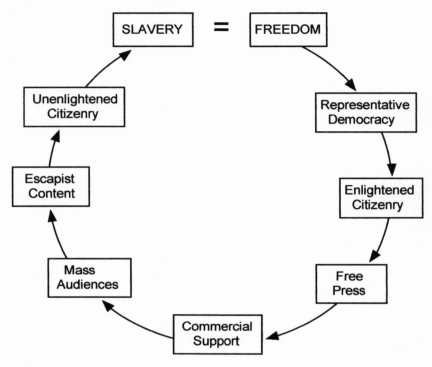

modern *Freedom Dilemma* (see Figure 5). Freedom is dependent upon a representative democracy, which in turn rests on an educated citizenry. As their source for information and enlightenment, the voters rely on the free press, which—in order to remain independent of government funding and control—is supported by commercial revenue. However, to attract a large enough audience to be financially profitable, the media have to provide popular content—stuff that is increasingly trivial and escapist. Thus, the audience—the citizenry—does not glean the information and enlighten-ment it must have in order to engage in collective decision-making. As a result, we do not have an enlightened citizenry. In effect, we use our free-dom to liberate ourselves from the necessity of thinking independently—thus creating a form of voluntary enslavement to the establishment.

In embracing the electric media, we have marginalized the written word. Neil Postman emphasizes that "the modern conception of democ-racy was tied inseparably to the printed word. All the Enlightenment political philosophers—none more explicitly than Locke, Madison, and Jefferson—assumed that political life would be conducted through print."[6]

Postman then goes on to ask, "Can a representative democracy, even a participatory democracy, function well if its citizens' minds are not disciplined by the printed word?"[7] In an age when our political issues are becoming increasingly sophisticated and complicated, we find that our vocabulary is deteriorating as we rely on oral/pictorial means of communication. One recent study, for instance, indicates that Lincoln and Douglas, in their mid-nineteenth-century debates, used a vocabulary suitable for eleventh and twelfth graders. However, recent politicians (Clinton, Gore, both Bushes) have been using a vocabulary aimed at sixth and seventh graders.[8]

William J. Lederer observed more than forty years ago: "This is the law of functioning democracies. A nation operates honestly and well as long as citizens show interest. But when citizens become apathetic, then dictatorship, ignorance, and national decline take over."[9] Except for the Clinton-Bush-Perot hullabaloo in 1992, the percentage of voters who have bothered to cast a ballot in a presidential election has hovered around 50 percent since 1984. State and local elections in off years often drop down to around 20 percent or even less. The decision not to vote is, in effect, self-excommunication from the system. In a democracy, the citizenry must remain involved and pay attention to what the government is up to, or the government will take on a direction of its own. Leave the decision-making up to the technocrats and the trains may run on schedule, but they may be headed in a direction that you didn't want to go.

The Overspecialized Citizenry

As the individual becomes increasingly specialized—concerned with his or her own professional microcosm—how can he or she maintain a balanced perspective on our entire intellectual enterprise? How do all these specialists and narrowly focused professionals—the corporate attorneys, interior decorators, insurance agents, chemical engineers, English professors, farmers, and brick layers—gather all the information they need to make informed decisions on international treaties and economic controls, environmental protection, and welfare reform? We work independently shaping the various specialized pieces of the socioeconomic jigsaw puzzle. But how can we make sure the pieces fit? Who knows enough to put all the pieces together? How can we expect to manage a global enterprise so complex that no one can grasp the whole? Even Adam Smith expressed concern about the effects of overspecialization. After warning that the specialist will become "as stupid and ignorant as it is possible for a human creature to become," he writes,

The torpor of his mind renders him not only incapable of relishing or bearing a part in any rational conversation, but of . . . forming any just judgment concerning many even of the ordinary duties of private life. Of the great and extensive interests of his country he is altogether incapable of judging. . . . His dexterity at his own particular trade seems, in this manner, to be acquired at the expense of his intellectual, social, and marital virtues.[10]

Information overload contributes to our political gridlock. Access to too many data renders a population incapable of making reflective and rational decisions—analysis paralysis. In comparing Aldous Huxley's *Brave New World* and George Orwell's *1984*, Postman observes, "Orwell feared those who would deprive us of information. Huxley feared those who would give us so much that we would be reduced to passivity and egoism."[11] Thus we submit to a system of governance with decisions being made by lobbyists, the Federal Reserve Board, government commissions, the corporate consultants, the lawyers, engineers, technocrats, bureaucrats, and congressional staffers. As Rousseau put it, "the State is governed by clerks."[12]

THE ENFEEBLED GOVERNMENT

One problem with representative democracy is that voters are concerned primarily with their parochial interests—as members of local communities, specific occupations, victimized groups, hog farmers, and soccer moms. Rather than worry about the abstract nature of cultural maintenance (which has escalated beyond their comprehension), they are concerned with potholes, local jobs, and immediate budget shortfalls. Therefore they will vote for representatives who promise to look after their neighborhood problems. Plato wrote 2,400 years ago that any leader of a popular government would have to answer to the *motley multitude*: "For when a man consorts with the many, and exhibits to them his poem or other work of art or the service which he has done the State, making them his judges . . . [he will be obliged] to produce whatever they praise."[13] *Please the motley multitude or face a recall election.*

Also, in order to keep our politicians grounded in the needs of their constituents, we elect our congressional representatives every two years. They must then satisfy the needs of their constituents within a relatively short time frame. We ignore Edmund Burke's eloquent argument against bowing to electoral pressure: "Your representative owes you, not his industry only, but his judgment; and he betrays instead of serving you if he sacrifices it to your opinion."[14] But the system does not allow elected representatives to focus on anything beyond immediate and local interests; they have to get re–elected right away. Even our senators and governors cannot do much better. Our elected politicians are not allowed to make the best decisions in terms of long-range interests of the country; they are forced to sacrifice their judgment to their constituents' immediate concerns.

Another problem is the autonomy of government bureaucracy. We create an agency or a bureau as a solution to some specific problem—to build roads, fight crime, or issue drivers' licenses. But the more successful a bureaucracy is—as a problem-solving technology—the more likely that it can generate more support and institutional backing to expand and spread its influence. We no longer function *as a nation*—working towards our long-term good—because every department, every bureau, must look out for itself. The continuation and growth of the bureaucracy becomes an end in itself. It is a form of technological determinism.

Weakened Authority

Authority is to be challenged—not eradicated. To question authority is healthy; to wipe it out is anarchy. A free press constantly struggles to define that blurry line between demolishing the establishment and strengthening the democracy. The mass media have consistently eaten away at the veil of secrecy and executive privilege that has traditionally protected government bureaucracy from the prying eyes of the public. Despite government attempts to control the media's perception of what was going on in Vietnam, Grenada, Panama, Iraq, or Afghanistan, muckraking reporters have shredded executive and legislative integrity in instance after instance. Which is as it must be. This is one of the inherent tensions of an intellectual society. We don't automatically accept what our leaders tell us about the safety of nuclear reactors, the security of Social Security, the advisability of a tax cut, and what the administration did or did not know before September 11. Authority must be questioned. But how do we keep it from cracking apart?

Joshua Meyrowitz, in his eye-opening 1985 book *No Sense of Place*, documents how "the new patterns of relatively open information flow have led to a general distrust of authority in America."[15] The more information the populace has access to, the less authority the government can exert over the populace. Information breeds contempt. With the ensuing deceptions over the Gulf War, the stalemates and scandals of the Clinton administration, the irregularities in the 2000 election, the uncertainties of the war on terrorism, and the volatility of our financial mechanisms, the public places less and less faith in its elected leaders. We have been led astray by Corporate America, religious leaders, and political opportunists. What do we do with the presidency once we have enfeebled, or even dethroned, the president? The Wizard of Oz turns out to be an old man manipulating a machine behind a curtain. Where do we turn now for inspiration and guidance?

We question not only the future of democracy, but also the viability of any kind of large-scale governmental authority. Due to the communications revolution, no government can any longer keep information out of the hands of the people. Radio and television transmissions, satellites, the Internet, photocopiers, fax machines, and cell phones all greatly accelerate the flow of chaotic and jumbled information across porous national borders. Political boundaries can no more halt the free flow of information than a chain-link fence can muffle thunder. Media and the unrestricted flow of information have undermined traditional authoritarianism. Thus, totalitarianism, as well as democracy, becomes increasingly difficult to maintain.

THE AUTHORITARIAN ALTERNATIVE TO DEMOCRACY

As people experience the uncertainties and chaos of a postmodern age, they become more willing to sacrifice freedom and independence for order and stability. The populace conceivably could deliberately seek out some type of benevolent authoritarianism. Not a despotic tyrannical oppressive regime—a Stalin or Hussein—but rather an elitist, and presumably gentle, totalitarianism. Huxley, not Orwell. We may ultimately choose the security of the zoo over the freedom of the jungle. Contrary to Francis Fukuyama's analysis of the end of history and the inevitability of liberal evolution, maybe democracy was just a temporary aberration between two stages of authoritarianism. In the words of historian John Lukacs, it is "quite possible that in the history of mankind the democratic period may have been an episode."[16] The prospect for a true intellectual democracy may have peaked and now grows fainter with each technological incursion.

The Corporate Oligarchy

One form of an authoritarian oligarchy is a political-economic system in which elitist corporate interests dominate and, in effect, run the government. Robert Kaplan concludes that "An elite with little loyalty to the state and a mass society fond of gladiator entertainments form a society in which corporate Leviathans rule and democracy is hollow."[17] In decades past, most politicians came from the ranks of lawyers and party operatives. However, in recent years more and more of our elected representatives and leaders have come from the business community. Historian Bruce J. Schulman points out that "Career politicians now work closely with bankers, developers, and corporate executives, stressing 'private-public partnerships' and emphasizing their hospitality to business interests."[18]

For instance, virtually all members of President Bush's inner circle and all but two of his initial cabinet appointees came from a strong corporate background.[19] They sat on corporate boards; they think like company

CEOs; they see a lucrative profit-loss balance sheet as the ultimate test of good government. Former Secretary of Labor Robert Reich states simply, "There's no longer any countervailing power in Washington. Business is in complete control of the machinery of government."[20] To cite just one example out of hundreds: In drawing up the energy policy for the Bush administration, Energy Secretary Spencer Abraham met with 36 representatives of Corporate America—including those from the National Association of Manufacturers, the Independent Petroleum Association, the Nuclear Energy Institute, and others from coal, oil, nuclear, and utility industries—and not one representative of consumer or environmental interests.

What we have is a corporate-government fusion so thoroughly a part of our governance culture that those most intimately involved see no wrongdoing. This is a hyper-intellectual mindset at its clearest. Those in charge sincerely believe that by promoting corporate greed they are doing what is best for America. However, a governmental system whose highest priority is corporate gain and materialistic success cannot help but foster a political climate of manipulation and corruption. The whole Wall Street fiasco (Enron, WorldCom, and all the rest) is symptomatic of this government-corporate union.

DEMOCRACY IS AN INTELLECTUAL UNDERTAKING. It demands an intellectual electorate—involving all citizens in information-gathering, analysis, critical thinking, debate, and voting. But what we have today is a large number of borderline illiterates who are ignorant about political realities, an election process dominated by image-makers and manipulators, a prevailing sense of cynicism and apathy among would-be voters, a suffocating bureaucracy, an enfeebled government, a tacit trend toward technocracy, and an implicit acceptance of corporate rule.

Freedom is possible in a high-tech culture only with a high degree of personal responsibility and rational decision-making. We understand that the right to make individual decisions depends upon personal freedom and independence—freedom of the press, freedom of inquiry, and freedom of association. Without freedom we are not allowed to engage in decision-making. But we often fail to see the flip side—that continued freedom is possible only with *successful* decision-making. Otherwise—if we fail to make responsible decisions, if we fall short in our problem-solving efforts—others will make our decisions for us. If you do not assume personal responsibility for critical, rational participation in the collective decision-making process, you will lose your independence. It's that simple. Yet today, in our postmodern torpor, we are moving in the opposite direction—toward less individual responsibility and more reliance on the bureaucracy and technocracy to handle our governmental decision-making.

PART IV

Solutions: Several Outlandish Proposals

All the dangers we have examined—population growth, war, environmental damage, scientific technology—are social problems, originating in human behavior and capable of amelioration by the alteration of that behavior.
—Robert Heilbroner

The problem to be solved in the twenty-first century is . . . how to transform information into knowledge, and how to transform knowledge into wisdom. If we can solve that problem, all the rest will take care of itself.
—Neil Postman

In the first three parts of the book, we have been defining the problem, probing the causes, and looking at some of the effects. This last part of the book offers some thinking about solutions. As H. G. Wells observed, "Our poverty, our restraints, our infections and indigestions, our quarrels and misunderstandings, are all things controllable and removable by concerted human action."[1] In Chapter 19, I argue that we need a sense of balance, an affirmation of the Chinese concept of yin and yang. Chapters 20 through 23 look at specific remedies to be considered in the areas of educational reform (a return to the liberal arts), environmental restoration (starting with strong population control measures), economic restructuring (devising a no-growth economic model), and political action (consideration of globalization and worldwide federalism). Some of these proposals are rather platitudinous and can easily be embraced by all virtuous souls. Others are quite radical and are guaranteed to raise the hackles of conservatives and liberals alike.

CHAPTER 19

The Search for Values

We need to restore some remnants of a cultural narrative—some guide-book to determine how we should conduct our affairs. Western civiliza-tion has discarded religion as the ideational basis for our culture; it no longer is the essential foundation of society. And in our postmodern dis-array we have undermined our faith in Enlightenment science and mod-ern empirical reason. What are we left with? By whose rules do we conduct our affairs? We need some sort of explanation of what we are all about. Materialism appears to be our one common goal. But our material acquisition of *stuff* falls short of satisfying our deeper yearnings. Surely there is more to life than faster Intel chips or a BMW convertible.

THE BASIS FOR A MORAL CODE

Humans can try to live together under a code of ethics that *transcends human authorship* or we can try to live together under a code that is *created by mortal men and women*. As E. O. Wilson puts it, "Centuries of debate on the origin of ethics come down to this: Either ethical precepts, such as justice and human rights, are independent of human experience or else they are human inventions."[2] The first possibility—moral guidelines exist outside of the human mind—is the choice of all devoted religious believ-ers, of Sorokin's ideational culture, and of most philosophers through the ages. The second possibility—we can write our own secular code—is what has been advocated by Enlightenment thinkers and secular humanists who argue that moral guidelines are creations of the human mind.

Let's consider first the feasibility of a secular, humanistic man-made code of ethics. The essence of humanism is the intellectual assertion that men and women can live a decent and righteous life without recourse to formal religious directives. We don't need God alternately offering us a heavenly carrot or a brimstone stick. We can figure how to behave in a rational manner because it is in our enlightened self-interest to do so. The argument against such a humanistic value system is that each person or tribe may create his or her or its own individual code. There is no Supreme Authority to which we can turn. So then we ask, *Why should my tribe accept the secular code written by your tribe?* Your code might include a proscription against homosexual orientation; and mine doesn't. Maybe your code tolerates a little wine; but mine advocates complete abstinence. Do you approve of capital punishment? Polygamy? Euthanasia? Cannibalism? Sexual relations outside of marriage? Treating women as second-class citizens? Does your code allow you to exceed the speed limit by 5 miles per hour if conditions permit? How about fudging just a little on your IRS deductions? It becomes difficult for any man-made code to claim unanimous authority that would apply to all citizens.

It is therefore argued that in order to be universally accepted, a code of ethics must come from a Higher Authority. We must adopt a moral system based on The Absolute Word from Above. Adoption of The Word as handed down by God is the only way to ensure acceptance of a transcendent rulebook. But with more than 4,000 sects to choose from, exactly which voice of God do we listen to? Does *your* God condone homosexuality? Alcohol? Capital punishment? Polygamy? Euthanasia? Cannibalism? Sex-before-marriage? Maybe we should just start with the Ten Commandments. Okay, which version do you want—what you find in Exodus 20 or Deuteronomy 5? (And don't forget to check the variations in Exodus 34, Leviticus 19, and Deuteronomy 27.) We are asked to rely on The Word as it has been revealed to individual theologians, shamans, seers, messengers, priests, prophets, and popes. But they all seem to have received different Words. Whose Absolute Word are we to believe? Jewish Zionists? Islamic fundamentalists? Jerry Falwell? The mystery and awe of the inspired Absolute Word from Above is clouded by the passions and perversions of the clergy down below.

We reject a theocracy. Yet we feel the need for some sort of spiritual lodestar. Wilson sums up this craving: "People need more than reason. They need the poetry of affirmation, they crave an authority greater than themselves at rites of passage and other moments of high seriousness. A majority desperately wish for the immortality the rituals seem to underwrite."[3] The American founders, following the precepts of most of the leading thinkers of the Enlightenment, believed in the existence of God— although their God was often envisioned as the Omnipotent Creator who set the cosmos in motion (Newton's clockwork universe), and then left it up to His/Her human creations to run things the best they could. Oswald

Spengler refers to "those men of the Age of Enlightenment . . . who disregarded the rites of the Church but never doubted the 'fundamental truths of faith.'"[4] This quasi-secular belief system encompasses a variety of religious and philosophical positions—existentialists, transcendentalists, Universalists/Unitarians, deists, and millions of nominal church-goers who espouse belief in a Supreme Being, but not necessarily of a personal God. *God exists, but He/She does not run the daily affairs of individual persons.*

Society cannot be governed solely by reason and scientific humanism. Neither will we embrace a culture dominated by religious zealots and state-mandated religious institutions. Science alone cannot tell us how to conduct our affairs. Religion by itself cannot define for us who we are. It's up to us to devise our own cultural narrative—some way to include both scientific reason and transcendent moral values.

Reconciling Reason and Faith

Intellectualism is the belief that Truth can be determined scientifically and logically; all knowledge can be established and proved by reason. Faith, on the other hand, is the belief in that which *cannot* be proven empirically: *God exists. Evil is ultimately punished. My spouse is faithful to me.* These beliefs cannot be proved by conducting scientific experiments. You take them on faith. A successful culture must find a way to reconcile these two conflicting systems of epistemology—reasoned inquiry and blind faith. We must accept the findings of science at the same time that we incorporate some sort of moral system that transcends human invention. Back to Wilson's need for the "poetry of affirmation."

Our country was founded on a pragmatic mix of religious and humanistic principles. De Tocqueville observed that the unique character of the "Anglo-American civilization . . . is the result . . . of two distinct elements, which in other places have been in frequent hostility but which in America have been admirably incorporated and combined with one another. I allude to the spirit of Religion and the spirit of Liberty."[5] One need not subscribe unquestioningly to a complete set of religious tenets and institutional rituals; but one must agree that it is necessary to live as if there is a higher authority, a transcendent intelligence beyond our rational comprehension. Francis Fukuyama adds that "Lockean liberals who made the American Revolution like Jefferson or Franklin, or a passionate believer in liberty and equality like Abraham Lincoln, did not hesitate to assert that liberty required belief in God."[6] This has been the bedrock of much of our philosophizing during the next two centuries. Both John Stuart Mill's *Religion of Humanity* and Albert Einstein's *Cosmic Religious Feeling*, for example, recognize the need for transcendent inspiration, but they do not subscribe to any specific religious credo or doctrine. Einstein stated, "Science without religion is lame, and religion without science is blind."[7]

Our attempt to balance reason and faith comes up with something like this: Each of us, individually, is guided by our own transcendental values and beliefs. This is the core of our personal system of faith. This personal code or faith may be either God-centered or secular humanistic. We recognize, however, that no single religious or moral code will satisfy all persons. Nor should it. Thus we rule out a theocracy—even while recognizing the importance of individual transcendent values. And we guarantee that all persons should be able to follow their own religious beliefs (insofar as they do not deny the human rights of other individuals). Then we superimpose some sort of rational, secular, humanistic legal structure—our social contract—over our individual faith-based values. We agree to live within a secular system of laws and governance by consensus (collective decision-making). Once we have debated a given policy or course of action (guided by our personal values) and we have enacted a particular law, we agree to abide by the societal norm—whether or not it reflects totally our personal religious faith, whether or not it is compatible with our individual beliefs about abortion, capital punishment, polygamy, liquor, extramarital sex, or IRS deductions. However, guided by our personal values, we reserve the right to work—within the framework of our system of laws—to challenge authority and try to change any particular part of the societal code. And in the meantime, we will find moral sustenance within our religious institutional haven.

SEEKING A BALANCE

The human brain has two hemispheres. A person cannot exist only as a left-hemisphered rational, scientific, yang creature. Neither can anyone be solely a right-hemisphered sensitive, intuitive, yin being. We must be able to demonstrate the mindset of the BENs (bureaucrats, engineers, and number-crunchers) to navigate our political and economic quagmire; and we must be able to enjoy the soul of the PAMs (poets, artists, and musicians) to live life to the fullest. One must be able to reason logically and analytically; and one must be able to be passionate and spontaneous. The key to surviving in a post-postmodern world is to find the balance between intellectual discipline and nonintellectual fervor, between objective analysis and mountaintop insights, between profit-and-loss sheets and Beethoven symphonies.

Balancing Print and Pictorial Media

In the mid-twentieth century, the modern print-oriented scientific world of BENs was confronted by the TV generation that cried *Love, Peace, and Tolerance*. In our postmodern times, television and other electric media challenge our Western mindset with a return to a right-hemisphere pictorial culture influenced by PAMs. This is the essence of our postmodern web culture—the clash between the hyper-intellectual emphasis on continued print domination and the counter-intellectual pull toward an oral/pictorial culture.

Wistfully, we flirt with the romantic fantasy of a revitalization of an oral culture—a deliberate refutation of print and a return to halcyon days of bucolic meadows and pictorial pleasures. But with our dependence upon contemporary technology, and more than six billion people on the planet, such a fanciful dream simply can't be pursued today. Print—and science and bureaucracy—are an integral part of any scheme one wishes to draw up. To the extent that print literacy facilitates abstractions and critical thinking—and modern Western civilization is based on abstractions and critical thinking—print literacy is indispensable to a continuation of our culture. What we must seek today is a balance between print and pictures, between rhetorical analysis and pictorial immersion, between the structured library and the anarchistic Internet.

The most serious impact of excessive TV viewing is the rewiring of the brain. Disproportionate use of the right hemisphere for oral and pictorial communication physically alters the way the brain works; some neural connections are strengthened, and others wither. The TV-saturated brain functions differently from the print-oriented brain. Pictorial media condition youngsters to not think and reason clearly. We are raising a generation geared to intuition and impulse rather than analysis and deliberation. To weaken the analytic linear capabilities of the left hemisphere is to undermine the foundation of Western civilization. Under the heading of *solutions,* parents must assume more responsibility for directing their offspring towards a more balanced media experience.

Balancing Progress and Tradition

It was the philosopher Heraclitus who said 2,500 years ago, "All is flux. . . . Nothing endures but change."[8] What would he have to say today—while defragmenting his hard drive, pondering the politics of the Middle East, surfing through unknown Internet waters, and trying to follow the debate over stem cell research? Change does happen; and it isn't all bad. We cannot stand still. To hold on to all from the past is folly. There is nothing sacred about preserving the status quo for its own sake. Our institutions must accept change and adapt in order to provide us with a functional framework for coping in a shifting world.

But neither can we abandon all the wisdom, tradition, and philosophical perspectives that we have inherited from our intellectual forebears. To discard all from the past is suicide. Let us not embrace change for change's sake. In order to maintain some emotional stability, it is more important than ever to hold on to a sense of continuity and tradition. We need some anchors, some guidelines, to remind us of who we are, where we came from, and where we want to be going. We use our institutions—religion, the courts, government, and our schools—to provide stability and tradition, to buttress us against overwhelming change.

In this era of accelerating change, there is more than ever a need to maintain an open mind, to be flexible, to consider rationally what it is we should change and what we should be holding on to. We must seek a balance between progress and tradition, between innovation and stability. It is essential to maintain both a readiness for change and a determination to hold on to some sense of the past.

Balancing Freedom with Law-and-Order

By living in a civilized society, humans have sacrificed much of their freedom for structure and security. To live in a natural state is to enjoy the freedom of the jungle; but there are no traffic lights or social safety nets. When humans evolved into a civilized state, we agreed to live under the social contract. We are then guaranteed a certain degree of civil equality and social support; we benefit from the security of the zoo—but we must comply with the general will. Rousseau explains, "What man loses by the social contract is his natural liberty and an unlimited right to everything he tries to get and succeeds in getting; what he gains is civil liberty and the proprietorship of all he possesses. . . . We must clearly distinguish natural liberty, which is bounded only by the strength of the individual, from civil liberty, which is limited by the general will."[9]

We compromise. We want protection by the local police, but we don't want them in our bedrooms. We want the freedom to roam where we please, but we don't want others trespassing on our private space. With the increasing population crush and with the ever-expanding complex technological web we live in, further concentrations of state control are inevitable. Fareed Zakaria writes, "Around the world we will see governments become more powerful, more intrusive and more important. This may not please civil libertarians and human-rights activists, but it will not matter. The state is back, and for the oldest Hobbesian reason in the book—the provision of security."[10]

After 9/11, there is a concerted push for tighter security and stronger law enforcement powers. As necessary as this emphasis might be, there is substantial danger that we will lose sight of the freedoms and liberties that have gotten us this far. We must remain ever alert to the struggle to maintain the optimum balance between freedom and security.

Balancing Rationality and Passion

According to Enlightenment thinkers, pure reason was to save the day. We could engineer our way to a better future. That promise has faded, however. We recognize today that a completely rational cultural paradigm is beyond realistic expectations. And anyway, the world would probably be somewhat better off with a little more yin, more softness and sensitivity. We acknowledge the need for balance between intellectualism and non-intellectual pursuits.

Many of our intellectual leaders have championed the causes of passion and pleasure. For all his dour analysis, Spengler observes that "Materialism would not be complete without the need of now and again easing the intellectual tension, by giving way to moods of myth, by performing rites of some sort or by enjoying the charms of the irrational, the unnatural, the repulsive and even, if need be, the merely silly."[11] Wilson states simply: "Pure reason is unappealing because it is bloodless."[12] Finally, Ben Stein, that articulate popularizer of conservative and capitalistic values, writes of the need for fervor and frivolity in one's life:

Eat that gourmet food, and buy that art, and take up that karate or birding, or that Corvette, or that cottage on the Eastern Shore. Life is an unbelievable rip-off, . . . You do all of that work, and act prudent, and sacrifice, and you're a good boy or girl, and then . . . you awaken to find out that you're fresh out of passion. One small way to make the balance right is to seize the moment and do the passionate thing when you can.[13]

THERE ARE MANY OTHER AREAS where we need to further a sense of balance. Sociologist Amitai Etzioni, promoting the concept of *communitarianism*, argues that contemporary values "have overemphasized the importance of rights and underestimated the significance of responsibilities, fostering selfishness and self-absorption rather than an awareness of the needs of others."[14] This is the theme of Robert Putnam's *Bowling Alone:* "A society of many virtuous but isolated individuals is not necessarily rich in social capital."[15] In our hyper-intellectual hubris, we push for ourselves—our liberties, our right to pursue whatever personal dream we want. *And the rest of society can fend for itself!* Rather, we must strive for a balance between individualism and community. We must find the commitment to nurture the greater human society of which we are a part.

We need to reconcile the need for tribal cohesiveness while maintaining the nation-state. As with other aspects of post-intellectualism, some elements of retribalization are to be encouraged. Despite the divisive intolerance that characterizes so many of our inter-tribal relationships, there certainly are positive—even needed—benefits of belonging to a group, sharing concerns and myths, gathering strength and security from those around you. In this shrinking but muddled global environment, we must have both a sense of tribal identity and a commitment to the larger rational nation-state.

We just can't sit still and let the system continue to run down. I reject the position that one student expressed several years ago: *If ecosystem destruction is inevitable, wouldn't the most rational thing to do be just to enjoy what we have left? We can't do anything about it, so let's party!* Rather, I subscribe to the position of Jacques Ellul in his insightful 1964 book, *The Technological Society:* "If man—if each one of us—abdicates his responsibilities with regard to values; if each one of us limits himself to leading a trivial existence in a technological civilization, with . . . increasing [material] success as his sole objective; if we do not even consider the possibility of making a stand against these determinants" then everything will continue to disintegrate.[16] Should we not at least make a stand against these determinants? Should we not try to move in that direction? There are steps we can take.

CHAPTER 20

Educational Restructuring

Numerous solutions and reforms are put forth for improving America's schools: charter schools, magnet schools, vouchers, dress codes and uniforms, better teachers' salaries, merit pay, upgraded teacher training, upgraded textbooks, universal preschool, making large schools smaller, making large school districts smaller, consolidating small districts into larger ones, instituting nationwide standards and testing, technological innovations, more local control, more federal control, and so forth. Rather than debating these particular proposals and innovative tinkerings, let me begin by looking at the basic functions of any schooling system—the curriculum. What is it we need to be teaching our young people? Before we try to reform a system, we should understand what it is we want the system to do. (*Before we can solve any problem we need to establish our objectives or criteria.*)

FOUR FUNCTIONS OF SCHOOLING

Basically all curricular purposes of education (from preschool through graduate school) can be divided into four functions: (1) *Education for Continued Learning,* the essential academic skills needed to pursue lifelong education—reading, writing, 'rithmetic, research skills, computer literacy, and so forth. (2) *Personal and Social Development,* needed social skills and character education. (3) *Preparation for Citizenship,* a broad liberal-arts orientation, giving students breadth and perspective so that as citizens they can participate in collective decision-making. (4) *Preparation for Earning a Living,* vocational and professional education.

Education for Continued Learning

At all stages of education, students must learn the academic skills needed to pursue their learning at the next grade level. Preschoolers learn their letters so that they can learn words in kindergarten so that they can write sentences in first grade so that they can make paragraphs in the second grade. Thus we keep acquiring higher levels of skills in reading, composition, mathematical computation, and research. This process never stops. Adults are still involved in continuing education as they fulfill in-service training requirements, learn new computer skills, dig into new professional demands, and perfect new research techniques.

Research proficiency becomes increasingly important as students progress through their studies: how to use a dictionary, read a map, look up simple facts in an almanac, dig through an encyclopedia article, and utilize the resources of a library, as well as how to ask questions and interview people and how to search through government or corporate files to dig out hidden facts. Especially needed are the discrimination skills for sorting out valuable information from the trash. Nowhere is this more critical than in learning to use the resources of the Internet. Skillful use of search engines and hyperlinks open the doors to unimaginable worlds of information. The danger is that so much of the stuff out there is garbage—worthless, if not downright dangerous. Even second-graders can be taught to ask, *Where did this information come from?* And by middle school, students should be asking, *What cultural biases are evident in this work? How could these data have been distorted?*

Education for Personal and Social Development

Students need to learn how to interact with their peers, how to give and take, how to share, how to relate to authority figures, how to work on a team, when to push and when to pull back. In the past, most socialization skills were learned in the home, in the neighborhood, at church or temple, and on the playing fields. But by the late twentieth century, much of the responsibility for instilling these skills had been turned over to the schools.

When one ventures into the realm of *affective* learning (dealing with feelings, attitudes, and values)—as opposed to *cognitive* education (dealing with facts and formulas)—the question of morals and ethics invariably arises. How does one explore social relationships without getting into values? Whose values do we teach? How do we go about teaching morality while maintaining separation of church and state? How are we to find a secular basis for character education?

There are numerous curricular approaches to teaching values or character education without getting into specific religious indoctrination. One of the most successful is the *Character Counts* program developed by the Josephson Institute of Ethics.[1] This nationwide project, with hundreds of participating school districts and other youth organizations, has identified six attributes that can be taught in the classroom: trustworthiness, responsibility, respect, fairness, caring, and citizenship. Certainly there are ways to teach moral values—including honesty, objectivity, and tolerance—outside of a religious framework. *Time* magazine writer Andrew Ferguson observes, "Across the country, schools both public and private are turning to programs of character education in hopes of inoculating kids with the values of civility and integrity, against the depredations of a popular culture that often seem to reward neither."[2] Some form of character education has been incorporated into the curricula of schools in all fifty states.

Education for Citizenship

Americans are so preoccupied with their specialized vocations and institutional entanglements that few of us—even among the educated elite—have really taken time to delve into the philosophers, essayists, poets, and other thinkers of the past. Consequently we have but a limited grasp of the journey of mankind. We must renew our commitment to a liberal-arts foundation, to the acquisition of a broad base of knowledge, to rational thinking, and to responsible social criticism. The citizenry must be educated to participate in collective decision-making. We need to strengthen—at all grade levels—social sciences, literature and the arts, science and mathematics for the citizen.

The problem is not the lack of subject matter details; it is the lack of coherence and the lack of critical reasoning. We need not more data, but more deliberation. We must be concerned with wisdom rather than information processing. Neil Postman laments, "The problem to be solved in the twenty-first century is not how to *move* information, not the engineering of information. We solved that problem long ago. The problem is how to transform information into knowledge, and how to transform knowledge into wisdom. If we can solve that problem, all the rest will take care of itself."[3] That is the task of a liberal-arts education.

We must teach problem-solving skills, scientific methodology, and decision-making stratagems at all grade levels. Historian John Hope Franklin writes, "It is the goal—and advantage—of a liberal arts education to appreciate learning, and indeed to love it, for its own sake. It is important to learn HOW to think, as well as WHAT to think. This is the foundation of an educated man or woman."[4] The pitfalls outlined in Chapter 15 need to be studied in our classrooms.[5]

We must teach students to be skeptical, to learn to respectfully question authority. The challenge is to facilitate social criticism when the system, from preschool through doctoral education, is so grounded in orthodoxy and convention. The intellectual mindset will always run into opposition from the established bureaucracies. One crucial area where critical thinking must be cultivated is the questioning of technological progress—technopoly or megatechnology. Postman writes that one of the most important things for any student to learn is that "all technological change is a Faustian bargain."[6]

Education for Earning a Living

Professionals must receive their specialized training somewhere. However, must vocational education be the dominating influence on the college campus? As the university curriculum is increasingly turned over to pre-professional education, the function of higher education has become virtually synonymous with job training. Communication Studies Professor Lawrence Grossberg writes, "The implicit assumption is that the responsibility of the university begins and ends with teaching students skills defined by the present and future job market. . . . But education is not about training people for jobs, although that may be one of its responsibilities."[7]

On the campus of virtually every large public or private university across the nation, this professional training is dictated by the corporate and professional world. The departments and colleges of business, science, engineering, economics, medicine, law, and other professional disciplines are governed by the demands of their respective fields. It is the requirements of these professions and their national associations that mandate the accreditation specifications for our nation's curricula. Academic departments have little choice but to design their curricula to meet those requirements if they want to remain accredited—as they must.[8]

Many educational critics decry the liberal influence in our colleges and universities—affirmative action preferences, left-wing activism, politically correct policies, and so forth. In reality, a much more pervasive influence comes from the right—from the corporate establishment. Higher education receives financing through corporate-sponsored research, the use of professors as consultants, endowed professorships, corporate officers serving as department and curriculum advisors, business contacts for fund-raising and development efforts, support for specific departmental programs, and the underwriting of buildings—as well as individual grants to deserving faculty members. Stroll through any major campus and gape at the edifices named for corporate benefactors, industrial kingpins, aerospace firms and pharmaceutical companies. The campus resembles more an industrial research park than it does a site of higher education. This is a clear manifestation of hyper-intellectual specialization—the professional tail wagging the educational dog.

Larry Soley, in his incisive *Leasing the Ivory Tower: The Corporate Take-over of Academia*, writes, "The story about universities in the 1980s and 1990s is that they will turn a trick for anybody with money to invest; and the only ones with money are corporations, millionaires, and foundations. These investments in universities have dramatically changed the mission of higher education; they have led universities to attend to the interests of their well-heeled patrons, rather than those of students."[9] Corporate funding has increased about ten-fold from 1980 to 2000. Soley continues "Corporate, foundation, and tycoon money has had a major, deleterious impact on universities. Financial considerations have altered academic priorities, reduced the importance of teaching, degraded the integrity of academic journals, and determined what research is conducted at universities."[10]

REDESIGNING SECONDARY AND HIGHER EDUCATION

Might there not be a better way to handle these several educational functions? Let me suggest a fundamental restructuring of America's secondary education and higher education systems—my "outlandish proposal" for this chapter. Maybe we can't realistically implement the following proposal as presented herein. But we can start thinking. Stretch your critical facilities a bit. What initial steps might we take?

High School Preparation

The fundamental job of secondary education should be the first function mentioned above—preparation for continued learning. Specifically, preparation for college work. Add to this a healthy dose of liberal-arts education for citizenship (our third function). This returns the high school to a solid core of "basics" in English, mathematics, science preparation, social studies, and so forth.[11] Eliminate most of the social-development electives and extracurricular offerings—sex education, driver training, family economics, drug-awareness programs, and the like.

At the same time, we must provide for the personal and social education of teenagers (our second function). There must be a place for family issues and sex education, athletics and physical education, multicultural sensitivity training, driver education, anti-drug programs, concert bands, drama presentations, and chess clubs. I would suggest a parallel secondary education institution. Turn these socializing and enrichment functions over to something other than the academic high school. Set up a corresponding institution that might mirror the enrollments of its associated high school. Call it, for lack of a better term, a *Community School*.

Let this Community School handle the nonacademic functions of preparation for adulthood.

Think creatively about how such a parallel system might be implemented. The Community School might certify student accomplishment with a pass/fail system, for example, rather than academic grades. What about using the same physical buildings—but with different administrations and pedagogical structures? Schedule the two schools on alternate days of the week (academic programs on a Monday-Wednesday-Friday schedule; activities and social programs on Tuesdays and Thursdays)? What about evening or weekend opportunities? All sorts of innovative possibilities and permutations might be worked out. Parents might choose to home-school their child for the academic requirements (first and third functions), and then send their kids to a public Community School for social and personal development. Or parents may choose to send their offspring to a public academic high school and then pack them off to a private Community School—where religious indoctrination of one's choosing might be included in the curriculum.

The Liberal-Arts Program

Once students are truly prepared for the college experience, they would enroll in a three-year *General Education* liberal-arts program. There would be no specialized majors (as we know them today). No professional training. There would be three years of literature, history and geography, philosophy, cultural studies, classics, communication skills, computer literacy, foreign languages, arts and music, research skills, economics, a wide range of social sciences, and consumer sciences and mathematics. This three-year college program might also incorporate opportunities for overseas study or fieldwork to round out one's perspective.

The curriculum would consist of 90 units of prescribed coursework, with little opportunity for substituting peripheral courses of tangential value. It would be administered by some sort of college of liberal studies—a truly interdisciplinary team whose primary allegiance would not be to any traditional academic fiefdoms. The resulting three-year certification would be a B.L.A. degree, *Bachelor of Liberal Arts*. It would certify that the recipient was truly an educated person, ready to step into the community of cultured persons and accept the responsibilities of citizenship.

The Academic Major

In addition to the B.L.A. degree, there would be a college program for academic majors—allowing students to pursue an in-depth study of medieval French literature, cosmology, philosophy, archeology, visual arts, opera, or whatever else they desired. Such a major—which might involve

30 or 40 units (another year of study)—could conceivably be offered under the same roof as the B.L.A. program, for administrative and institutional efficiency. But the *major* program (which might result in a *Master's* degree) would be handled entirely outside of the structure of the B.L.A. program. Different departments. Different faculty. No overlapping jurisdictional empires. Two separate and distinct programs. Upon receiving the M.A. degree, the person would be an acknowledged expert in some particular area of human culture.

It would be generally recognized that the B.L.A. degree is what is required to earn one's place in society. It would be the continuation of one's public education. The M.A. would be optional; it reflects a mastery of some specific academic area. The M.A. would normally be earned following the B.L.A.—although the two degrees could be pursued concurrently. Such an M.A. program might or might not eventually lead to a career. It could well prepare one for moving on in teaching or law or science or journalism. But it would not be geared to meet professional requirements and accreditation.

Specialized Professional and Technical Training

Now comes the part about preparation for earning a living. I propose that vocational training and professional education would not be pursued at the same institutions as the B.L.A. or the M.A. These are very different kinds of educational functions. And the more we can keep them distinctly separated, the clearer are our educational roles and our institutional responsibilities. Let the student pursue his or her B.L.A. or M.A. at the local public college—or private college of one's choice—and then work for his or her veterinary degree at the specialized school that is set up to handle that training.

Better yet, let specialized professional education be handled by the professions themselves.[12] Let IBM and General Motors and Microsoft train the specific managers, designers, programmers, and executives they need. Let the American Bar Association get into the business of training lawyers. The American Medical Association could set up a system of professional schools for its myriad specialties. The industries and professions certainly know best the requirements for their jobs. They can swiftly adapt to the changing needs of the corporate world. They can train the young aspirants exactly the way they want. The industries can design the best balance of classroom lectures, lab projects, practical training, apprenticeships, and research experience they need from their workers. Such a shifting of institutional responsibilities would tie in the job training much more closely with the industries that need the workers.

And the job of liberally educating young people to be responsible citizens would be left to public education as well as to private colleges and universities. One advantage of this arrangement is that industries would be getting students who are better prepared to train for today's real-world needs—well-rounded thinkers who are truly educated. The B.L.A. would be a prerequisite for most professional programs. Writing for *The Futurist*, Roger E. Herman, a strategic business futurist, emphasizes,

Insightful leaders now recognize that a liberal arts education prepares graduates to think more broadly, to conceptualize at a multidisciplinary level that's more responsive to the increasingly broad issues confronting people in all walks of life. . . . [In] the years ahead we'll need more and more workers who can think, collaborate, create, solve problems, communicate, and lead. Demand will be high for people who have learned how to learn; who have a strong multidisciplinary education; and who can adapt easily to whatever comes their way.[13]

The liberal-arts students have the perspective, the communication skills, and the critical-thinking abilities to move forward and adapt. Let the schools educate young people to think, to understand their culture, and acquire the skills to keep on learning. And let the industries design their own job-training programs.

THERE ARE TWO BASIC PROBLEMS with all these educational proposals. First we have the inbred aversion to change. There are too many politicians and professional educators with their own fiefdoms at stake. Irving Buchen writes, "Their political platform is always the same: Maintain the status quo, keep privilege for those who already have it, and regularly frighten the public by invoking apocalyptic visions of the chaos that will ensue if they give up any power or control."[14] A major roadblock to any real innovation is going to be the closed minds of the establishment—including educators, politicians, parents, and students. This is anti-intellectualism at its clearest.

The second problem is that virtually every proposal is going to cost money. The actuality is that *if we wanted to*, we could fund any educational innovation we felt worthwhile. In any kind of intellectual, rational society, education would be one of the top priorities. We could do it—if we simply had the collective will to do so. If we wanted to spend our resources on things other than ostentatious displays of personal affluence. Begin by rethinking the absurdity of funding schools out of local property taxes. Does it really make sense any longer to predetermine that those localities that have the weakest economies, the poorest housing, the highest rates of unemployment, and the least educated parents, shall therefore have the poorest schools? William Raspberry asks, "Why on earth should public education, a state function, be funded primarily on the basis of local property taxes? Or to put it more practically, why should there be within a single state rich public schools and poor ones?"[15] Even more to the point: Why, in the United States of America in the twenty-first century, should there be such a large discrepancy among the states? Why should school children in New Jersey and New York enjoy an annual per-capita budget that is twice as much as what the kids have in Utah or Mississippi?[16] Is the sacred cow of local control enough of a justification to perpetuate an outdated and inequitable schooling system?

Why not do what is rational, what is logical—instead of repeating what we have been doing for the last couple centuries? We are living in a completely different world than what we had at the turn of the last century. We need to rethink our needs and our ways of solving our problems. We certainly aren't doing a very good job of managing our schooling the way we are going about it today. Here's an exercise: Try to envision how you would design a society's total educational system if you were starting with a blank slate—if you could set it up any way you wanted. From scratch. Start with a fresh planet. The chances are that you wouldn't do it the way we are doing it now. Think about what we should be doing.

CHAPTER 21

Environmental Restoration

Many of the issues we have explored are topics where we need to seek a balance—science versus religion, privacy versus security, reason versus spontaneity, individualism versus tribalism. But when it comes to the environment, there are no two sides to be debated. Our topmost priority must be to leave the planet as we found it—to leave the ecosystem intact for future generations. Period. This is the overriding intellectual responsibility of mankind; this is our foremost obligation. To lose the planet's biosphere is to lose everything.

CONSERVATION AND ANTI-POLLUTION MEASURES

There are steps we can take to reverse much of our environmental devastation—if we simply resolve to do so. For example, we are beginning to see the undoing of public projects that have had detrimental environmental impact: the dismantling of vast hydroelectric dams, curtailing the use of certain pesticides, eliminating some urban freeways, and the de-canalizing of the Everglades.

On the international level, there are encouraging signs that worldwide conservation cooperation can be attained. Hundreds of environmental meetings and conferences have taken place over the last few decades—typically under the auspices of the United Nations or other regional multi-nation pacts. And dozens of international treaties have been drafted and implemented. Parochial self-interest often thwarts the best intentions of these conventions—such as the United States pulling out of the 1997

Kyoto Protocol on Climate Change or President Bush refusing to join other world leaders at the 2002 Johannesburg World Summit for Sustainable Development. But generally there is emerging a global awareness of the perilous plight of our biosphere.

Non-polluting renewable energy sources can be developed.[1] Both for the sake of the planet and to restore sanity in the Middle East, let's kick our oil addiction and get on with finding and implementing alternative energy sources. We know we are going to have to do it sometime. One way or another, we will find non-petroleum solutions. The question is, *How long will we wait, and how much more environmental and cultural damage will we inflict before we turn to some rational answers?* Numerous technologies have proven themselves either in the lab or in the field: passive solar energy, solar photovoltaic cells, wind turbine farms, hydroelectric power (much of which can be tapped without massive dam projects that wipe out natural flowing rivers), tidal energy, ocean thermal energy conversion, geothermal energy, thermal depolymerization, hydrogen and hydrogen fuel cells. Most of these energy sources can be developed and harnessed with relatively little impact on the earth's ecosystem—generally resulting in much less pollution than burning fossil fuels. There is no excuse for not utilizing these sources as quickly as possible (*We know what we should do!*) All it takes is a change in attitude—an intellectual shift—to make feasible the consideration of such solutions.

Conservation Efforts

Conservation works. For example, the amount of electricity used by refrigerators dropped by about two-thirds during the 1980s and 1990s—even while the boxes were getting bigger and features were added. We have just about doubled the average fuel efficiency of our new cars since 1974—although Americans still embrace an irrational lust for massive SUVs. Upgrading to highly efficient new high-tech lighting bulbs could eliminate almost half of America's commercial electrical consumption for illumination.

Another solution would be environmental taxes. We should be taxing heavily both resource-depleting activities (mining, logging, fishing) and pollution-causing activities (manufacturing, refining, and so forth). Industries should pay the true costs of their operations—including pollution of the biosphere, killing individual animals, wiping out entire species, and destroying complete ecosystems. Rather than making businesses pay the true costs of their industrial activities, however, we are doing just the opposite: doling out government subsidies for mining and logging on federal lands—even building the logging and mining roads for the industries engaged in resources depletion. And city after city routinely encourages polluting industries to locate in their areas—with tax breaks, special housing considerations, favorable zoning changes, and so forth.[2] Such policies are contrary to reason and to our best long-term interest.

If we were to tax such industries, rather than subsidize them, this would increase the overall cost of manufacturing and providing products and services to the public—which costs would then be passed on to the consumers. Which is as it should be. In order to reflect the true costs of steel, water, lumber, paint, batteries, aluminum, or electrical energy, we consumers should have to pay the actual price—including environmental damage. If lumber were to cost twice as much as it does now, we would use it much more carefully and wisely. The same is true for concrete, plastic, glass, or gasoline. Such measures would factor the costs of environmental destruction into any economic planning.[3]

Let's rethink the way we define the Gross Domestic Product. The costs of digging resources out of the earth, cleaning up polluted lakes and rivers, and pollution-related medical expenses are all counted as assets in totaling up the Gross Domestic Product—that is, jobs are created. In actuality, these activities should properly be factored in as negative charges against our planetary health. E. O. Wilson states that we must seek "an accurate balance sheet, one that includes a full accounting of the costs to the planet incurred by economic growth."[4] Let us be honest and label environmental destruction as a negative in our overall Gross Domestic Balance Sheet. Wilson encourages consideration of the *Genuine Progress Indicator* "which includes estimates of environmental costs of economic activity."[5] Economic viability cannot be measured only in terms of growth and development. The negative costs must be subtracted.

POPULATION CONTROL

Of all the global problems we are concerned with, overpopulation far outranks everything else. Indeed, population pressures exacerbate all the rest of our eco-woes. Pollution, global warming, resources depletion, deforestation, desertification, extinction of flora and fauna species, and hyper-urbanization: these are all made worse by the increasing numbers of people trying to survive on this planet. For the best of humanitarian motives, we do everything we can to protect and promote human life. We want to decrease infant mortality, increase the life expectancy of the elderly, conquer life-threatening diseases, and provide genetic and test-tube miracles for infertile couples. But if we are going to increase the chances for every couple to have children and for our senior citizens to live long and healthy lives, we must also be intellectually responsible in limiting our profligate procreation.

The attempt to cope with growth by planning to accommodate more growth never works. Widening a freeway, in the long run, never alleviates traffic congestion. And, as pointed out in Chapter 16, feeding the starving masses, in the long run, is not the answer to widespread starvation. In both cases we are just facilitating continuation of the problem—prolonging the crisis. Garrett Hardin emphasizes, "People are repeatedly surprised when building more roads merely makes traffic jams worse. They are also surprised when giving food to a starving population today increases the number of the starving in future years."[6] Twenty years after his prophetic *Essay on the Principles of Population*, Malthus wrote, "It is not easy to conceive a more disastrous present, one more likely to plunge the human race in irrecoverable misery, than an unlimited facility for producing food in a limited space."[7] We cannot accommodate more growth by growing more food; we must stop irresponsible reproduction.

Defining the Carrying Capacity

A given ecosystem can support only so many bluebirds, or field mice, or deer, or houseflies. Or human beings. At some time we simply will not be able to cram any more bodies into the planet's biosphere. We may burrow into the ground, stack high-rise apartments miles into the air, and build underwater cities. But at some point, we simply will not be able to squeeze any more beings into habitable spaces. In fact, numerous biologists and ecologists would argue that we have already greatly exceeded the human carrying capacity of the planet.[8]

However, for the sake of argument, let's say that with technological miracles—super fertilizers, desalinization, and genetically engineered crops—we will greatly increase the number of humans we can squeeze onto the planet. Arbitrarily pick an ultimate planetary carrying limit. Choose any number you want. Fifteen billion? A hundred billion? Five-hundred billion? Six trillion? We do not need to agree on the actual number. We need only agree that at some time we will reach the planet's maximum population density. All open space, parklands, and wilderness preserves will have been eliminated. All rivers, wetlands, and lakes have dried out or have been drained and paved over. Every acre of dry land and ocean has been cultivated with high-tech agriculture and aquaculture processes until there is no more conceivable room to grow our designer crops. Our physical environment consists of asphalt, concrete, metal, and glass. The great outdoors is replaced by television nature programs and virtual-reality holograms. Wildlife has been wiped out. No more scenic vistas. No more elbow room. No more privacy. And we have embraced a high degree of state control—it is axiomatic that the denser the population, the more regulations and restraints there must be. *There. Are we happy now?* As Wilson points out, "long before that ultimate limit was approached, the planet would surely have become a hellish place to exist."[9] The question is, *What can we do to halt our population explosion before we reach that hellish place?* We're going to stop growing once we reach the ultimate carrying capacity. Why not do it sooner?

Americans are fond of proclaiming that we want the rest of the world to enjoy our standard of living. This is admirable, humane, and gloriously impossible. The number of people to be supported on the planet and the quality of life are incontrovertibly inversely related. The more people the Earth tries to support, the lower the standard of living for all. If we want all the peoples of the planet to enjoy the American standard of living, we are going to have to reduce the population of the Earth to well under one billion persons!

Programs for Population Control

In a pure libertarian framework, neither the government nor any other social agency would have the right to interfere with a woman's child-bearing decisions—whether she wants to have ten children or if she wants to abort every pregnancy. However, this libertarian freedom exists only when people exercise their decision-making with responsibility. Responsible couples would recognize that if they have more than two children they would be doing more than just providing for their replacements; they would be adding to the planet's population burden. Bringing more children into the world than the ecosystem can support is not responsible. And since we have not been conducting our reproductive affairs in a responsible fashion, we therefore relinquish our freedom to decide how many offspring we want; we simply have been having too many babies.

One of the clearest justifications for society getting involved in reproductive control was voiced almost 150 years ago—by one of our strongest champions of individual liberty, John Stuart Mill: "The fact itself, of causing the existence of a human being, is one of the most responsible actions in the range of human life. To undertake this responsibility—to bestow a life which may be either a curse or a blessing—unless the being on whom it is bestowed will have at least the ordinary chances of a desirable existence, is a crime against that being."[10] As we look at the starving babies of Africa, the urban urchins wandering our city streets, the abandoned foundlings in our orphanages, the abused children with no stable home, it is all too apparent that the globe has been overrun with those who have not had "at least the ordinary chances of a desirable existence." We have not only the right, but also the moral imperative, to do what we can to alleviate the suffering of overpopulation.

Some will argue that it is a sin to use any form of birth control: condoms, diaphragms, IUDs, sterilization, or any manner of before-or-after pills. *Anything that interferes with fertilization of the ovum is morally wrong.* Extending this line of reasoning to the extreme, it could be argued therefore that every month that goes by without a fertile woman becoming pregnant is somehow contrary to God's Great Design—and therefore is a sin. *Get pregnant this month or go to Hell!* Such an argument is, of course, preposterous. But where do we draw the line? Either we practice rational family planning of some sort, or we resort to unrestrained procreation—like the spider and the mosquito. And we accept that most of our babies, like those of the spider and mosquito, will never make it to adulthood.

Education and Family Planning

Our primary focus should be birth-control information and contraceptive assistance. Organizations such as Population Connection (formerly Zero Population Growth) and Planned Parenthood represent the most effective and most humane answer to the problem of population pressures. Education and family planning work. One early irresponsible act of George W. Bush's administration was the edict that the United States would ban aid to overseas nonprofit family planning agencies that even mentioned abortion counseling. Nothing could be more damaging to the future of the planet. If we are going to assist underdeveloped countries with famine relief and agricultural assistance, do we not also have the right—indeed, the obligation—to advise those countries on population control and family planning? Joseph Fletcher writes, "As some forgotten wag once put it, our aid should be offered on condition that contraceptives and vasectomies 'go with the groceries.'"[11]

There are many other specific steps that the government could take to encourage a lower population rate: support both celibacy and late marriages with tax incentives, strengthen financial liability laws in divorce cases, restrict public housing to smaller families, and so forth. (One solution *not* worth considering is planetary colonization.[12]) But there are also more intrusive means of government coercion and control—short of China's draconian one-child-per-family mandate.

One approach would be to reward young women for postponing motherhood. In the 1950s the ecologist Raymond B. Cowles suggested a plan whereby every young woman would be given a substantial cash reward every year that she postpones having her first baby. Sort of a reverse welfare incentive system. The rate of population increase would slow merely because of the greater age gap between generations. Also, studies indicate that the older a woman is before having her first baby, the fewer children she will ultimately have.[13] One variation on this approach is offered by one of our more iconoclastic social critics, Edward Abbey, who suggested that we offer a brand-new Ford Mustang convertible to every girl who consents to having her fallopian tubes tied.[14]

Resorting to a stronger measure, society could dictate how many children a woman should bear—two would be the obvious limit. If the woman (or the married couple in conventional families) wanted more children, she would have to pay a really hefty fine—say the equivalent of a year's salary. This should be enough to make a couple think twice before deciding to raise a large family; but it would still allow a couple to have more children—if they could afford it. A variation on this proposal was offered by the economist Kenneth Boulding in 1964. Every young girl would be issued a given number of transferable birth licenses or "baby rights"—entitling her to bear, say, two children. These rights (or fractions thereof) could then be traded on some national *reproductive rights market*. The wealthy who wanted to have more babies would purchase rights from those who, either for financial or other personal reasons, would be willing to sell their rights (nuns, lesbians, non-maternal professionals, and old maid aunts). This would help to stabilize the nation's population while offering a modicum of free-market choice.[15] One advantage of such extreme measures would be the propaganda value. By instituting this negative incentive, society would be sending out a strong message to all its citizens: *We cannot afford to increase our population any further. Having more than two children is socially irresponsible.*

Many objections can be raised to such a quota system. First, it is coercive; we start with Big Brother telling us how many babies we can have. Second, there would have to be some sort of penalty for those who exceed their quota; this raises the specter of forced abortions or even mandated sterilization. This approach to oppressive government control is indeed abhorrent. But unlimited freedom—including reproductive freedom— cannot be allowed if it is not handled with responsibility. One must demonstrate accountability for one's actions. And, given today's ecological realities, planning on having more than two children simply cannot be accepted as responsible behavior.

Tax Disincentive For Large Families

Without getting into draconian quota systems, here is my one outrageous proposal for this chapter: *Eliminate the IRS tax exemption for all but the first two children born to any woman.* The mother (and male partner) will continue to get tax deductions for the first two children she has. But third and subsequent children will not warrant any more tax breaks. Such a tax revision states, in effect, that we will no longer encourage couples to have big families.

All current large families would be exempted so the program would not penalize any current families with more than two children. (Also, to be fair, such a regulation should not take effect until a year after it has been enacted. If such a tax disincentive were to be approved today, for example, it would apply only to third and subsequent children born to any woman a year after next January First.) This proposal would not condone abortion or any specific means of birth control. It would not violate any religious doctrines. And it would not prohibit anyone who really wanted three children from going ahead; they just wouldn't be subsidized. This would simply be an unmistakable and practical way to say that society no longer is encouraging large families.

While this tax plan would not provide any direct legal or financial incentive to other nations, it would be a clear message to other countries. As Herman Daly points out, "A definite U.S. policy of population control at home would give us a much stronger base for preaching to the underdeveloped countries about their population problem."[16] It has to be done some time; we—our cities, our nation, our planet—cannot continue to expand forever. And the sooner we commit ourselves to a stable population policy, the better off we all will be.

Lest you think that even this proposal for a tax disincentive is too proscriptive for today's sensitive mindset, let me return to Mill: "The laws which, in many countries on the Continent, forbid marriage unless the parties can show that they have the means of supporting a family, do not exceed the legitimate powers of the State; and whether such laws be expedient or not . . . they are not objectionable as violations of liberty."[17] If men and women do not make responsible family-planning decisions then they will lose some of their reproductive freedom. Society will have to make the decisions for them. Use your freedom responsibly or lose it.

IN ANY GIVEN DEBATE where the central issue is development versus environmental preservation, we should err on the side of environmental conservation. If we are wrong—and we decide at some point in the future that development would have been the proper alternative—we can always initiate the development at a later date. We can start pouring concrete at any time. If we err on the side of too much development, however, we are in trouble. A natural ecosystem cannot be restored. Do we not want to leave some of the natural environment for our grandchildren? And their grandchildren? Let us heed the Great Law of the Iroquois Nation: *In our every deliberation, we must consider the impact of our actions on the next seven generations.*

It is much easier to cope with a sudden catastrophe—a hurricane, an earthquake, a terrorist bombing—than it is to deal with a slowly evolving disaster. Especially one of the magnitude of our planet's population explosion. But in a world governed by reason and responsibility, we would accept that we have to face our growing global population crisis. Hardin observes, "Anything to be *done* about human populations necessarily depends on the will to do it."[18] We do have a choice. Do we want a world in which a healthy population can enjoy a reasonable measure of the earth's resources, open spaces, wilderness areas, and a modicum of comfort? Or do we want a world filled with wall-to-wall impoverished people, struggling to find the meager resources to barely stay alive?

CHAPTER 22

Economic Reform

Robert Heilbroner is an economist who believes we can change our patterns of exploitation and hyper-capitalism: "As we have repeatedly sought to emphasize, all the dangers we have examined—population growth, war, environmental damage, scientific technology—are *social* problems, originating in human behavior and capable of amelioration by the alteration of that behavior."[1] Nowhere is this truer than with economics. Economics is a human invention. We created it, and we should be able to restructure the basic economic rules we live by. The rules, however, have become rather obscured. Economics has clothed itself in a mystical shroud of abstract concepts and impenetrable jargon designed to keep outsiders at bay. Herman Daly, former economist with the World Bank, writes that from the early nineteenth century, "the structure of economic theory became more and more top-heavy with analysis. Layer upon layer of abstruse mathematical models were erected higher and higher above the shallow concrete foundation of fact."[2] It is time to bring economics back down to the "concrete foundation of fact." One of those facts is that we live in a finite world. By ignoring this reality, classical economists have built their intricate models on the fantasy of perpetual growth.

THE CONCEPT OF STEADY-STATE ECONOMICS

Unending physical growth is not possible. We must devise a plan for evolving into a sustainable, steady-state economy.[3] A zero-growth or steady-state economy means simply that we no longer can plan, year after year, on having more taxpayers, more factories, and more SUVs than the year before. A steady-state economy does not mean a stagnant culture; intangible assets need not be limited—cultural entertainments, works of art, religious services, and interpretive nature programs can continue to expand. It merely recognizes that we cannot count on infinite physical growth.

As argued in Chapter 21, the earth does have a finite carrying capacity. At some point—when our environment has deteriorated unimaginably—we will have to stop adding more bodies to the planet's census. The question is, *What do we do once we have reached this ultimate capacity*—whether twenty years from now or two hundred years from now? The answer is that at that point we will have to come up with a viable economic system that does not depend on continuing physical growth. A zero-growth plan. No more industrial expansion. No increasing number of consumers every year. Ultimately, we will have to develop a steady-state economic model.

The next question is, *Why don't we do that now?* Whatever the ultimate paradigm might be—whatever kind of eventual zero-growth economic system we must devise—why not start working on that system now? Why wait? This is not altogether a new thought to forward-looking political economists. In 1848, John Stuart Mill wrote the following in his *Principles of Political Economy:*

There is room in the world, no doubt, and even in old countries, for a great increase of population, supposing the arts of life to go on improving, and capital to increase. But even if innocuous, I confess I see very little reason for desiring it. . . . Nor is there much satisfaction in contemplating the world with nothing left to the spontaneous activity of nature; with every rood of land brought into cultivation, which is capable of growing food for human beings; every flowery waste or natural pasture ploughed up, all quadrupeds or birds which are not domesticated for man's use exterminated as his rivals for food, every hedgerow or superfluous tree rooted out, and scarcely a place left where a wild shrub or flower could grow without being eradicated as a weed in the name of improved agriculture.[4]

How much longer do we ignore Mill's prophetic passage? Do we wait until we have reached the absolute final finite frontier? Or do we have the intellectual courage to start planning now for a rational zero-growth economy?

TWO STEPS TO A STEADY-STATE ECONOMY

There are two reasons why we have not started to work on a zero-growth economic model. First, we have a problem with rational decision-making. Rather than look at the problem afresh, we fall back on tradition. *This is the way classic economics has always worked.* This response—continuing to do what we have always done—reflects a failure of *reason*. Second, there is the matter of greed, the desire for immediate short-term gains. This second factor demonstrates a lack of *responsibility*. We simply refuse to consider the greater societal needs. These two components, the failure of reason and the disregard of responsibility, are what define post-intellectualism. Let us look first at the failure of our rational planning process.

Adding Critical Thinking to Our Planning Processes

Most planning agencies today concern themselves with guiding development, projecting trends, fighting congestion, and encouraging "smart growth" or "managed growth." In other words, they are *reacting*. This is not critical thinking. We accept as a given that we (at the city, county, state, national, and global levels) will continue to grow. All of our "planning" agencies are in actuality *response* agencies—concerned with how to accommodate growth, how to adjust and adapt. This is nothing more than accepting a projection, recognizing a pattern, acknowledging a trend, and then saying, *What do we do about it?*

One of the best examples of this line of thinking is the widening of freeways. Whenever any urban area faces a traffic congestion crisis (every half-hour or so), city planners and state highway commissioners immediately jump on the obvious solution: *widen the freeway!* After we add a couple more lanes, traffic does flow more freely—for a short time. But the higher capacity of the freeway merely makes it possible for commuters and other travelers from farther away to take advantage of the freeway. *If you build it, they will come.* Traffic expands to fill the available roadway. In congested urban areas, the traffic will always try to increase to about 110 percent of the capacity. You never catch up by increasing the capacity. John Norquist, the Mayor of Milwaukee, once observed that "Trying to fight urban congestion by building more highways is like trying to fight obesity by loosening your belt."[5]

Here's a proposal for urban planners—city councils, county supervisors, zoning commissioners, state legislatures, regional planning boards, and the like. A truly radical idea. *Plan!* Actually plan. I'm not saying *manage, project, accommodate,* or *react.* I mean PLAN. The essence of planning is this: start with a *goal,* a specific measurable objective that you want to achieve. This is what we do with business models, military operations, scientific research, instructional design, and church-building programs (back to the Analytic Thinking Pattern). Start with a goal.

In the case of urban planning, a reasonable place to start would be to decide what size your ultimate population should reach. This is your goal. Establish an ideal number—your target. Maybe 250,000? Maybe a million? What number will give you an optimum balance of educational, cultural, and medical facilities, job opportunities, municipal services, open space, and civility—while minimizing congestion, pollution, and urban sprawl? Decide on that number and then plan on how best to achieve it. Listen to what the demographers and the economists have to say, but don't let their projections dictate your goals. Don't ask, *What numbers do we anticipate in five years? Ten years?* That is not planning. That is reacting. Plan by stating, *These are what numbers we* want *in five years. And in ten years.* Then curtail unwanted growth by using your planning tools—zoning restrictions, taxing authority, urban service boundaries, impact fees, watershed protection legislation, pollution controls, traffic patterns, development fees, building permits, and other land-use strategies.

It is possible to avoid unwanted growth. Start by refusing to authorize new residential or industrial development; then don't build any new highways, water-storage facilities, schools, hospitals, and sewage treatment plants. This sounds severe. But it will work. And we will enjoy clean air, open space, more community involvement, less congestion, lower levels of pollution. And probably less crime. While Genesis exhorts us to "be fruitful and multiply," a much less quoted biblical passage is found in Isaiah: "Woe unto them that join house to house, that lay field to field, till there be no place that they may be placed alone in the midst of the earth!"[6]

Such an idealistic approach will not work in isolation at the city level, of course. Nor at the state level. Nor even at the national level. No municipality can build a medieval wall around its perimeter. National immigration policies must reflect real-world needs and pressures. We ultimately must deal with steady-state economic policies on a global scale. Economists and politicians and global leaders will eventually have to quit relying on population growth and development as an easy path to economic viability. We must recognize that unending growth is not physically possible.

Reversing the Image of Greed as Good

Turning to the second factor that promotes continuing growth—greed— we ask on what principles should society base its value system? The religious moralities of Moses, Buddha, Christ, and Mohammed? The philosophies of classical Greece? The visions of the Enlightenment thinkers? The republican politics of our Founding Fathers? Or the principles and goals of Wall Street arbitragers and corporate CEOs? Our present hyper-intellectual system proclaims, *Wealth is to be coveted. Greed is good.* Such a policy says, in effect, our system is so philosophically bankrupt that we have no way of motivating people except to promise them they can become filthy rich. A culture cannot permanently endure if its overriding obsession—its cultural narrative—is short-term material gratification. If it cannot dedicate itself to the greater societal good (Rousseau's General

Will), if it cannot think intellectually and responsibly about the seventh generation (the Great Law of the Iroquois Nation), then it is doomed to eventual decay and dissolution.

Actual material worth doesn't necessarily determine your happiness, anyway. Former corporate executive Axel Granered writes, "Our incomes don't noticeably influence our satisfactions with marriage, family, friendships, or ourselves. If not wracked by hunger or hurt, people on all income levels can enjoy one another and experience comparable joy. . . . Once beyond poverty, further economic growth does not appreciably improve human morale."[7] Money does not buy a feeling of community or a sense of purpose. If your only goal in life is to acquire more material wealth, you are poor indeed. If on the other hand, you endeavor in your life to develop your personal talents, to cultivate good friendships, to read some good books, to contribute something of value to your chosen vocation, to cherish a loving relationship with your family, to find spiritual or philosophical peace, to help build a community, then you are indeed a wealthy person. We embrace greed only because we are so intellectually shallow.

Several things can be done. Let's start in school. We could incorporate into our schools' curricula a different set of values. Under the discussion of character education in Chapter 20, could we not include an anti-greed component in the curriculum? How can we reverse the degree to which greed is held to be a universal cultural value? Schools certainly should support the underlying merits of capitalism—*the profit motive is the best avenue to ensure the highest-quality products at the most competitive prices; individuals certainly need sufficient material success to guarantee a comfortable and secure lifestyle.* But at the same time, can we not question the credo that *greed is good* to the detriment of other values such as honesty, compassion, and intellectual satisfaction? How can we support the profit motive while downplaying excessive greed as an unqualified good? Allan Sloan, Wall Street Editor for *Newsweek*, writes, "Greed—defined as an inordinate desire for wealth—is not good, and it doesn't drive markets. Greed drives people to cut corners for short-term gain. . . . Greed replaced self-interest, which by definition has a long-term horizon, rather than gaming the system for a quick hit."[8] We must aim not for short-term profits, but for long-term stability and for advancement of the greater societal good. Once we have lessened the role of materialism as our highest cultural goal, we are on our way toward figuring out how to achieve a steady-state economy.

SOME TAXING ALTERNATIVES

As our Byzantine political and economic environment becomes even more complex and convoluted, the government must play ever-more intrusive roles. George Will observes that "a mature capitalist economy is a government project. A properly functioning free-market system does not spring spontaneously from society's soil as dandelions spring from suburban lawns. Rather, it is a complex creation of laws and mores."[9] One direct way that government can play a role is with specific tax reforms.

Tax Relief for Vacant Land

Municipalities generally tax property at its highest potential use. Why? If you own a vacant acre, or a city block, in the middle of a congested urban area, it is potentially a very valuable piece of real estate—and therefore you are going to be taxed heavily. The reasoning is straightforward: you *could* be making lots of money from the property, so the taxing authority is going to hit you as if you *were* pulling in big bucks. Your only fiscal recourse is to develop the property and turn it into a commercial money-maker. You cannot afford to let the vacant property remain unproductive—while you pay stiff taxes on it.

But looking at our affairs from an intellectual perspective, is that really the most rational thing to do? Why must every square foot of "property" be developed? Why not devise a system that can keep vacant land undeveloped? What if you wanted to turn your empty property into a mini nature preserve; let the trees and flowers provide a little green oasis in the midst of the congestion. But, no, you're still paying substantial taxes. Of course you could donate the land to the city or to the state as a park. Or you could turn it into a permanent nature preserve through some environmental trust fund. But then you would lose your capital investment in the property.

Instead of levying a steep tax on unused land, why don't we declare that every landowner pays *nothing* on his or her vacant land? The tax laws could allow you to hold on to the property, tax-free, until such time as you or your heirs might want to turn it into a money-making venture. If the property sits undeveloped, attracting nothing but gophers and wildflowers, you pay no tax at all! It is only when you develop it—when you turn it into a housing development, an industrial park, a shopping mall—that you start paying taxes. And then you pay big time. Tax the actual income, not the potential.

The same principle could apply to residential property. If you buy three building sites, and then build your house on one of the sites—keeping the other two lots as undeveloped open space—you would be taxed only on the one lot that has been developed. Taxes would have to be adjusted so that the total tax revenue would be the same; you pay more for your house and less for your empty property. Somewhere along the line we must start thinking in different terms. Taxing policies, zoning regulations, rules and permits are all man-made bureaucracies. They can be changed.

Highly Progressive Income tax

One final outrageous proposal for this chapter is this: amend the IRS code to levy a highly progressive income tax of 100 percent on all income above a given rather-comfortable level—say, $500,000 a year (including bonuses, stock options, corporate perks, and other benefits). Sam Pizzigati, a trade-union journalist, argues in his 1992 book, *The Maximum Wage*, that the time has come for us to reconsider the idea of a maximum wage. A 100 percent tax bracket would create such a maximum ceiling. Daly ties in such a proposal with steady-state economic theory: "In the growth paradigm there need be no upper limit. But in the steady-state paradigm there must be an upper limit to the total, and consequently an upper limit to per-capita income as well."[10]

This proposal argues that any income above a designated amount is superfluous. A half-million dollars a year will provide any American family with all the material blessings and elevated standard of living that anyone can reasonably justify. Offering top athletes, entertainment stars, and corporate executives extravagant salaries and stock options worth tens of millions of dollars serves only to establish one's ranking in the capitalistic pecking order. *Since I make fifty million a year and so-and-so is paid only forty million, obviously I am more important!* What a sad distorted sense of values!

A person whose highest goal is the acquisition of material possessions is a person who does not have very high goals. Jonathan Swift in the early eighteenth century argued, "In all well-instituted commonwealths, care has been taken to limit men's possessions; which is done for many reasons, and, among the rest, for one which, perhaps, is not often considered; that when bounds are set to men's desires, after they have acquired as much as the laws will permit them, their private interest is at an end, and they have nothing to do but to take care of the public."[11] Isn't that a nice thought—as unrealistic as it may sound at first? Once "bounds are set to men's desires" (by creating a ceiling on one's income), from that point on they gladly will "have nothing to do but to take care of the public."

Such thinking is not limited to flaming left-wing politicians. Even John Locke, the ultimate defender of the right to hold on to one's private property, recognized the danger of amassing too much wealth. There are inherent limits to the very notion of property.

Whatsoever, then, a man removes out of the state that nature hath provided and left it in, he hath mixed his labor with it, and joined to it something that is his own, and thereby makes it his property. But how far has God given property to us to enjoy? As much as anyone can make use of to any advantage of life before it spoils, so much may he by his labor fix his property in. Whatever is beyond this is more than his share, and belongs to others.[12]

That's quite a statement—coming from Locke: *Whatever is beyond as much as anyone can make use of is more than his share, and belongs to others.* We also could heed the words of a contemporary conservative. William F. Buckley—as strong a free-enterprise advocate as you will find—agrees there may be a point beyond which executives are over-compensated. He wrote of the "implications of preposterous salaries" five years before the Enron debacle: "There is a point at which one stares at the salary and should ask oneself: Is this thing looking ugly? What do we have here, voluptuary greed? . . . . The super-rich CEOs should pause just for a minute and ask whether, comparative advantage to one side, there isn't a sensibility in modern capitalism they'd just as soon not scorn."[13]

The idea behind a 100 percent tax bracket would be simply to instill a moral climate that says: *Outrageous avarice and ostentatious displays of wealth are to be frowned upon. It's not cool to be flagrantly rich.* Perhaps, again, we could benefit from the values of the Iroquois Nation. Doug George-Kanentiio writes, "Traditional Iroquois morality frowns upon the accumulation of personal wealth while others are in need: generosity, humility, and simplicity are held in highest regard."[14]

A proposal for a maximum wage seems simplistically naïve. It is as naive as is the expectation that the masses can govern themselves by participating in a rational democracy. Kathleen Dalton, Theodore Roosevelt biographer, points out that Roosevelt favored such a heavily progressive tax because "political democracy would have no meaning without government intervention to cushion the poor and tame the excesses of the rich."[15] In addition to refocusing our national goals, such a ceiling can be healthy for the functioning of a democratic society.

THERE ARE MANY STEPS THAT COULD BE TAKEN to encourage the creation of a steady-state economic system. Let's start by setting up a Presidential Commission on Non-Growth. Call together some of the most respected and innovative thinkers in a variety of fields—economics certainly, but also in labor, history, literature, philosophy, social work, media, education, and the arts. Charge them with coming up with a far-seeing economic plan that would not be dependent upon annual physical expansion and exploitation. Define how a zero-growth economy is going to work. Develop the outline for a steady-state economy. It's got to happen sometime. Let's be rational and start planning for it now. The sooner the better.

We devised the economic rules by which we play the game. For a couple hundred years, the rules laid down by Adam Smith served us well. But the world is different now. The game has changed. There are more players; and the planetary playing field has shrunk. We now must change the rules. We will have to do it sometime. The global well is running dry. The longer we wait, the more desperate our position becomes.

CHAPTER 23

Global Transformation

Recall Einstein's comment about "how small an influence reason and honest good-will exert upon events in the political field." Looking at our domestic politics, there is no end to the inanities and irrationalities that dominate our political playing fields. Start with the concept of *states*—an outdated legacy from British trading colonies established almost four hundred years ago. Why is Rhode Island a separate political entity? Or Kansas, for that matter? Why should Nevada have as many U.S. senators as California? Due to the weighted representation of small states, it is possible to have half of the Senate controlled by just sixteen percent of the population. Why should metropolitan areas such as New York City or Chicago each sprawl into three different state jurisdictions? While we're at it, why do we have overlapping county and city governments?

Why do we still stick with the Electoral College? There have been four presidential elections in which the candidate receiving the most popular votes was not elected.[1] In effect, the *states* elect the president. This may have made sense in 1800; does it make sense in 2000? The "winner take all" system used by 48 states is patently unfair. With the *district plan* used by Maine and Nebraska electoral votes are divided according to winners of the individual congressional districts—considerably fairer. Better yet would be the "popular electoral vote" or *proportional* system, in which electoral votes are divided according to the percentage of votes won by each candidate.

One needed area for genuine reform is campaign financing. Elected office-holders are not serving as our representatives and executives; they are first and foremost money-grubbers—attending fund-raisers, on the phone dialing for dollars, meeting the movers and shakers, and making promises. You learn to serve business interests or you don't get a chance to serve. Although the Campaign Reform Act of 2002 limits the amount of "soft money" flowing into the political coffers, it increases the amounts of "hard money" that can be contributed directly to candidates. Accounting procedures become increasingly convoluted; the line between hard money and soft money grows hazy and irrelevant; and the potential for corruption increases proportionately. If we really wanted to do so, meaningful ceilings on obscene political spending could be instituted: short broadcast spots could be eliminated; air time for substantial messages could be made available free of charge to candidates; PBS and cable channels could be utilized; third-party candidates could be assured a voice; real debates could be structured. If we wanted to be rational about it.

A WORLD COMING TOGETHER

Our primary concern in this chapter, however, is not domestic reform, but the need for a reformed planetary outlook. I have no doubt but that if an expeditionary force of extra-terrestrial aliens were to actually visit Earth in their flying saucers, their first observation would be, *What in heaven's name are you Earthlings doing by carving your planet up into 200 separate sovereign nations? For Jupiter's sake, you have but one people, one race, inhabiting one small celestial body.* It makes no sense to divide the globe among numerous kingdoms, sheikdoms, fiefdoms, assorted dictatorships, and democracies.

Less than ten years after adopting the Articles of Confederation, the thirteen original colonies realized that their loose alignment was not adequate to protect their security and economic interests. The states then agreed, somewhat reluctantly, to a binding national government. Now it is time for the 200 nation-states of the planet to consider a comparable federation. Only 125 years ago, it took about a week to travel from New York to California by train. High-speed communication was possible only by sending dots and dashes along telegraph wires. Today we can physically get to virtually any civilized spot on the globe in less than twenty-four hours. And any individual can instantaneously send moving color images to anyone else in the developed world. In terms of travel and communication, America today is much closer to India than Oregon was to Indiana 125 years ago. Whatever justification there was for consolidating the thirteen colonies into one nation, there certainly is much more reason—in this shrunken globe—to consider ourselves today all citizens of one small planet.

If human beings can, indeed, participate in self-government, if they can come together and engage in civil deliberation and collective decision-making, they should be able to do so at all levels—from the town hall to the global forum. *Homo sapiens* in Afghanistan or Zimbabwe are no less capable of thinking and acting reasonably than are humans in America or Estonia. To condone the crazy patchwork of independent countries we have on this globe is utterly irrational.

What is it we really revere—the symbols and icons of America, the flag, the bald eagle, the *Star Spangled Banner?* Or the values and principles for which those symbols stand—human dignity and justice, freedom of speech and religion, respect for all persons, equal economic opportunities for all, and citizen participation in self-government? Why support democratic objectives only for citizens of the United States? Why not pursue such goals on a global scale? Should not the United States of Earth be even more of a noble goal than the United States of America? Let us work for the betterment of all peoples.

The Case for Global Cooperation

World War I was fought to make the world safe for democracy. We are engaged today in a much larger battle to make the world safe for modern civilization. Isolationism is no longer an option. We have little choice but to coexist and work for some degree of peace and security in a larger global order. We must find a way to cooperate on a worldwide basis. This is our only rational alternative. Despite their provincial defensiveness, many world leaders sense the day is approaching when the logic of a global federation can no longer be ignored. In his last public reflections on the role of the United Nations, in September 1988, Ronald Reagan said, "A change that is cause for shaking the head in wonder is upon us . . . the prospect of a new age of world peace. The U.N. has an opportunity to live and breathe and work as never before."[2] And Mikhail Gorbachev, in 1992, spelled out his vision of a new world government: "Humanity is at a major turning point. We live in a watershed era. One epoch has ended and a second is commencing. . . . What is emerging is a more complex global structure of international relations. An awareness of the need for some kind of global government is gaining ground, one in which all members of the world community would take part."[3]

Transportation advances, instantaneous global communication, and multinational financial webs all demand that we create a supernational worldwide federation of some sort. Common sense dictates that we do no less. There are many areas of governance and jurisprudence where global cooperation and federalism make sense—the global economy, telecommunications regulation, environmental protection, welfare and medical concerns, cultural preservation, humanitarian measures, nuclear controls, international drug police action, and the war on terrorism.

Economic Globalization

For all practical purposes, the world is one integrated economy. Let us recognize it and regulate it as such. Trying to make globalization go away is as futile as the Luddites' thrashing against mechanization two centuries ago. Agencies such as the World Bank, the World Trade Organization, and the International Monetary Fund are needed for a rational international economy—to deal with tariff agreements, export quotas, food-safety standards, protection of intellectual property, the allocation of radio-spectrum frequencies, and like matters.[4] Such issues cannot be arbitrarily decided by 200 sovereign states.

However, global economic rules must be controlled not by the multinational corporations, but by the democratic policies of participating states. Corporate profits cannot be the primary driving force in global relationships. The more intertwined our economic culture becomes, the more need there is for regulation. Much of our corporate deception, for example, could be eliminated if financial manipulators no longer had access to banking in places such as the Bahamas, Barbados, and Bermuda. The Cayman Islands, with a population of 35,000, now ranks as the fifth largest financial center in the world. Enron set up 43 subsidiaries in Mauritius—a tiny Indian Ocean island country that requires no corporate taxes. These are not rational and responsible ways to structure our global economy. Just as there is need for increased corporate regulation at the domestic level, so is there need for increased regulation on the international level. There must be intellectual and humanitarian global regulations put in place by thinking citizens, not by multinational corporate profiteers. Wayne Ellwood adds that "political reforms need to be combined with particular mechanisms for structural reform. In combination these should put meaningful employment and human rights at the heart of economic policy, boost local control and decision-making, and restore the ecological health and natural capital of our planet."[5]

Clearly there must be reform of the economic institutions charged with controlling the global economy. In a thoughtful analysis, Tina Rosenberg points out that the WTO "has become an unbalanced institution largely controlled by the United States and the nations of Europe, and especially the agribusiness, pharmaceutical and financial-services industries in these countries" and the IMF "has become a champion of market supremacy in all situations, echoing the voice of Wall Street and the United States Treasury Department."[6] The heavy-handed pressures of the IMF have forced many underdeveloped countries to adopt economic "reforms" that serve only to dig themselves deeper into unmanageable debt.

Rosenberg goes on to outline numerous proposals that could reform the global economic market into a more equitable force for international structure and progress: promote democratization, institute appropriate market regulations, increase technology transfer and high-tech sophistication in the Third World, reign in the lobbyists from richer countries, set up more equitable tariffs, legalize short-term migration, soften the IMF's harsher reform dictates, consider debt-forgiveness for the poorest countries, and similar measures.[7] Ellwood adds the need for increasing citizen participation, establishing a global financial authority, honoring the earth, taxing international financial speculation, and controlling capital for the public good.[8] While we're at it, why not start working towards merging the dollar and the euro into a global currency?

Planetary Environmental Cooperation

We must move toward more effective planetary cooperation in conserving natural resources and controlling pollution—problems that recognize no political boundaries. Global environmental troubles cannot be dealt with at the national level. Smog and acid rain don't acknowledge lines drawn on a map. Desertification and deforestation in one country affect the entire planet. It is imperative that all nations work together in a coordinated effort to tackle our ecological deterioration.

As mentioned in Chapter 21, during the past three or four decades, nations of the globe have demonstrated that they can come together to deal with these problems. They have met in hundreds of environmental conferences—dealing with population, agriculture, ocean depletion pollution, dwindling resources, global warming, desertification, biodiversity, and other environmental issues. Despite the fact that America is one of the greatest foot-draggers in accepting and implementing these agreements and accords, there is nevertheless an undeniable worldwide trend toward global consensus on what needs to be done.

Worldwide Medical and Humanitarian Efforts

Numerous humanitarian crises can be dealt with only on a global level: widespread poverty, major natural disasters, women's rights, refugee settlement, the spread of AIDS, the need for smallpox and other vaccinations, migration pressures, the global resurgence of tuberculosis and other diseases, infant mortality, regional famine and drought, and global overpopulation. These problems cannot be handled individually on a nation-by-nation basis.

In 1960, the average income in the richest 40 countries was 30 times greater than the income of those living in the poorest 40 countries. By 1990, the gap had increased to 60 to one. By 2000, it was about 75 to one.[9] This global destitution can be addressed only with coordinated worldwide efforts. If society doesn't like the way that globalization is working, a rational society would institute the reforms needed to make it work right.

Much of the battle against terrorism hinges on humanitarian relief. Tackle the underlying causes for terrorism—many of which stem from poverty, ignorance, inequitable squandering of resources—and you eliminate much of the basis of the problem Thomas Friedman argues that "countries that are globalizing sensibly but steadily are also the ones that are becoming politically more open, with more opportunities for their people, and with a young generation more interested in joining the world system than blowing it up."[10] If America were as good at restoring electricity, water, and medical support as it is at taking out tyrranical regimes, the globe would be a much safer place. People cannot contribute to the world economy, or even to their own family's subsistence, until they are whole persons, medically and educationally.

Global Peace-Keeping

International terrorism, drug smuggling, global financial scams, civil and religious wars, Internet fraud, crimes against humanity (genocide, torture, piracy, slavery), deteriorating nuclear stockpiles and burgeoning nuclear proliferation: these all demand international law enforcement. Until all nations are united under a common police umbrella with worldwide enforcement authority, separate sovereign states will continue to arm themselves and fight to define and defend their boundaries. But without national borders, there can be no national warfare. Global law enforcement also would be considerably less expensive than our present medieval system of national fortresses; there would be substantial resources freed up for welfare, education, medical programs, and economic development.

Worldwide aggression and terrorism will lessen as we experience the spread of democratic self-government. In the last two centuries there have been virtually no instances of freely elected democratic states going to war against other free democratic states. Until the world is democratized, however, we still do need to be concerned with unruly sovereign nation-states. Every culture has to deal with its mad dogs and rouge elephants. How do you live rationally on a planet inhabited by a sizable population that is irrational? How do you exist peacefully with a neighbor who wants to blow you up (basically because you drive a Lexus and you don't go to his church)? How do you reconcile the modern West with the premodern tribal culture? Some sort of international peacekeeping police structure has to be in effect.

From any perspective, Saddam Hussein was unquestionably a bad character. As such, he should not have been allowed to continue in power. However, the United States does not have the right to unilaterally attack another sovereign state—any more than any other country has the moral authority to attack America because it doesn't like our germ warfare stockpiles. For a nation to take matters into its own hands is to condone vigilantism. That in essence is the doctrine of preemptive strikes against another country. Extend such thinking to other trouble spots where despots or terrorists are doing things we do not like—Iran, Syria, Libya, Indonesia, North Korea, Palestine, Columbia, and the Philippines—and pretty soon we have 20 or 30 individual wars of preemption going on.

We had no more ethical legitimacy to unilaterally attack Hussein than the governors of Illinois or Pennsylvania had to attack George Wallace or Orville Faubus or Lester Maddox 50 years ago because the northerners didn't like what these southern governors were doing to people in their states. It had to be up to the federal authorities to call in the National Guard and tell the errant governors how to run their precincts. On the global level, the U.N. is the only body we have with the authority and power (as limited as it is) to maintain international order. And that body must be the one to handle outlaw regimes. Without global law enforcement, we are left with only quarreling sovereign military states determining their own rules of engagement.

One must consider the moral inconsistencies of setting oneself up as the world's policeman—especially when that self-appointed law enforcer has rejected the international land-mine treaty, refused to accept the convention banning germ warfare, diluted the U.N. agreement to reduce illegal trafficking in small arms, unilaterally abandoned the Antiballistic Missile Treaty, and refused to ratify the treaty creating the International Criminal Court. Such self-righteous hubris does not add to the authority of the nation that purports to be the world's model for moral and intellectual leadership. Our military incursions have been based on *our* definition of what is right and *our* declaration that *we* know what is best for the rest of the world. As *The New York Times* editorializes, "This is not a productive role for the world's leading country and the architect of much of the international law created over the last half-century. Contempt for the concerns of other countries will only erode American influence."[11]

The Initial Steps

Shortly after the United Nations was created, H. G. Wells wrote, "Whatever be the fate of the United Nations, there can be little question that the attainment of a federation of all humanity, together with a sufficient measure of social justice, to ensure health, education, and a rough equality of opportunity to most of the children born into the world, would mean such a release and increase of human energy as to open a new phase in human history."[12] Isolationist cries to the contrary, the time has come to accept that we are one people inhabiting this planet.

Today, there are hundreds of international organizations of one kind or another: the United Nations, the North Atlantic Treaty Organization, the

International Court of Justice at the Hague, the North American Free Trade Agreement, the World Bank, the European Union, the World Trade Organization, the International Monetary Fund, numerous U.N. agencies, multinational pacts, regional alliances, economic unions, non-governmental groups, and on and on. Not all these agencies are functioning perfectly. Not all espouse the same humanitarian or liberal agenda. But they do exist. Objectives change as needs are redefined. For instance, an expanding NATO now functions more as a political entity than as a mutual defense alliance—serving as a forum for America and Europe on issues ranging from stabilization of the Balkans to the modernization of Central Asia. The infrastructure is in place.

These are all mutual associations wherein the individual member states have agreed to certain deliberate limitations on their sovereignty in order to forge a stronger and more secure world community—as opposed to those kingdoms of past millennia which relied upon religious or military dominance to hold together a global empire by force. These instances of nations coming together voluntarily for the greater good are not unlike the original thirteen colonies which, after trying to work together under the loose Articles of Confederation, finally agreed to surrender much of their sovereignty in order to establish the United States of America as one nation.

Even as we watch the efforts of small ethnic enclaves (Basques, Gypsies, or Kurds) trying to break away from the political states that contain them, we also see movements towards multinational pacts growing into real political unions. Colin Nickerson of *The Boston Globe* writes of the gradual economic fusing of the United States and Canada: "Notions once dismissed as the paranoid fantasies of Canadian ultranationalists—an end to border controls, the U.S. dollar as common currency, the undercutting of Canada's tax codes and cherished social policies to align with those of the superpower next door—are now bandied about as the way of the future in corporate strategy sessions and policy thinkfests."[13] For all practical purposes, nothing separates the two countries but irrelevant nationalistic pride. Nickerson continues, "Many U.S.-Canada watchers are convinced that formal divides between the countries will vanish within a decade or two, the border becoming just a mark on the map."[14] Better yet, why not include Mexico and form the United States of North America?

THROUGHOUT THE BOOK SEVERAL THEMES HAVE EMERGED. Democracy is an intellectual idea; it can be sustained only by a population that has the intellectual tools to make decisions and the determination to act responsibly. We must have a system of ethics and values, humanistic in nature but based on an underlying faith in transcendental and religious values. Runaway population growth must be brought under control; the environment must be protected; a steady-state economic system will eventually be set into place. And there must be recognition of the interrelatedness of our little blue planet. To continue with the globe split into 200 separate sovereign realms is suicidal.

With our concerns about an apathetic citizenry, amorality, runaway technology, environmental devastation, predatory greed, and all the other symptoms of the Progress Paradox, let us not overlook this crucial fact: The United States of America is the most successful system of government ever conceived on this planet. The United States of Earth will be even a greater accomplishment. Francis Fukuyama rhetorically asks if critics of the Enlightenment were right that anarchy was the inevitable product of the modern thrust, and then he responds, "The answer, in my view, is no, for the very simple reason that we human beings are by nature designed to create moral rules and social order for ourselves."[15]

Many of the ideas and proposals suggested in these final chapters may seem too outrageous and preposterous for serious consideration. Restructure higher education? Eliminate tax breaks for large families? Stop growing? Place a limit on salaries? Promote world federalism? Before replying with a knee-jerk, *We could never seriously consider such suggestions,* stop and think about them. These are fantastic times we are facing. And they demand some drastic rethinking.

What would it take for us *Homo sapiens* to see ourselves as citizens of the Planet Earth—rather than as Brazilians, Ethiopians, Koreans, Texans, or Maori? Try to visualize a world without military borders, a planet where freedom and equal opportunity are made available to all peoples, a globe where mankind's energies can be focused on humanitarian relief, medical progress, and economic equality—rather than on military confrontations and petty squabbling over lines on a map. Visualize a planet where all men and women can live and work and play together with respect for their cultural diversity. This is an intellectual vision. A vision that can become reality if we but determine to reclaim our intellectual heritage. If we decide that we will structure our affairs with reason and act with responsibility.

Notes

INTRODUCTION

1. *Post-Intellectualism and the Decline of Democracy: The Failure of Reason and Responsibility in the Twentieth Century* (Westport, CT: Greenwood/Praeger, 1996). Those who have read that book will forgive me if I go over some familiar material. In fact, the discerning reader will find a few passages reprinted from the earlier work (although not many).

2. Obviously the seeds were planted much earlier, in the days of classical Greece and the Roman Empire, but it was during the Enlightenment that the idea of modern liberal democracy took hold.

3. Saul, 1992, p. 17.

4. Hardin, 1993, p. 5.

CHAPTER 1

1. Numerous critics and social observers could be cited. Here are three. In the *Decline of the West*, written in 1918, Oswald Spengler wrote, "The future of the West is not a limitless tending upwards and onwards for all time towards our present ideals, but a single phenomenon of history, strictly limited and defined as to form and duration, which covers a few centuries . . ." (Spengler [1918], 1991, pp. 29–30).

One of the most clear-sighted of our cultural critics was the sociologist Pitirim A. Sorokin who wrote in 1941, "The present crisis is not ordinary but extraordinary. It is not merely an economic or political maladjustment, but . . . it is a crisis involving almost the whole way of life, thought, and conduct of Western society. More precisely, it consists in a disintegration of a fundamental form of Western culture and society dominant for the last four centuries" (Sorokin, 1941, pp. 16–17).

Jacques Barzun opens his monumental *From Dawn to Decadence* with the statement that as the twentieth century comes to an end, "a wider and deeper scrutiny is needed to see that in the West the culture of the last 500 years is ending at the same time." (Barzun, 2000, p. ix.)

2. Thoreau [1854], 1942, p. 30.

3. One report, by psychologist Martin Seligman, concluded that "the rate of depression over the last two generations has increased roughly tenfold." (Seligman, 1988, p. 50.)

4. The number of children born to unwed mothers climbs each year. In 1970 the percentage of babies born to single mothers was 10.7 percent. In 1980 it was 18.4 percent. In 1990 it was 28 percent. And in 2000 the figure was 33.2 percent.

5. See Phillips, 2002, p. 167.

6. By contrast, J. P. Morgan decreed that the chief executives of his companies should be paid no more than twenty times the lowest worker's pay. (See Phillips, 2002, p. 395.)

7. See Allan Sloan, "The Brainteaser of Deficit Math," *Newsweek*, 8 September 2003, p. 37.

8. Naisbitt, 1984, p. 25.

9. For an extended discussion, see Wood, *Post-Intellectualism*, 1996, pp. 69–70.

10. Functional illiteracy is defined as the inability to handle such tasks as addressing a letter, filling out a job-application form, reading the warnings on a pesticide can, or understanding a want ad.

11. See Fukuyama, 1999, pp. 55–56.

12. Within the space of a few months, questions were raised about the works of Stephen Ambrose, Michael Bellesiles, Joseph Ellis, Doris Kearns Goodwin, and David McCullough.

13. Berman, 2000, p. 1.

14. Ibid., pp. 159–160.

15. Wilson, 1998, p. 6.

16. Crowther, 1995, p. 2.

CHAPTER 2

1. Milton [1644], 1952, p. 409.

2. Barzun, 2000, p. 362.

3. Kurt Vonnegut, *God Bless You, Dr. Kevorkian* (New York: Seven Stories Press, 1999), p. 9.

4. Hardin, 1993, p. 23.

5. Fukuyama, 1992, p. 4.

6. Ibid., p. xi. In support of this theory of Universal History, and the ultimate triumph of liberal democracy, Fukuyama points out that even most totalitarian states and military dictatorships today say that they are holding on to power *only until the people are ready to vote and assume responsibility for self-government.* In other words, even the autocrats concede that ultimate political legitimacy lies with some sort of representative government.

7. Wilson, 1998, p. 8.

CHAPTER 3

1. Tocqueville [1835], 1956, p. 103.

2. For a mnemonic reminder of these four concepts, I think of my Danish

friend, LARS—Liberal arts, Acquisition of knowledge, Rational problem-solving, and Social criticism.

3. Quoted in Berman, 2000, p. 122.

4. *Random House Webster's College Dictionary* (New York: Random House).

5. Bennahum, 1998.

6. *Encarta World English Dictionary* (New York: St. Martin's Press).

7. The "Reflective Thinking Pattern" is loosely based on John Dewey's *How We Think* (New York: D.C. Heath & Company, 1933). This pattern is the starting point for the Analytic Thinking Pattern described in this chapter.

8. For a detailed examination of this process, see Wood, *Designing the Effective Message: Critical Thinking and Communication*, 1996, Chapter 3.

9. For mnemonic assistance, think of how to *POSE* a problem: Problem, Objectives, Solutions, and Evaluation.

10. Lincoln, 1958.

11. Berman, 2000, p. 55.

12. Barrett, 1958, p. 17.

13. Mill [1859], 1952, p. 294.

14. Crowther, 2000.

15. Quoted in William Ophuls, "Locke's Paradigm Lost: The Environmental Crisis and Collapse of Laissez Faire Politics." Paper presented at the 1973 Annual Meeting of the American Political Science Association, New Orleans, September 1973.

CHAPTER 4

1. Postman, 1999, pp. 68–69.

2. Paraphrased in Best and Kellner, 1997, p. 7.

3. Technology consultant George Rebane writes: "The important point here is that some time in the 1980s scientists began to admit that there exist domains of human knowledge and understanding that will *never* be informed by science. This is an enormous blow and arguably the *coup de grace* to the Enlightenment mind" (Personal correspondence, 3 April 2002).

4. Van Iten, personal communication, 8 December 2000.

5. Postman, 1999, p. 71.

6. Wallace Jackson, personal correspondence, 29 June 2000.

7. Wilson, 1998, p. 214.

8. Barzun, 2000, p. 725.

9. Best and Kellner, 1997, p. 146.

10. Ibid., p. 179.

11. John 8:32.

12. Breen, 2000.

13. Berman, 2000, p. 50.

14. Gray, 1995, p. 146.

15. Ibid., p. viii.

16. In describing the proliferation of "junk courses" on college campuses today, critic John Leo notes, "The junk courses creep in because much of the professoriate now believes that nothing can truly be known, so nothing truly matters" (John Leo, "The New Trivial Pursuit," *U.S. News & World Report*, 30 August 1999, p. 20).

17. Personal correspondence, 29 June 2000.
18. Quoted in Crowther, 1995, p. xvi.

CHAPTER 5

1. For mnemonic assistance, think of the other *SIDE* of the equation (**S**peciali-zation, **I**gnorance, **D**umbth, and **E**stablishmentism).
2. Saul, 1992, p. 121.
3. Wilson, 1998, pp. 38–39.
4. Taken from a famous 1959 essay entitled "The Two Cultures and the Sci-entific Revolution," quoted in Wilson, 1998, p. 126.
5. Adam Smith, *Lectures on Jurisprudence* (Indianapolis: Liberty Classics, 1982), p. 541.
6. The survey, sponsored by the American Council of Trustees and Alumni, was given to 556 randomly selected college seniors by the Center for Survey Re-search and Analysis at the University of Connecticut in early 2000.
7. From the Associated Press, "Only 25% of American Adults Get Passing Grades in Science Survey, " *Los Angeles Times*, 24 May 1996, p. A22.
8. Berry, 1977, p. 20.
9. Quoted in Rick Vanderknyff, "Creating Drama with History in One Easy Lesson," *Los Angeles Times*, 23 March 1994, p. E6.
10. T. S. Eliot, *The Rock*, 1934.
11. Gearino, 2000, p. 25A.
12. Einstein, 1994, pp. 160–61.
13. Adams, 1996, p. 2.
14. Allen, 1989, p. 15. Steve Allen updated this book with the revised title, *Dumbth: The Lost Art of Thinking With 101 Ways to Reason Better and Improve Your Mind* (Buffalo, NY: Prometheus Books, 1998).
15. Mill [1859], 1952, p. 292.
16. Mill defines the essence of establishmentism in terms of conformity and preserving one's public image: people "ask themselves, what is suitable to my position? what is usually done by persons of my station and pecuniary circum-stances? or (worse still) what is usually done by persons of a station and circum-stances superior to mine? . . . It does not occur to them to have any inclination, except for what is customary." (Mill [1859], 1952, p. 296.)
17. Postman and Weingartner, 1969, p. 24.
18. Sullivan, 2001, p. 46.
19. Jacoby, 1987, pp. 107, 108.

CHAPTER 6

1. Stavrianos, 1982, p. 9.
2. We must be careful in using the terms *libertarian* or *liberal* in a political sense. Our definition of intellectualism (or, sometimes, *liberalism*) can encompass both a liberal (left-leaning) political outlook and a conservative (right-leaning) political position. The intellectual is one who is open to questioning the establishment—whether the ensuing response is to continue the status quo (the conservative) or to try a new approach (the liberal). Properly speaking, anyone with an open mind

represents a liberal or intellectual mindset. The closed-minded individual will be considered the non-intellectual—both the right-wing pre-intellectual reactionary and the left-wing post-intellectual radical.

3. Not all "progress" toward the modern lifestyle has necessarily been positive. Noted physiologist Jared Diamond refers to agriculture as "the worst mistake in the history of the human race." He writes that "with agriculture came the gross social and sexual inequality, the disease and despotism, that curse our existence." (Diamond, 1987, p. 64.) He proceeds to build a strong argument that we never have been up to the intellectual task we undertook when we started walking behind the plow.

4. Barzun, 2000, p. 714.

5. For example, we are taking down numerous hydroelectric dams in order to restore natural ecosystems; at the same time, our national energy policy calls for the building of more hydroelectric dams. *Whatever.*

6. Endicott, 1998, p. 38.

7. McLuhan and Fiore, 1967, p. 48.

8. See McLuhan, 1964.

9. Sorokin, 1941, p. 19.

10. Ibid., pp. 19–20.

11. Ibid., p. 20.

12. Postman, 1992, p. 23.

13. Ibid., p. 45.

14. Ibid., p. 52.

15. Mander, 1991, p. 51.

CHAPTER 7

1. See Foster, 1983, and Ebert, 1996.

2. Best and Kellner, 1997, p. 137.

3. Ibid.

4. In *Post-Intellectualism and the Decline of Democracy* (1996), I labeled this aspect of post-intellectualism as "Distended Intellectualism." However, I believe the term *hyper-intellectualism* more clearly conveys the intent and thrust of the phenomenon.

5. Fukuyama, 1992, p. 244.

6. Toulmin, 1990, p. 167.

7. Ibid., p. 168.

8. Ibid., p. 167.

9. Fukuyama, 1992, p. 83.

10. See Nicholas Kristof, "Taking Religion on Faith," *Raleigh News & Observer,* 17 August 2003, p. 27A.

11. FitzGerald, 1979, p. 171.

12. Putnam, 2000, p. 72.

13. Ibid., p. 76.

14. Postman, 1985, p. 51.

15. Shlain, 1998, p. 72.

16. Berlin, 1997, p. 267.

17. See David Bennahum's discussion of *Technorealism,* 1998.

18. Fukuyama, 1999, p. 80.

CHAPTER 8

1. Fukuyama, 1992, p. xxi.
2. Herbert Spencer, "The Americans" in *Essays*, 1891.
3. Quinn, 1999, p. 171.
4. For an extended discussion of degradation of the gene pool, see Wood, *Post-Intellectualism*, 1996, pp. 52–54.
5. Hofstadter, 1963, p. 233.
6. Mander, 1978, p. 45.
7. Allen, 2001, p. 86.
8. Figures are from the Congressional Budget Office. See Phillips, 2002, p. 137.
9. Rousseau [1762], book 2, ch. 11, 1952, p. 405n.
10. Lasch, 1978, p. 145.
11. George Will, "Writing Isn't Taught Anymore," *Honolulu Advertiser*, 3 July 1995, p. A10.
12. Postman, 1985, p. 135.
13. Smith [1776], 1952, p. 340.
14. Al Koning, personal correspondence, 25 August 2000.

CHAPTER 9

1. Capra, 1982, p. 201.
2. Gleick, 2001, p. 64.
3. For a delightful and overwhelming account of the television torrent of trivia, see Bill McKibben, *The Age of Missing Information*.
4. Postman, 1985, p. 77.
5. Cited in Moyers, 1989, p. 182.
6. Wurman, 1989, p. 37.
7. The term *blip culture* comes from futurist Alvin Toffler who wrote: "On a personal level, we are all besieged and blitzed by fragments of imagery, contradictory or unrelated, that shake up our old ideas and come shooting at us in the form of broken or disembodied 'blips.' We live, in fact, in a 'blip culture.'" (Toffler, 1980, p. 165.)
8. Quoted in René Dubos, "The Despairing Optimist," *The American Scholar*, Winter 1974–75, p. 8.
9. Gleick, 2001, p. 62.
10. Quoted in W. Stanley Jevons, *The Coal Question*, 2nd ed. (London: Macmillan, 1866), p. 331.
11. George Johnson, "This Time, the Future Is Closer Than You Think," *The New York Times*, 31 December 2000, section 4, pp. 1, 4.
12. Crichton, 2002, p. 6.
13. Bart Kosko, "Brain-Implant Chips Will Upstage 'A. I.,'" *Raleigh News & Observer*, 18 July 2001, p. 17A.
14. Lemley, "Machines That Think," 2001, p. 79.
15. Charles Krauthammer, "A Surgeon General Who Grasps the Future," *Raleigh News & Observer*, 29 April 2001, p. 29A.
16. See Justin Gillis, "Scientists to Attempt Creation of New Life Form," *Raleigh News & Observer*, 21 November 2002, p. 8A.

17. The interview was released in early September 2001 for the newsmagazine *Focus*. See the AP release at <http://sns.dailypress.com/news/nationworld/sns-ap-a.i.-humans0901sep01.story?coll = sns-newsnation-headlines>.

18. Quoted in Crichton, 2002, p. 8.

CHAPTER 10

1. Berlin, 1997, p. 243.
2. Best and Kellner, 1997, p. 28.
3. Ibid., p. 28.
4. Plato (1942), book 8, p. 453.
5. Wilson, 1998, p. 35.
6. Quoted in Berlin, 1997, p. 258.
7. Quoted in Barrett, 1958, pp. 111–112.
8. Davis and Schleifer explain that the Marxist literary critic demonstrates "the dehumanizing and fragmenting effect of capitalist culture and, further, [shows] how a modernist novel can promote the acceptance of underlying social principles and values" (Davis and Schleifer, 1989, p. 370).
9. Barrett, 1958, p. 28.
10. Zakaria, "Why Do They Hate Us?" 2001, p. 29.
11. Spong, 1998, p. 37.
12. Spong also points out the impact that Freud had on established religious thinking: "Freud brought to consciousness the infantile nature of so much of the language of the Christian religion, which had portrayed believers as children dependent upon the good favor of the divine heavenly father figure. He exposed the neurotic elements in religion, the childlike desire to win divine reward and to avoid divine punishment" (Spong, 1998, p. 38).
13. One 1991 survey indicated that about 40 percent of the American populace believed that "God created man pretty much in his own image at one time during the last ten thousand years" (cited in Winchester, 2001, p. 15 [footnote]). Winchester goes on to add, "and anecdotal evidence now suggests that this number is climbing."
14. Ehrenfeld, 1978, pp. 16–18.
15. Sanneh, 2001.
16. Saul, 1992, p. 17.
17. Lukacs, 1984, p. 7.

CHAPTER 11

1. Although we commonly refer to *The Sixties* as if this were a cleanly delineated ten-year period bracketed by years ending in zero, it should be recognized that this period started in the late 1950s and lasted well into the 1970s. If you want specific dates, let's arbitrarily pick 1955 (the year of Rosa Parks's bus ride) and 1974 (the year of Richard Nixon's resignation). For convenience, I shall continue to use *The Sixties* as a shorthand for this twenty-year period.

2. See, for example, John Kenneth Galbraith, *American Capitalism: The Concept of Countervailing Power*, 1956; William J. Lederer, *A Nation of Sheep*, 1961; C. Wright Mills, *The Power Elite*, 1956; David Riesman, *The Lonely Crowd*, 1950; and William H. Whyte, Jr., *The Organization Man*, 1956.

3. Farewell radio and television address, 17 January 1961.
4. Brokaw, 1998, p. 11.
5. See Toffler, 1980, p. 10.
6. Gleick, 1999, pp. 9, 10.
7. Linton Weeks, "We Do Everything At Once, But Are We Forgetting Something?" *Raleigh News & Observer*, 25 July 1999, p. 5D.
8. Shari Lewis with Lan O'Kun (Garden City, NY: Doubleday, 1982).
9. Wilson, 1998, p. 271.
10. Historian J. H. Plumb writes "There was no separate world of childhood. Children shared the same games with adults, the same toys, the same fairy stories. They lived their lives together, never apart." (Quoted in Postman, 1988, "The Disappearance of Childhood," pp. 149–50.)
11. Postman, 1999, p. 124.

CHAPTER 12

1. See McLuhan, 1964, Chapter 1.
2. McLuhan and Fiore, 1967, p. 8.
3. Shlain, 1998, pp. 71–72.
4. Ong, 1982, p. 184.
5. Crossman, 1999, p. 42.
6. Bradbury [1953], 1991, p. 84.
7. Ibid., p. 55.
8. Postman, 1985, p. 92.
9. Cornish, 1999, pp. 11–12.
10. There are several problems with much of the discussion regarding violence and the media. First, many studies show that violence on TV may trigger aggression. But aggression (which is actually an intellectual attribute) is not necessarily the same as antisocial violence. Second, it is easy to mistake *correlation* for *causation*. Many studies show that youngsters who watch an inordinate amount of violence on TV are violent or aggressive—there is a correlation. But which is the cause and which is the effect? Third, it is easy to point to copycat crimes (*modeling theory*), but we must ask what price we are willing to pay in order to make sure that a few unbalanced individuals are not exposed to any suggestive behavior in the media that might trigger a violent outburst. Let's start by censoring all Shakespeare and all fairy tales—they can get pretty gruesome. For a detailed discussion of the arguments condemning violence in the media, see Wood, *Post-Intellectualism*, 1996, pp. 177–182.
11. Medved, 1992, p. 243.
12. Much of the classic research conducted by Pennsylvania State University's George Gerbner over the years has dealt with what he has labeled the "mean world syndrome." His studies have shown repeatedly that people who view a lot of television tend to see the world as a much more hostile and mean place than do people who watch less television.
13. Meredith, 1999, p. 29.
14. Postman, 1985, p. 62.
15. Meredith, 1999, p. 29.

CHAPTER 13

1. Mill [1859], 1952, p. 295.

2. Ibid.

3. Rand [1943], 1993, pp. 682–683.

4. Fukuyama, 1992, p. 315.

5. Attributed to an interview in *Playboy*, March 1969.

6. Watchdogs, such as James X. Dempsey of the Center for Democracy and Technology, point out that "The FBI is placing a black box inside the computer network of an ISP [Internet Service Provider], [and] not even the ISP knows exactly what that gizmo is doing." Quoted at <http://www.stopcarnivore.org/>.

7. See William Safire, "Not a Lifelong Friend," *Raleigh News & Observer*, 6 June 2003, p. 15A.

8. Rosen, 2001, p. 41.

9. Ibid., p. 42.

10. Quoted in Anthony Lewis, "War That Puts Liberty At Risk," *Raleigh News & Observer*, 12 March 2002, p. 13A.

11. Rosen, 2000, p. 51.

12. Quoted in Rosen, 2002, p. 49.

13. Rosen, 2002, p. 51.

14. Ibid.

15. The statement, by the cofounder of Sun Microsystems, was at a Stanford University forum entitled *Will Spiritual Robots Replace Humanity by 2100?* (Quoted in Cave, 2000.)

CHAPTER 14

1. Zakaria, "Why Do They Hate Us?" 2001, p. 22.

2. Raspberry, 1999.

3. Allen, 2001, p. 73.

4. Cheshire, 2001, p. 57.

5. In 2000, Eminem released his album, *The Marshall Mathers LP*. One reviewer, Jim Fleming, writes that "Listeners will find they are constantly subjected to explicit details regarding acts of violence against women. . . . Numerous sexual perversions such as sodomy, incest, bestiality, and sexual abuse with a tire iron are also part of this heinous tripe that some call art." The full review is available at <www.gradingthemovies.com/html/music/eminem_mathers.shtml>.

6. Quoted in Tassel, 1999, p. 66.

7. Spong, 1998, p. 40.

8. Postman, 1992, p. 160.

9. Quoted in Ellwood, 2001, p. 17.

10. Berman, 2000, p. 49.

11. George Will, "Dignity For Sale on America's Auction Block," *Raleigh News & Observer*, 15 February 2001, p. 15A.

12. Oliver Stone and Stanley Weiser, screenwriters; Oliver Stone, producer and director; *Wall Street*, 1987. The film was released by Twentieth Century Fox.

13. Quoted in "Enron Report Details Greed, 'Overreaching,'" *Raleigh News & Observer*, 3 February 2002, p. 8A.

14. Paul Krugman, "Classic Case of System Failure," *Raleigh News & Observer*, 20 January 2002, p. 29A.

15. Ibid.

16. See Berenson, 2002, p. 1.

17. Warren E. Buffet, "Getting to the Bottom Line," *Raleigh News & Observer*, 25 July 2002, p. 13A.

18. Paddy Chayefsky, screenwriter; Howard Gottfried, producer; Sidney Lumet, director; *Network*, 1976. The film was released by Metro-Goldwyn-Mayer.

19. See Bill Mann, "The Threat of Bad Consumer Debt," *The Fool on the Hill*, 19 January 2001. For the full text, see <http://www.fool.com/news/foth/2001/foth010119.htm>.

20. Russell, *Principles of Social Reconstruction*, 1917.

21. Rushkoff, 1999.

CHAPTER 15

1. For a brief discussion of these and other alternatives to rational problem-solving, see Wood, *Designing the Effective Message: Critical Thinking and Communication*, 1996, p. 47.

2. Gearino, 2000, p. 25A.

3. Ong, 1982, p. 189.

4. Toulmin, 1990, p. 12.

5. This is the theme of John Ralston Saul's *Voltaire's Bastards: The Dictatorship of Reason in the West* (1992). He documents in painstaking detail how we have used rational means to pursue morally questionable ends—gaining political power, waging warfare, and exploiting our natural resources.

6. Barrett, 1958, p. 239.

7. Bernard Avishai, quoted in *Discover*, September 2000, p. 18.

8. For instance, the falsehood that 4,000 Jews were warned not to go to the World Trade Center on September 11 was a fabrication that was spread entirely over the Internet—and is still widely believed throughout much of the Muslim world.

9. Daly, 1977, p. 7.

10. Roszak, 1994, p. xlvi.

11. Unintended consequences abound in all areas: the early adoption of Thalidomide, Fen phen, and human growth hormones; the evolution of superbugs; nuclear wastes; major forest fires as a result of suppressing smaller fires; the potential of the Y2K crisis; gasoline additives such as MTBE (methyl tertiary butyl ether) leading to future pollution; and we are just beginning to see some of the unanticipated results of animal cloning.

12. In looking at any program to increase traffic flow (for example, by widening highways), we conveniently do not consider costs such as environmental damage from increased petroleum usage, added insurance premiums, additional law enforcement burdens, taxes to support the accompanying bureaucracy, and so forth.

13. Mill [1859], 1952, p. 292.

14. Quoted in Wurman, 1989, p. 39.

CHAPTER 16

1. Genesis 1:28.
2. Quoted in Daly, 1977, p. 2.
3. For documentation, see the annual Worldwatch Institute's *State of the World* reports, edited by Lester Brown. See also Robert D. Kaplan's *The Coming Anarchy*; Eugene Linden's *The Future In Plain Sight*; and Martin Ree's *Our Final Hour: A Scientist's Warning*.
4. Quoted in Hardin, 1993, p. 191. Even earlier, Rufus Miles had written, "Anyone who believes that exponential growth can go on forever is either a madman or an economist." (Miles, 1976, p. 11.)
5. Gray, 1995, pp. 107–108.
6. Commission on Population Growth and the American Future, 1972, p. 1. The Commission (appointed by Richard Nixon) continued its summation in *Population and the American Future*: "Our country can no longer afford the uncritical acceptance of the population growth ethic that 'more is better'."
7. "Environment: Nasty, Brutish, and Dirty." *Discover*, February 1999, p. 30.
8. Hardin, 1985.
9. See Malthus (1798), 1965, pp. 139–140.
10. For a more detailed discussion of hyper-urbanization, see Wood, *Post-Intellectualism*, 1996, Chapter 9.
11. Spengler [1918], 1991, p. 249.
12. Braile, 2000.
13. See McClintock, 2000, p. 65. See also Powell, 2000, p. 54. Wilson estimates conservatively that we are losing 27,000 species a year. See Manning, 1999, p. 178.
14. See Braile, 2000.
15. Turney, 2002.
16. Ibid.
17. Fisher and Fisher, 2001, p. 57.
18. President Bush's environmental insensitivity was readily apparent. Shortly after he took office, he had issued a gag order on overseas population-control counseling that might mention the possibility of abortion, weakened arsenic standards in drinking water, loosened standards for carbon dioxide emissions by power plants, renounced the Kyoto Protocol on global warming, imposed a ban on private lawsuits to add new entries to the endangered species list, loosened controls on toxic runoff from mining sites, announced support for additional logging roads in 58 million acres of national forest land, proposed oil exploration in the Arctic National Wildlife Refuge, taken steps to abolish the White House Council on Environmental Quality, and proposed reducing the EPA budget by over six percent. All this in just 75 days.

CHAPTER 17

1. McLuhan, 1964, p. 87.
2. Jefferson's letter to Francis Hopkinson, 13 March 1789, reprinted in Peterson, 1975, p. 435.
3. Quoted in Whyte, 1956, p. 59.
4. Sullivan, 2001, p. 47.

5. Wiesel, 2002, p. 5.

6. Zakaria, "Why Do They Hate Us?" 2001, p. 24.

7. Sullivan, 2001, p. 45.

8. Postman, 1999, p. 113.

9. Isaacs, 1975, p. 25.

10. Address to the NAACP (Baltimore, MD), 10 July 2000.

11. President John F. Kennedy's Executive Order Number 10,925 required all employers who were government contractors to "take affirmative action to ensure that the applicants are employed, and that employees are treated during employment without regard to race, creed, color, or national origin." Nothing was said initially about numerical ratios, equal balance, or racial quotas. That all came later.

12. Address to the Duke Institute for Learning in Retirement (Durham, NC), 10 September 2000.

13. The Southern Poverty Law Center is actively tracking more than 500 designated hate groups. The Simon Wiesenthal Center says it has found more than 2,000 hate sites on the Internet.

14. Thomas L. Friedman, "A Traveler to Saudi Arabia," *The New York Times*, 24 February 2002, section 4, p. 13.

15. Samuelson, 2001.

16. McLuhan and Fiore, 1967, p. 63.

17. McLuhan, 1964, p. 263.

18. See Richard Reeves, "Fighting the Good Fight, for Peace on Earth," *Raleigh News & Observer*, 10 March 2001, p. 18A.

19. Quinn, 1999, p. 185.

CHAPTER 18

1. Tocqueville [1835], 1956, p. 156.

2. Rousseau [1762] (book 1, ch. 4), 1952, p. 389.

3. Benjamin Franklin, *Historical Review of Pennsylvania*, 1759.

4. Zakaria, "Why Do They Hate Us?" 2001, p. 30.

5. George Will, "Blair's Universal Soldiers," *Raleigh News & Observer*, 19 August 2003, p. 9A.

6. Postman, 1999, pp. 144–145.

7. Ibid., p. 150.

8. See Diane Ravitch, "Dumbing Down Our Civic Debate," *Raleigh News & Observer*, 27 December 2000, p. 13A.

9. Lederer, 1961, p. 183.

10. Smith [1776] (Book 5, Ch. 1, Part 3, Article II), 1952, pp. 340–341.

11. Postman, 1985, p. vii.

12. Rousseau [1762] (book 2, ch. 9), 1952, p. 403.

13. Plato, "Republic" (Book. VI), 1942, p. 379.

14. Speech to the Electors of Bristol, 3 November 1774.

15. Meyrowitz, 1985, p. 166.

16. Lukacs, 1984, p. 7.

17. Kaplan, 2000, p. 93.

18. Bruce J. Schulman, "Is the Business of America Business?" *The New York Times*, 13 May 2001, section 4, p. 4.

19. Only Mel Martinez (Department of Housing and Urban Affairs) and Rod Paige (Department of Education) did not have strong corporate ties.

20. Robert B. Reich, "Corporate Power in Overdrive," *The New York Times*, 18 March 2001, section 4, p. 13.

CHAPTER 19

1. Wells [1920], 1956, p. 942.

2. Wilson, 1998, p. 238.

3. Ibid., p. 247.

4. Spengler [1918], 1991, p. 209.

5. Tocqueville [1835], 1956, p. 47.

6. Fukuyama, 1992, p. 326.

7. Quoted in Harold Koenig and Karl Giberson, "The Great Scientist's Faith," *Raleigh News & Observer*, 14 March 2002, p. 21A.

8. From Diogenes Laertius, *Lives and Opinions of Eminent Philosophers* (book IX, section 8).

9. Rousseau [1762] (book 1, ch. 8), 1952, p. 393.

10. Zakaria, "The End of the End of History," 2001.

11. Spengler [1918], 1991, p. 346.

12. Wilson, 1998, p. 33.

13. Stein, 2001, p. 36.

14. "The Left in Western Europe," *The Economist*, 11 June 1994, p. 19.

15. Putnam, 2000, p. 19.

16. Ellul, 1964, p. xxix.

CHAPTER 20

1. For details see the Character Counts Web site: <http://www.charactercounts. org>.

2. Andrew Ferguson, "Character Goes Back to School." *Time*, 24 May 1999, p. 68.

3. Postman, 1999, p. 98.

4. From an address to Phi Beta Kappa members, excerpted in "Money Isn't the Value of Education," *Raleigh News & Observer*, 24 October 2000, p. 11A.

5. Postman offers five steps to the teaching of critical thinking: teach children how to ask questions; beef up the teaching of formal *logic* (scientific and critical thinking) and *rhetoric* (especially semantics); develop a scientific mindset, a critical, questioning habit of perceiving and wondering; stress *technology education*, the impact of technological determinism; and institute the study of comparative religions. (See Postman, 1999, pp. 161–164.)

6. See Postman's *The End of Education* for ten principles of technological education that should be included in the school curriculum. (Postman, 1996, pp. 192–193.)

7. Lawrence Grossberg, "Higher Education: Accept No Substitute," *Raleigh News & Observer*, 26 March 2000, p. 29A.

8. At one time, I was teaching in the School of Communication and Professional Studies at California State University, Northridge, where the curricula of our nine

different departments were dictated by more than twenty-five different professional associations and accrediting agencies.

9. Soley, 1995, p. 5. See also Eliot Marshall, "When Commerce and Academe Collide," *Science*, 13 April 1990, p. 152.

10. Soley, 1995, p. 145.

11. Some sort of remedial "special education" institutional structure would obviously have to be established for the truly incorrigibles and educationally retarded.

12. Jeanne Meister, president of Corporate University Xchange, Inc., reports that there are in existence more than 1,600 organizations titled "corporate universities" and that this number will shortly rise to over 2,000. See *Vision: The Technology Source*, available at <http://horizon.unc.edu/TS/vision/2000-07.asp>.

13. Herman, 2000, p. 16.

14. Buchen, 2000, p. 34.

15. William Raspberry, "Hunting Up Equal Resources for Equal Students," *Raleigh News & Observer*, 6 April 2001, p. 17A. The innovative "Michigan Plan," for example, reduced the dependence on local property taxes for school funding from 65 percent to 20 percent. In so doing, local property taxes were cut by $400 million, yet with a two-cent boost in the state sales tax, school funding was increased by $300 million.

16. According to the National Center for Education Statistics, in 1998–99 the average per pupil expenditures in New Jersey and New York were $10,233 and 9,970 respectively; in Utah and Mississippi the figures were $4,256 and 4,575.

CHAPTER 21

1. For a quick overview and World Wide Web portal to more than 600 links and 80,000 documents concerning alternative energy sources, see the Department of Energy's Renewable Energy Network at <http://www.eren.doe.gov/>.

2. See Daly, 1977, pp. 61–68.

3. Economist Herman Daly spelled out a quarter-century ago a detailed proposal for both a tax on pollution and a depletion quota. (See Daly, 1977, Chapter 3, "Institutions for a Steady-State Economy.")

4. Wilson, "The Bottleneck," 2002, p. 85.

5. Ibid., p. 86. See also Hardin, 1993, pp. 57–60.

6. Hardin, 1993, p. 309.

7. Malthus [1820], 1836, p. 227.

8. See Burke, 2000.

9. Wilson, "The Bottleneck," 2002, p. 88.

10. Mill [1859], 1952, p. 319.

11. Fletcher, 1991, p. 4.

12. As Jerry Mander facetiously states the position, "Space is the answer. Use up this planet; go find another." (Mander, 1991, p. 145.) Examination of the exponential mathematics involved reveals that such a scheme would result in our colonizing every possible planet in the Milky Way in less than 2,000 years—assuming that each of the 100 billion stars in our galaxy has a solar system with at least one habitable planet, that each world will have a maximum population of six billion persons, and that our human population will keep doubling every fifty

years. (In 500 years we will have doubled ten times; that's a one-thousand-fold increase. In 1500 years, thirty doublings, we will have increased the population one billion times. Do the math yourself.) Also we have to assume the whole enterprise is indeed practicable from an economic and engineering standpoint. At the present rate of population growth we would need to send over 200,000 people into space every day!

13. See Hardin, 1993, p. 272.
14. Abbey, 1988, p. 67.
15. See Boulding, 1964, p. 136.
16. Daly, 1977, p. 75.
17. Mill [1859], 1952, p. 319.
18. Hardin, 1993, p. 187.

CHAPTER 22

1. Heilbroner, 1980, p. 77.
2. Daly, 1977, p. 3.
3. For a detailed technical description of how a steady-state system would work, see Daly, 1977, Chapter 2, "The Concept of a Steady-State Economy."
4. Quoted in Hardin, 1993, p. 118.
5. Quoted on *ABC World News with Peter Jennings,* 10 August 1999.
6. Isaiah 5:8.
7. Personal correspondence, 11 December 2000.
8. Allan Sloan, "The Jury's In: Greed Isn't Good," *Newsweek,* 24 June 2002, p. 37.
9. George Will, "A Chance to Fix the System," *Raleigh News & Observer,* 17 January 2002, p. 15A.
10. Daly, 1977, p. 54.
11. Jonathan Swift, "Thoughts on Various Subjects," in G. B. Woods, et al., eds., *The Literature of England.* (Glenview, IL: Scott, Foresman, 1958), p. 1003.
12. Quoted in John McClaughry, "The Future of Private Property and Its Distribution," *Ripon Quarterly,* Fall 1974, p. 31.
13. William F. Buckley, "CEO Salaries, Like Sausages, Aren't Pretty," *Los Angeles Times,* 11 April 1996, p. B15.
14. See <http://www.natv.org/other_voices/new_doug.html>.
15. Kathleen Dalton, "For T. R., Government Was the Solution," *The New York Times,* 14 July 2002, section 4, p. 5.

CHAPTER 23

1. Andrew Jackson in 1824, Samuel Tilden in 1876, Grover Cleveland in 1888, and Al Gore in 2000.
2. Quoted in Jonathan Power, "United Nations Moving Toward a New Age," *Los Angeles Times,* 19 January 1990, p. B15.
3. Quoted in Eric Harrison, "Gorbachev Backs World Government," *Los Angeles Times,* 7 May 1992, pp. A1, A38.
4. Such international cooperation is not a new thing. The International Telecommunication Union, now an arm of the United Nations, actually grew out of

the International Telegraphic Convention that was established by 25 European countries in 1865.

5. Ellwood, 2001, p. 107.

6. Rosenberg, 2002, p. 30.

7. See Rosenberg, 2002, pp. 30–33, 50, 74–75.

8. See Ellwood, 2001, Chapter 7, "Redesigning the Global Economy."

9. See Molly Ivins, "Clock Ticking on Economic Meltdown," *Raleigh News & Observer*, 14 February 2002, p. 13A.

10. Thomas Friedman, "Globalization, Alive and Well," *The New York Times*, 22 September 2002, section 4, p. 13.

11. *The New York Times*, 29 July 2001, section 4, p. 14.

12. Wells [1920], 1956, p. 938.

13. Nickerson, 2000, p. 27A.

14. Ibid., p. 28A.

15. Fukuyama, 1999, p. 76.

Selected Bibliography

Abbey, Edward. *One Life At a Time, Please.* New York: Henry Holt and Company, 1988.

Adams, Scott. *The Dilbert Principle.* New York: HarperCollins Publishers, Inc., 1996.

Allen, Steve. *Dumbth: And 81 Ways to Make Americans Smarter.* Buffalo, NY: Prometheus Books, 1989.

———. *Vulgarians at the Gate: Trash TV and Rauch Radio—Raising the Standards of Popular Culture.* Amherst, NY: Prometheus Books, 2001.

Altschull, J. Herbert. *From Milton to McLuhan: The Ideas Behind American Journalism.* White Plains, NY: Longman, 1990.

Armstrong, Karen. *The Battle for God.* New York: Alfred A. Knopf, 2000.

Auchincloss, Kenneth. "Fanfare for the Common Man." *Newsweek,* 20 December 1999, pp. 48–54.

Barrett, William. *Irrational Man: A Study in Existential Philosophy.* New York: Doubleday Anchor Books, 1958.

Barzun, Jacques. *From Dawn to Decadence: 500 Years of Western Cultural Life, 1500 to the Present.* New York: HarperCollins Publishers, 2000.

Begley, Sharon. "The Battle for Planet Earth." *Newsweek,* 24 April 2000, pp. 50–53.

Bennahum, David S. "Technorealism," *MEME,* 11 March 1998, <http://memex.org/meme4–02.html>.

Berenson, Alex. "The Biggest Casualty of Enron's Collapse: Confidence." *The New York Times,* 10 February 2002, section 4, pp. 1, 6.

Berger, Arthur Asa. *Cultural Criticism: A Primer of Key Concepts.* Thousand Oaks, CA: Sage Publications, 1995.

Berlin, Isaiah. *The Age of Enlightenment: The 18th Century Philosophers.* New York: Mentor Book/New American Library, 1956.

———. *The Proper Study of Mankind: An Anthology of Essays.* New York: Farrar, Straus and Giroux, 1997.

Berman, Morris. *The Twilight of American Culture*. New York: W. W. Norton & Company, 2000.

Berry, Wendell. *The Unsettling of America: Culture and Agriculture*. San Francisco: Sierra Club Books, 1977.

Best, Steven, and Douglas Kellner. *The Postmodern Turn*. New York: The Guilford Press, 1997.

Bloom, Allan. *The Closing of the American Mind: How Higher Education Has Failed Democracy and Impoverished the Souls of Today's Students*. New York: Simon and Schuster, 1987.

Boaz, David. *Libertarianism: A Primer*. New York: The Free Press, 1997.

Botstein, Leon. *Jefferson's Children: Education and the Promise of American Culture*. New York: Doubleday, 1997.

Boulding, Kenneth E. *The Meaning of the Twentieth Century*. New York: Harper & Row, 1964.

Bradbury, Ray. *Fahrenheit 451* [1953]. New York: Ballantine Publishing Group/ Random House, Inc., 1991.

Braile, Robert. "Group Forecasts Ecological Doom." *Raleigh News & Observer*, 16 January 2000, p. 11A.

Breen, T. H. "Enlighten Us," (book review of Roy Porter's *The Creation of the Modern World*). *The New York Times Book Review*, 24 December 2000, p. 6.

Brokaw, Tom. *The Greatest Generation*. New York: Random House, 1998.

Brooks, David. *Bobos in Paradise: The New Upper Class and How They Got There*. New York: Simon and Schuster, 2000.

———. "Time to Do Everything Except Think." *Newsweek*, 30 April 2001, p. 71.

Brown, Lester R., Christopher Flavin, and Hilary French. *State of the World 1999: A Worldwatch Institute Report on Progress Toward a Sustainable Society*. New York: W. W. Norton & Company, 1999.

Buchen, Irving H. "A Radical Vision for Education." *The Futurist*, May-June 2000, pp. 30–34.

Burke, Meredith. "America on the Path to Its First Billion." *San Diego Union-Tribune*, 25 October 2000, p. B7.

Campbell, Jeremy. *The Improbable Machine: What the Upheavals in Artificial Intelligence Research Reveal About How the Mind Really Works*. New York: Simon and Schuster, 1989.

Capra, Fritjof. *The Turning Point: Science, Society, and the Rising Culture*. New York: Bantam Books, 1982.

Carr, Caleb. *Killing Time*. New York: Random House, 2000.

Carson, Rachel. *Silent Spring*. Boston: Houghton Mifflin, 1962.

Cartmill, Matt. "Oppressed by Evolution." *Discover*, March, 1998, pp. 78–83.

Cave, Damien. "View From the Top." *Salon Magazine*, 10 April 2000 <http:// www.salonmag.com/tech/view/2000/04/10/joy>.

Cheshire, Godfrey. "Movies: Judgment Call." Durham-Raleigh *Independent Weekly*, 26 September 2001, pp. 55–57.

Commission on Population Growth and the American Future. *Population and the American Future*. New York: Signet Book, New American Library, 1972.

Commoner, Barry. *The Closing Circle: Nature, Man, and Technology*. New York: Alfred A. Knopf, 1971.

Cornish, Edward. *The Cyber Future: 93 Ways Our Lives Will Be Changed by the Year 2025.* Bethesda, MD: World Future Society, 1999.

Cose, Ellis. "The Prison Paradox." *Newsweek,* 13 November 2000, pp. 40–52.

Crichton, Michael. "Could Tiny Machines Rule the World?" *Parade Magazine,* 24 November 2002, pp. 6–8.

Crossman, William. "The Coming Age of Talking Computers." *The Futurist,* December 1999, pp. 42–48.

Crowther, Hal. "Why I'm not a Libertarian." Durham-Raleigh *Independent Weekly,* 14 June 2000, p. 9.

———. *Unarmed But Dangerous: Withering Attacks on All Things Phony, Foolish, and Fundamentally Wrong with America Today.* Atlanta: Longstreet Press, 1995.

Dalton, Kathleen. *Theodore Roosevelt: A Strenuous Life.* New York: Alfred A. Knopf, 2002.

Daly, Herman E. *Steady-State Economics: The Economics of Biophysical Equilibrium and Moral Growth.* San Francisco: W. H. Freeman and Company, 1977.

Davis, Robert Con, and Ronald Schleifer. *Contemporary Literary Criticism: Literary and Cultural Studies.* 2nd ed. New York: Longman, 1989.

Debord, Guy. *The Spectacle of Society* [1967]. Translated by Donald Nicholson-Smith. New York: Zone Books, 1995.

Dewey, John. *How We Think.* New York: D.C. Heath & Company, 1933.

Diamond, Jared. *Guns, Germs, and Steel: The Fates of Human Societies.* New York: W. W. Norton, 1997.

———. "The Worst Mistake in the History of the Human Race." *Discover,* May 1987, pp. 64–66.

Dubos, René. *Mirage of Health: Utopias, Progress, and Biological Change.* New Brunswick, NJ: Rutgers University Press, 1987.

Dye, Thomas R., and L. Harmon Zeigler. *The Irony of Democracy: An Uncommon Introduction to American Politics.* 4th ed. North Scituate, MA: Duxbury Press, 1978.

Easterbrook, Gregg. "America the O.K." *The New Republic,* 4 January 1999, pp. 19–25.

Eaton, S. Boyd, Marjorie Shostak, and Melvin Konner. *The Paleolithic Prescription: A Program of Diet and Exercise and a Design for Living.* New York: Harper and Row, 1988.

Ebert, Teresa. *Ludic Feminism and After.* Ann Arbor: University of Michigan Press, 1996.

Ehrenfeld, David. *The Arrogance of Humanism.* New York: Oxford University Press, 1978.

Einstein, Albert. *Ideas and Opinions.* Based on *Mein Weltbild* [1954]. Edited by Carl Seelig. New translations by Sonja Bargmann. New York: The Modern Library, 1994.

Ekelund, Robert B., Jr., and Robert F. Hébert. *A History of Economic Theory and Method.* 2nd ed. New York: McGraw-Hill Book Company, 1983.

Ellul, Jacques. *The Technological Society.* Translated by John Wilkinson. New York: Vintage Books, 1964.

Ellwood, Wayne. *The No-Nonsense Guide to Globalization.* London: Verso, 2001.

Endicott, Karen. "Post-What?!?" *Dartmouth Alumni Magazine,* December 1998, pp. 38–41.

Fisher, David E., and Marshall Jon Fisher. "The Nitrogen Bomb." *Discover,* April 2001, pp. 50–57.

FitzGerald, Frances. *America Revised.* Boston: Atlantic Monthly Press Book, Little, Brown and Company, 1979.

Fletcher, Joseph. "Chronic Famine and the Immorality of Food Aid: A Bow to Garrett Hardin," *Population and Environment,* Vol. 12, No. 3 (Spring, 1991). Available at <http://dieoff.org/page91.htm>.

Foster, Hal. "Introduction." In *The Anti-Aesthetic,* edited by Hal Foster. Port Townsend, WA: Bay Press, 1983.

Friedan, Betty. *The Feminine Mystique.* New York: W. W. Norton & Company, 1963.

Friedman, Thomas. "Global Village Idiocy." *The New York Times,* 12 May 2002, section 4, p. 15.

Fukuyama, Francis. *The End of History and the Last Man.* New York: Avon Books, Inc., in arrangement with The Free Press, 1992.

———. "The Great Disruption: Human Nature and the Reconstitution of Social Order." *The Atlantic Monthly,* May 1999, pp. 55–80.

———. "Their Target: The Modern World." *Newsweek* insert, 17 December 2001, pp. 14–24.

Galbraith, John Kenneth. *The Affluent Society.* 4th ed. Boston: Houghton Mifflin, 1984.

———. *American Capitalism: The Concept of Countervailing Power.* Rev. ed. Boston: Houghton Mifflin, 1956.

Gay, Peter. *Age of Enlightenment.* New York: Time Incorporated, 1966.

Gearino, G. D. "With So Many Opinions at Hand, Why Form Your Own?" *Raleigh News & Observer,* 13 February 2000, pp. 23A, 25A.

Gleick, James. *Faster: The Acceleration of Just About Everything.* New York: Vintage Books / A Division of Random House, Inc., 1999.

———. "Theories of Connectivity." *The New York Times Magazine,* 22 April 2001, pp. 62–67, 101, 108, 112.

Gore, Albert, Jr. *Earth in the Balance: Ecology and the Human Spirit.* Boston: Houghton Mifflin, 1992.

Gray, John. *Enlightenment's Wake: Politics and Culture at the Close of the Modern Age.* New York: Routledge, 1995.

Habermas, Jürgen. *Jürgen Habermas on Society and Politics: A Reader.* Edited by Steven Seidman. Boston: Beacon Press, 1989.

Halstead, Ted, and Michael Lind. *The Radical Center: The Future of American Politics.* New York: Doubleday, 2001.

Hardin, Garrett. "Feeding the World's Hungry Only Makes World Hunger Worse." *Los Angeles Times,* 3 November 1985, Part IV, p. 3.

———. *Living Within Limits: Ecology, Economics, and Population Taboos.* New York: Oxford University Press, 1993.

Heilbroner, Robert L. *An Inquiry Into the Human Prospect: Updated and Reconsidered for the 1980s.* New York: W. W. Norton & Company, 1980.

Herman, Roger E. "The Case for Liberal Arts." *The Futurist,* July-August 2000, pp. 16–17.

Hobart, Michael E., and Zachary S. Schiffman. *Information Ages: Literacy, Numeracy, and the Computer Revolution.* Baltimore: The Johns Hopkins University Press, 1998.

Hofstadter, Richard. *Anti-Intellectualism in American Life*. New York: Alfred A. Knopf, 1963.

Huntington, Samuel P. "Issues 2002: The Age of Muslim Wars," *Newsweek* insert, 17 December 2001, pp. 3–12.

Huxley, Aldous. *Brave New World* [1932]. New York: Harper and Row, 1969.

Isaacs, Harold R. *Idols of the Tribe: Group Identity and Political Change*. New York: Harper and Row, 1975.

Jacoby, Russell. *The Last Intellectuals: American Culture in the Age of Academe*. New York: Noonday Press/Farrar, Straus and Giroux, 1987.

Jennings, Peter, and Todd Brewster. *The Century*. New York: Doubleday, 1998.

Kaplan, Robert D. *The Coming Anarchy: Shattering the Dreams of the Post Cold War*. New York: Random House, 2000.

Kaufman, Walter. *Existentialism From Dostoevsky to Sartre*. Revised and Expanded. New York: Meridian/Dutton Signet. A division of Penguin Books USA Inc., 1975.

Koberg, Don, and Jim Bagnall. *The Universal Traveller: A Soft-Systems Guide to Creativity, Problem-Solving, and the Process of Reaching Goals*. Los Altos, CA: William Kaufman, Inc., 1974.

Kozol, Jonathan. *Illiterate America*. Garden City, NY: Anchor Press/Doubleday, 1985.

Krugman, Paul. "For Richer." *The New York Times Magazine*. 20 October 2002, pp. 62–67, 76, 77, 141, 142.

Kubey, Robert, and Mihaly Csikszentmihalyi. "Television Addiction Is No Mere Metaphor." *Scientific American*, February 2002, pp. 74–80.

———. *Television and the Quality of Life: How Viewing Shapes Everyday Experiences*. Hillsdale, NJ: Lawrence Erlbaum Associates, 1990.

Lapham, Lewis. "Modern Democracy: A State of Being Artfully Deceived." *Los Angeles Times*, 21 November 1993, p. M2.

Lasch, Christopher. *The Culture of Narcissism: American Life in an Age of Diminishing Expectations*. New York: W. W. Norton and Company, 1978.

———. *The True and Only Heaven: Progress and Its Critics*. New York: W. W. Norton and Company, 1991.

Lederer, William J. *A Nation of Sheep*. New York: W. W. Norton and Company, 1961.

Lemley, Brad. "Computers Will Save Us: The Future According to James Martin." *Discover*, June 2001, pp. 52–57.

———. "Machines That Think." *Discover*, January 2001, pp. 74–79.

Leonard, George B. *Education and Ecstasy*. New York: Delacort Press, 1968.

Lincoln, Abraham. Speech to the Republican State Convention. Springfield, Illinois, 16 June 1858.

Linden, Eugene. *The Future In Plain Sight: Nine Clues to the Coming Instability*. New York: Simon & Schuster, 1998.

Lukacs, John. *Outgrowing Democracy: A History of the United States in the Twentieth Century*. Garden City, NY: Doubleday and Company, 1984.

Malthus, Thomas Robert. *An Essay on the Principles of Population, as It Affects The Future Improvement of Society*. London: J. Johnson, in St. Paul's Church-Yard, 1798. New York: Reprints of Economic Classics, Augusts M. Kelley, Bookseller/Sentry Press, 1965.

———. *Principles of Political Economy* [1820]. London: Kelley, 1836.

Mander, Jerry. *Four Arguments for the Elimination of Television.* New York: William Morrow and Company, 1978.

———. *In the Absence of the Sacred: The Failure of Technology and the Survival of the Indian Nations.* San Francisco: Sierra Club Books, 1991.

Manning, Phillip. *Islands of Hope.* Winston-Salem, NC: John F. Blair, Publisher, 1999.

McClintock, Jack. "Twenty Species We May Lose in the Next Twenty Years." *Discover,* October 2000, pp. 62–66.

McGinn, Daniel. "Maxed Out." *Newsweek,* 27 August 2001, pp. 34–40.

McKibben, Bill. *The Age of Missing Information.* New York: Random House, 1992.

McLuhan, Marshall. *Understanding Media: The Extensions of Man.* New York: New American Library, Signet Books, 1964.

———, and Quentin Fiore. *The Medium is the Message: An Inventory of Effects.* New York: Bantam Books, 1967.

McWhorter, John H. *Losing the Race: Self-Sabotage in Black America.* New York: Free Press, 2000.

Medved, Michael. *Hollywood Vs. America: Popular Culture and the War on Traditional Values.* New York: HarperCollins Publishers, 1992.

Meredith, Geoffrey E. "The Demise of Writing." *The Futurist,* October 1999, pp. 27–29.

Meyrowitz, Joshua. *No Sense of Place: The Impact of Electronic Media on Social Behavior.* New York: Oxford University Press, 1985.

Miles, Rufus E., Jr. *Awakening from the American Dream: The Social and Political Limits to Growth.* New York: Universe Books, 1976.

Mill, John Stuart. *On Liberty* [1859]. In *Great Books of the Western World,* Robert Maynard Hutchins, general editor. Vol. 43: *American State Papers, Federalist, J. S. Mill.* Chicago: Encyclopædia Britannica, 1952.

Mills, C. Wright. *The Power Elite.* New York: Oxford University Press, 1956.

Milton, John. *Areopagitica* [1644]. In *Great Books of the Western World,* Robert Maynard Hutchins, general editor. Vol. 32: *Milton.* Chicago: Encyclopædia Britannica, 1952.

Moore, Michael. *Downsize This!* New York: HarperCollins, 1997.

Moser, Leo J. *The Technology Trap: Survival in a Man-Made Environment.* Chicago: Nelson-Hall, 1979.

Mowat, Farley. *Never Cry Wolf.* Boston: Little, Brown, 1963.

Moyers, Bill. *A World of Ideas: Conversations with Thoughtful Men and Women about American Life Today and the Ideas Shaping Our Future.* Edited by Betty Sue Flowers. New York: Doubleday, 1989.

Mumford, Lewis. *Sticks and Stones: A Study of American Architecture and Civilization,* 2nd ed. New York: Dover Publications, Inc., 1955.

Naisbitt, John. *Megatrends: Ten New Directions Transforming Our Lives.* 2nd ed. New York: Warner Books, 1984.

Neuman, W. Russell. *The Paradox of Mass Politics: Knowledge and Opinion in the American Electorate.* Cambridge, MA: Harvard University Press, 1986.

Newman, Judith. "Twenty of the Greatest Blunders in Science in the Last Twenty Years." *Discover,* October 2000, pp. 78–83.

Nickerson, Colin. "A Vanishing Border." *Raleigh News & Observer,* 5 November 2000, pp. 27A–28A.

Ong, Walter J. "Reading, Technology, and Human Consciousness." In *Literacy as a*

   Human Problem, edited by James C. Raymond. University, AL: University of Alabama Press, 1982.

Orwell, George. *1984* [1949]. New York: New American Library, 1961.

Packard, Vance. *The People Shapers*. Boston: Little, Brown, 1977.

Pask, Gordon, with Susan Curran. *Micro Man: Computers and the Evolution of Consciousness*. New York: Macmillan Publishing Co., 1982.

Peterson, Merrill D., ed. *The Portable Thomas Jefferson*. New York: Penguin Books, 1975.

Phillips, Kevin. *Wealth and Democracy: A Political History of the American Rich*. New York: Broadway Books, 2002.

Pizzigati, Sam. *The Maximum Wage: A Common-Sense Prescription for Revitalizing America—By Taxing the Very Rich*. New York: Apex Press, 1992.

Plato. "Republic." In *Five Great Dialogues*. Translated by B. Jowett. Edited by Louise Ropes Loomis. New York: Van Nostrand Company, 1942.

Porter, Roy. *The Creation of the Modern World: The Untold Story of the British Enlightenment*. New York: W. W. Norton, 2000.

Posner, Richard A. *Public Intellectuals: A Study of Decline*. Cambridge, MA: Harvard University Press, 2001.

Postman, Neil. *Amusing Ourselves to Death: Public Discourse in the Age of Show Business*. New York: Penguin Books, 1985.

———. *Building a Bridge to the 18th Century: How the Past Can Improve Our Future*. New York: Alfred A. Knopf, 1999.

———. *Conscientious Objections: Stirring Up Trouble About Language, Technology, and Education*. New York: Vintage Books/Random House, Inc, 1988.

———. *The End of Education: Redefining the Value of School*. New York: Alfred A. Knopf, 1996.

———. *Technopoly: The Surrender of Culture to Technology*. New York: Alfred A. Knopf, 1992.

Postman, Neil, and Charles Weingartner. *Teaching as a Subversive Activity*. New York: Dell Publishing Company, 1969.

Powell, Corey S. "Twenty Ways the World Could End Suddenly." *Discover*, October 2000, pp. 50–57.

Putnam, Robert D. *Bowling Alone: The Collapse and Revival of American Community*. New York: Simon & Schuster, 2000.

Quinn, Daniel. *Beyond Civilization: Humanity's Next Great Adventure*. New York: Harmony Books, 1999.

———. *Ishmael: An Adventure of the Mind and Spirit*. New York: A Bantam/Turner Book, 1992.

Rand, Ayn. *The Fountainhead* [1943]. 5th ed. New York: Signet Novel/Penguin Books, 1993.

Raspberry, William. "As Always, On the Road to Perdition." *Raleigh News & Observer*, 13 May 1999, p. 19A.

Rees, Martin. *Our Final Hour: A Scientist's Warning: How Terror, Error, and Environmental Disaster Threaten Humankind's Future in This Century—on Earth and Beyond*. New York: Basic Books, 2003.

Riesman, David. *The Lonely Crowd: A Study of the Changing American Character*. New Haven: Yale University Press, 1950.

Rosen, Jeffrey. "The Eroded Self." *The New York Times Magazine*, 30 April 2000, pp. 46–53, 66.

———. "Silicon Valley's Spy Game." *The New York Times Magazine,* 14 April 2002, pp. 46–51.

———. "A Watchful State." *The New York Times Magazine,* 7 October 2001, pp. 38–43, 85, 92-93.

Rosenberg, Tina. "The Free-Trade Fix." *The New York Times Magazine,* 18 August 2002, pp. 28–33, 50, 74–75.

Roszak, Theodore. *The Cult of Information: A Neo-Luddite Treatise on High Tech, Artificial Intelligence, and the True Art of Thinking.* 2nd ed. Berkeley: University of California Press, 1994.

Rousseau, Jean Jacques. "The Social Contract Or Principles of Political Right" [1762]. Translated by G. D. H. Cole. In *Great Books of the Western World,* Robert Maynard Hutchins, general editor. Vol. 38: *Montesquieu [and] Rousseau.* Chicago: Encyclopædia Britannica, 1952.

Rushkoff, Douglas. "A Talk with Douglas Rushkoff," *Edge,* 25 October 1999, <http://www.edge.org/documents/archive/edge61.html>.

Safire, William. "Prying Eyes Diminish Private Lives." *Raleigh News & Observer,* 19 February, 2002, p. 9A.

———. "The Wreck of Privacy: Never Out of Touch." *Raleigh News & Observer,* 2 June 1999, p. 13A.

Salins, Peter D. *Assimilation, American Style.* New York: BasicBooks, 1997.

Samuelson, Robert J. "Can America Assimilate?" *Newsweek,* 9 April 2001, p. 42.

Sanneh, Lamin. "Faith and the Secular State." *The New York Times,* 23 September 2001, section 4, p. 17.

Saul, John Ralston. *Voltaire's Bastards: The Dictatorship of Reason in the West.* New York: Vintage Books (A Division of Random House, Inc.), 1992.

Schlesinger, Arthur M., Jr. *The Cycles of American History.* Boston: Houghton Mifflin Company, 1986.

Schramm, Wilbur. *Responsibility in Mass Communication.* New York: Harper and Row, 1957.

Schulman, Bruce J. *The Seventies: The Great Shift in American Culture, Society, and Politics.* New York: Free Press, 2001.

Seligman, Martin E. P. "Boomer Blues." *Psychology Today,* October 1988, pp. 50–55.

Sheehy, Gail. "The Accidental Candidate." *Vanity Fair,* October 2000, pp. 164–196.

Shlain, Leonard. "The Curse of Literacy." *Utne Reader,* September-October 1998, pp. 71–75.

Siebert, Fred S., Theodore B. Peterson, and Wilbur Schramm. *Four Theories of the Press.* Urbana: University of Illinois Press, 1956.

Singer, Peter. *One World: The Ethics of Globalization.* New Haven: Yale University Press, 2002.

Smith, Adam. *An Inquiry Into the Nature and Causes of the Wealth of Nations* [1776]. In *Great Books of the Western World,* Robert Maynard Hutchins, general editor. Vol. 39: *Adam Smith.* Chicago: Encyclopædia Britannica, 1952.

Sokal, Alan, and Jean Bricmont. *Fashionable Nonsense: Postmodern Intellectuals' Abuse of Science.* New York: Picador USA, 1998.

Soley, Lawrence C. *Leasing the Ivory Tower: The Corporate Takeover of Academia.* Boston: South End Press, 1995.

Sorokin, Pitirim A. *The Crisis of Our Age: The Social and Cultural Outlook.* New York: E. P. Dutton & Co., Inc., 1941.

Spengler, Oswald. *The Decline of the West* [1918]. Abridged edition by Helmut Werner. Prepared by Arthur Helps. Translated by Charles Francis Atkinson. New York: Oxford University Press, 1991.

Spong, John Shelby. *Why Christianity Must Change or Die: A Bishop Speaks to Believers in Exile*. New York: HarperSanFrancisco, 1998.

Stavrianos, L. S. *The World to 1500: A Global History*, 3rd ed. Englewood Cliffs, NJ: Prentice-Hall, 1982.

Stein, Ben. "Slippery When 'Vette." *Modern Maturity*, July/August 2001, pp. 32–36.

Stoll, Cliff. *Silicon Snake Oil: Second Thoughts on the Information Highway*. New York: Doubleday, 1995.

Straubhaar, Joseph, and Robert LaRose. *Communications Media in the Information Society*. Belmont, CA: Wadsworth Publishing Company, 1997.

Sullivan, Andrew. "This *Is* a Religious War." *The New York Times Magazine*, 7 October 2001, pp. 44–47, 52–53.

Sykes, Charles J. *A Nation of Victims: The Decay of the American Culture*. New York: St. Martin's Press, 1992.

Tassel, Janet. "The 30 Years' War: Cultural Conservatives Struggle with the Harvard They Love." *Harvard Magazine*, September-October 1999, pp. 56–66, 99.

Thoreau, Henry David. *Walden: or, Life in the Woods* [1854]. New York: New American Library of World Literature, 1942.

Tocqueville, Alexis de [Charles Henri Maurice Clerel]. *Democracy in America, Part I* [1835], *Part II* [1840]. Edited and abridged by Richard D. Hefner. New York: Penguin Books/A Mentor Book, 1956.

Toffler, Alvin. *Future Shock*. New York: Bantam Books, 1970.

———. *The Third Wave*. New York: Bantam Books, 1980.

Toulmin, Stephen. *Cosmopolis: The Hidden Agenda of Modernity*. New York: Free Press, 1990.

Tuchman, Barbara, W. *The March of Folly: From Troy to Vietnam*. New York: Alfred A. Knopf, 1984.

Turney, Jon. "Of Mites and Men." *The New York Times Book Review*, 17 February 2002, p. 11.

Van Evra, Judith Page. *Television and Child Development*. Hillsdale, NJ: Lawrence Erlbaum Associates, 1990.

Weber, Max. *Max Weber on Capitalism, Bureaucracy and Religion: A Selection of Texts* [1889–1924]. Edited by Stanislav Andreski. Boston: George Allen & Unwin, 1983.

Wells, H. G. *The Outline of History: Being a Plain History of Life and Mankind* [1920]. New York: Garden City Books/Doubleday, 1956.

Whyte, William H., Jr. *The Organization Man*. New York: Simon and Schuster, 1956.

Wiesel, Elie. "How Can We Understand Their Hatred?" *Parade Magazine*, 7 April 2002, pp. 4–5.

Will, George F. "Are Children Little Adults?" *Newsweek*, 6 December 1999, p. 98.

Wilson, Edward O. "The Bottleneck." *Scientific American*, February 2002, pp. 82–91.

———. *Consilience: The Unity of Knowledge*. New York: Alfred A. Knopf, 1998.

———. *The Future of Life*. New York: Alfred A. Knopf, 2002.

Winchester, Simon. *The Map That Changed the World: William Smith and the Birth of Modern Geology*. New York: HarperCollins Publishers, 2001.

Winn, Marie. *The Plug-In Drug: Television, Children, and the Family.* Rev. ed. New York: Penguin Books, 1985.

Wolfe, Alan. "The Final Freedom." *The New York Times Magazine,* 18 March 2001, pp. 48–51.

Wood, Donald N. *Designing the Effective Message: Critical Thinking and Communication.* 2nd ed. Dubuque, IA: Kendall/Hunt, 1996.

———. *Post-Intellectualism and the Decline of Democracy: The Failure of Reason and Responsibility in the Twentieth Century.* Westport, CT: Greenwood/Praeger, 1996.

Wurman, Richard Saul. *Information Anxiety.* New York: Doubleday, 1989.

Zakaria, Fareed. "The End of the End of History." *Newsweek,* 24 September 2001, p. 70.

———. "Why Do They Hate Us?" *Newsweek,* 15 October 2001, pp. 22–37.

Index

Racial discrepancies, 6
Racism
  media, 115, 116
  tribalism, 161–62
Radical, discussion of term, 226–27
  (n.6-2)
Radio. *See* Electric media
Rand, Ayn, 121–22
Raspberry, William, 129–30, 161, 194
Rationality, balance with passion,
  184–85
  See also Reason
Reactionary, discussion of term,
  226–27 (n.6-2)
Reagan, Ronald, 79, 215
Realism, 34
Reason, 55
  distrust of, 139–40
  eight difficulties, 141–45
  Enlightenment legacy, xiv, 14, 15,
    184
  failure of, 138–45, 207
  faith, 181–82
  rational thinking, 24–26
  rejection of, xv, 46
  See also Analytic Thinking Pattern;
    Decision-making; Twin pillars
Rebane, George, 225 (n.4-3)
Rebellion, youth, 101, 105, 106
Recall election, 172
Reflection, time for, 45–46, 105
Reflective Thinking Pattern, 24, 225
  (n.3-7)
Reformation, 9, 12
Refrigerators, 198
Reich, Robert, 175
Relativism, 36
Relativity, Theory of, 32, 96
Religion, 55
  counter-intellectual, 67–68, 132, 157
  evangelistic, 67, 132
  extremism, 37
  fundamentalism, 48, 65, 98, 131,
    132, 138, 157–59
  hyper-intellectual, 67, 131–32
  Ideational society, 57
  intolerance, 158
  mainline denominations, 67, 131–32

racism, 161
  residual trappings, 132
  terrorism, 159
Renaissance, 12, 58
Renaissance Man, 22
Renewable energy sources, 198
Reproductive choice, 201–2, 204
Reproductive Rights Market, 203
Republican party, 66
Resentment, toward America, 76, 129
Resources, natural
  dwindling, 152–54
  tax policies, 198–99
Responsibility
  affective component of problem-
    solving, 27–29, 137
  Enlightenment legacy, xiv, 16, 17, 19
  failure of, xv, 132–33, 138–41, 207
  moral, 132–33
  need for, 74
  See also Freedom; Twin pillars
Retail ethnography, 125
Retribalism. *See* Retribalization
Retribalization, 55, 66, 70, 157–65
  assault on individualism, 159–60
  counter-intellectualism, 157
  definition, 157
  drift towards, 65
RFID (radio-frequency identification),
  125
Rhode Island, 213
Riesman, David, 229 (n.11-2)
Right hemisphere (brain), 69–70,
  110–11, 116, 182–83
Roark, Howard, 121–22
Robertson, Pat, 129
Roman democracy, 11
Romanticism, xv, 37, 92, 98
Romantics, 63
Roosevelt, Theodore, 212
Rootlessness, 54
Rosen, Jeffrey, 126, 127, 128
Rosenberg, Tina, 216–17
Roszak, Theodore, 143
Rousseau, Jean Jacques
  class gap, 76
  Enlightenment figure, 14, 22
  governance by clerks, 172

About the Author

DONALD N. WOOD is Professor Emeritus, Media Studies, California State University, Northbridge. He is the author of *Post-Intellectualism and the Decline of Democracy* (Praeger, 1996).